WHAT A LIBRARY
MEANS TO A WOMAN

WHAT A LIBRARY MEANS TO A WOMAN

Edith Wharton and the Will to Collect Books

Sheila Liming

University of Minnesota Press
Minneapolis
London

The University of Minnesota Press gratefully acknowledges the financial assistance provided for the publication of this book by the College of Arts and Sciences and the Office of the Vice President for Research at the University of North Dakota.

Published by the University of Minnesota Press
111 Third Avenue South, Suite 290
Minneapolis, MN 55401-2520
http://www.upress.umn.edu

ISBN 978-1-5179-0703-7 (hc)
ISBN 978-1-5179-0704-4 (pb)

A Cataloging-in-Publication record for this book is available from the Library of Congress.

Printed on acid-free paper

The University of Minnesota is an equal-opportunity educator and employer.

UMP KEP

In Memoriam
George Ramsden (1953–2019)

CONTENTS

· · · · · · · · · · · · · · · · ·

ACKNOWLEDGMENTS   ix

INTRODUCTION   1

1. The Library as Space
   Self-Making and Social Endangerment in
   The Decoration of Houses *and* Summer   29

2. The Library as Hoard
   Collecting and Canonicity in
   The House of Mirth *and* Eline Vere   71

3. The Library as Network
   Affinity, Exchange, and the Makings
   of Authorship   105

4. The Library as Tomb
   Monuments and Memorials in
   Wharton's Short Fiction   137

CONCLUSION   181

NOTES   207

INDEX   259

ACKNOWLEDGMENTS

· · · · · · · · · · · · · · · · · ·

THIS BOOK AND ITS AUTHOR HAVE BEEN NURTURED BY A GREAT many individuals, and by the institutions that bracket and benefit from their collective work. The Mount estate in Lenox, Massachusetts, for instance, was where it all began. When I first visited there during the summer of 2013, as eager and starry-eyed a graduate student as ever there was, I had no idea how my relationship with it would develop and deepen over the coming years, or how this project would sprout from those initial interactions. Susan Wissler, The Mount's executive director, has been there from the very start, recommending sources, providing introductions, and checking in with me each summer, even as the estate roared annually into its busiest season. The same is true of Nynke Dorhout, The Mount's librarian, who offered crucial and unyielding support at every stage of the library digitization project, from which this book emerged, and who introduced me to the works of Louis Couperus along the way. Dorhout plays her many roles at The Mount with enviable grace; I have benefited from her guidance as much as from her relentless cheer. Other Mount staff members (including Anne Schuyler, Ross Jolly, Patricia Pin, Rebecka B. McDougall, Nicole Williams, and Rebecca McBrien, in addition to the many knowledgeable docents and guides) helped smooth the way for this project, for which I am very grateful. Throughout it all, Julie Quain has been there as both my research assistant and my friend, combing the archives, fending off attic ghosts on my behalf, and lending continuous entertainment and encouragement.

The University of North Dakota provided another institutional basis of support for this project. I am grateful for the funding I received in support of the digitization project through the College of Arts and Sciences, particularly through its Early Career and First-Year Faculty Award programs, and for my receipt of summer salary funds through the Arts and Humanities Scholarship Initiative. Through the college, I met many colleagues who contributed individually to this project. My faculty writing group (including Chris Basgier, Cynthia Prescott, Elizabeth Scharf, Caroline Campbell, David Haeselin, Patrick Henry, and Rebecca Weaver-Hightower) encountered each chapter in its first and most humble state, and many of my immediate colleagues in the English department (including Eric Wolfe, Chris Nelson, Yvette Koepke, Sherry O'Donnell, Crystal Alberts, Sharon Carson, Adam Kitzes, and Lori Robison) supported my work in countless direct and indirect ways. I benefited from several truly wonderful undergraduate research assistants, including Luke Jirik, Lora Horner, Liesel Hauge, and Sandra Kruse. Other students at both the undergraduate and graduate levels helped to foster and expand my interest in the subject through their own research and through our ongoing conversations and classroom interactions. Research exists for the sake of students and for the sake of study; I am grateful to all the engaged and thoughtful students who, on a daily basis, remind me of this fact.

This project would never have gotten out of the gate if it weren't for the Edith Wharton Society, which awarded me the research fellowship that first sent me to The Mount in 2013. Since then, many Wharton Society members (including Donna Campbell, Emily Orlando, Carol Singley, Sharon Kim, Paul Ohler, Shafquat Towheed, Alice Kelly, and M. M. Dawley) have continued to support my research and work. Alan Price and Irene Goldman-Price, two "star" Whartonians, offered guidance and kindness along the way, making me feel more at home during my summers at The Mount.

Wharton's library might not exist today if it weren't for George Ramsden, whose decades of labor have resulted in a true archival treasure. I am personally grateful for the contributions that he made to this particular project in the form of interviews and for the hospitality that he and Lady Polly Feversham showed me during my visit to York. I owe thanks to Duane Watson at the Wilderstein estate, to Shelagh Hancox, and to Cornelia Brooke Gilder, all of whom furnished me with background information. Colleagues like Laura Fisher and Lee Konstantinou weighed in on parts of this project while they were still in the making, and I am grateful to them as well as to the many students, colleagues, and contacts I have come to know through Twitter. Doug Armato at the University of Minnesota Press has been an enthusiastic champion of the project, and Gabe Levin was helpful in shepherding it through the publication process. Colleagues and friends from Carnegie Mellon University contributed in important ways to this book's realization: they include David Shumway, who served on my dissertation committee and first introduced to me to Wharton, as well as Jeffrey J. Williams, Kathy M. Newman, Kristina Straub, Richard Purcell, Robert Kilpatrick, Matthew Lambert, and Dan Markowicz. The most important contact I made while at Carnegie Mellon was David Haeselin, who remains, in every way imaginable, my "ideal reader." I cannot adequately acknowledge the level of support that he has given and continues to give to me—I can only commit to repaying it in kind, forever.

INTRODUCTION

····················

At Home among Books

A thing's value becomes most clear in the event of its absence or its destruction. Where value is specious and abstract, loss bequeaths sudden, tragic impressions of weight and of heft. This is certainly true in the case of books, which succeed in appearing symbolically or sentimentally important even as their actual value has fluctuated over the centuries. The destruction of a book (or, worse, an entire library) is almost always viewed as a tragedy, regardless of the particularities surrounding its worth. It is in this way that books defy simple discussions of worth and value—discussions that are necessarily yoked to notions of contemporaneity, markets, and fashion—to emerge as objects that appear heavy with history and laden with a curious and irresistible sort of timelessness.

The English writer Rose Macaulay, for instance, reflects upon the experience of losing her personal library. Macaulay's books, along with the rest of her flat, were bombed in May 1941, during the last days of the London Blitz. Afterward, Macaulay found herself confronted with "a mass of wreckage smelling of mortality" that persisted in teasing her with "hints of what had been." In Macaulay's tender elegy for her library, which was published in the *Spectator* some months after the incident, the loss of material objects appears fused with the loss of self, or of "mortality." But while the essay starts in despair, it soon turns to the more pleasant task of listing the collection's contents. The overall effect is thus reparative: we see Macaulay taking steps to rebuild her collection and to heal herself, even in the midst of profound grief. "When the first stunned sickness begins to lift a little, one perceives that something must be done about lost books. One

1

makes lists; a prey to frenetic bibliomania, I made lists for weeks; when out, I climbed my ruins, seeking in vain; when in, I made lists." Though Macaulay admits that many items in her library can never be replaced, or else wouldn't mean much if they were, she finds consolation in the act of listing them and of fantasizing about their eventual retrieval.[1]

Macaulay's was not the only library that figured among the casualties of the blitz. About 2,500 volumes from the American writer Edith Wharton's library (roughly half of her collection) likewise suffered destruction at the hands of the German bombing campaign. Wharton had died a few years previously, in 1937, and did not have any children of her own. As such, she had willed the books to the children of two separate friends. One of them was William Royall Tyler, the son of Elisina Grant and Royall Tyler; Elisina and Wharton had grown close during the First World War, when they had worked together in connection with Wharton's various French charities. William Royall Tyler was twenty-seven when he inherited half of Wharton's books, and he elected to store them in a London warehouse. When it was bombed four years later, he had not yet had the chance to make a thorough inventory of the collection's contents. Like Macaulay, then, the story of Edith Wharton's library hinges on the articulation of absence, but unlike with Macaulay, absence was there all along, even from the beginning. It is a story that springs from historical voids and from conditions of misuse, neglect, destruction, and corrosion. Wharton never compiled a comprehensive list of her library books either, and her unwillingness to do so has resulted in many long-ranging questions regarding their value. But where topics of personal significance and professional growth are concerned, there can be no question: Wharton's library crucially informed her understandings of herself and played a vital role in shaping the narrative of self-development that emerged in concert with her identity as an author. That narrative, which was only ever partially true, is as much a part of the story of Wharton's success as the fictional ones that she presents in her novels.

This book mounts a claim for libraries as technologies of self-making in late nineteenth- and early twentieth-century America. It focuses, as its primary case in point, on Wharton, though it is less about Wharton than it is about the books that she collected. Wharton was "not a bibliophile": this is according to William Royall Tyler, a man who ought to have known, since he inherited half of the products of her bibliophilic tendencies. But if one spends any time among the 2,700-plus books that, today, are housed at The Mount, her historic Massachusetts estate, a different impression of Wharton's identity as a collector is likely to emerge. Wharton's library, in addition to offering a window onto her development as a thinker and writer, offers contemporary scholars and readers glimpses of another world—one wherein owning thousands of books does not distinguish one as a collector, for example, and where claims to autodidacticism are valorized to the point where attending actual school looks a bit like cheating. This is not the world that we live in today, but it was hers, and it was a world in which attitudes toward book owning and book collecting were shaped by evolving discussions of access, inheritance, and capital.

Bibliophile or no, Wharton viewed her library collection as an indispensable companion, even from an early age. In an 1880 letter to her former governess, for instance, she agonizes over the prospect of packing for an impending trip to Europe. "I am going to '*cram*' before we start," she tells Anna Bahlmann, "for you know it is impossible to take many books with one and I want to know as much as possible about what we *may* be going to see."[2] Though she had been to Europe several times before, Wharton had, throughout the course of her studious teenage years, come to depend upon the company of books. Her burgeoning personal library, which during this time still resided, like her, under her parents' roof, had already helped to explain so much of the world to her. Works by favorite writers like Emerson and Stendhal, for example, embroidered meaning upon her own experiences and served as guides to aid in the interpretation of life's realities and mysteries alike. Books had also helped to impart standards of taste upon the young Edith, spurring her toward the establishment of her own taste-based judgments (as when she casually derides her parents' taste in travel literature). Wharton's anxieties in this letter show how, for her, and for like-minded readers during this era, books were often recruited to the task of constructing tenuous lifelines between a bafflingly frenetic modern present and a distant but comparatively more stable-looking past. In preparing for her family's journey to Europe, Wharton appears eager to see her modern travels embedded within, and thus made more meaningful by, a network of historical associations. And she is counting on books to grant her access to that history, as when she tells Bahlmann, "Milton, Shelly, and Browning must certainly go—and Wordsworth of course. Think of reading Shelley's 'Evening' at Pisa where it was written—think of seeing the Campo Santo, and the pine woods where Byron rode near Ravenna, and Tintoretto's fresco in the Council Chamber (isn't it?) at Venice."[3] Edith Jones depended upon books for a curated sense of history—one that she could take with her as she perambulated, with the ease that was as much a product of her economic privilege as it was a condition of her modern era, all about the globe. Yet what also emerges from this letter to Bahlmann is an indication of Wharton's growing apprehensions concerning the meaning of her own mobility, and her distress regarding modern conceptions of home.

Edith Wharton's childhood was defined by experiences of transatlantic migration, as her parents shuttled their youngest child back and forth between the European continent and their various American addresses in New York and Rhode Island. Too, in 1880 Wharton was still young, just eighteen years old, yet she had recently received public designation as an adult. This meant that she could no longer afford to labor under the delusion that her parents' house was her own, or that it might afford any guarantees of permanence. Wharton's "coming out" forced her to prepare for a set of marital eventualities that, for a woman like herself, necessarily included relocation and resettlement. Home, then, had looked like a fraught concept from the start for Wharton, in contrast to which books offered a kind of solid, material ballast that helped to offset the ephemeral and fleeting qualities of a life lived among a shifting assortment of spaces. For while the idea of home has, arguably, always been an unstable one, in the late-nineteenth century, *home* reached new heights of conceptual instability in light of the multitudinous adjustments made to acts of social living under the auspices of modernity. Home, for example, became a thing that could exist in more than one place, as it did for the Jones family, or else a thing that could be forsaken and left behind entirely, thanks to the growth of transportation technologies and, in America, to the continuing enlargement of national borders as well. Consider, then, that Wharton, though she would eventually settle into a suite of permanent French addresses many years later, would cross the Atlantic Ocean as much as seventy times throughout her seventy-four years of life.[4] The frequency of her international travels suggests the extent to which, for her, the concept of *home* remained negotiable and subject to constant revision.

4

Wharton's attachments to her books—even those exhibited here, at a young age—thus foretell a set of synecdochal relations between her personal library and her understandings of inhabited space, or home. More than any house she ever owned (and there were many of them), her library became a kind of conceptual home base, a vessel for the containment of the stories that she would tell both to the world and to herself *about* herself. As George Ramsden puts it in the introduction to his self-published *Edith Wharton's Library* catalog, "[her books] provided the stable counterpoint to a bewilderingly active life."[5] This was as much true for the young Edith Jones as it was for the mature Edith Wharton: her anxious words to her former governess find their echo, for instance, in a fastidiously detailed set of packing lists created many decades later, in the early 1920s. One of them, labeled "Liste des Livres à Jean-Marie," is a typewritten, multipage document that carefully specifies and describes the library volumes that Wharton selected for shipment to "Jean-Marie," also known as "Pavillon Colombe," her newly purchased house in the Paris suburbs. This "Liste des Livres" is part of a larger set of packing lists that, collectively, help us to see how Wharton went about splitting up her library books among multiple residences during her lifetime. Another, for example, is titled "Volumes à Relier," which translates to "Volumes to be Rebound," and which likely refers to books that needed to have their bindings repaired prior to being installed (either at Pavillon Colombe or else at Wharton's other French residence, Sainte-Claire-du-Château, on the French Riviera). This list features physical descriptions of the items in question, including handwritten instructions for custom bindings ("papier," "toile," "peau") and colors ("peau marron," "toile bleue" [*sic*]). Notes in Wharton's hand show her preparing her library for relocation and, likewise, for posterity. At the end of the list of "Volumes à Relier," Wharton has sketched some handwritten calculations about the total number of books that are to be included in the shipments, stipulating eighty-two in one and ninety in another.[6]

Together with her youthful letters to her former governess, then, these library packing lists—which were probably dictated by Wharton but typewritten by a servant—appear like a functional inversion of Walter Benjamin's ruminations in his landmark essay "Unpacking My Library." We get an image of Wharton "packing up" in the early 1920s just as we get an image of Benjamin doing the reverse ten years later, in 1931.[7] Indeed, the reinforcement of such unlikely connections between these two writers—who were contemporaries of a kind, and who had plenty to say on the subject of book collecting and were furthermore saying such things during the same era—constitutes a sort of byproduct of the discussion that follows in this book. Benjamin's essay has proven to be crucially instructive for scholars working within veins of both historical materialism and object-oriented critique. But while Benjamin is only too happy to apply the term "bibliomania" to his own actions as a collector,[8] it is worth mentioning that his library, which, according to Joseph D. Lewandoski, contained about two thousand volumes,[9] amounts to only a fraction of Wharton's, which probably contained closer to five thousand at the time of her death. What's interesting, then, is how Benjamin claims the title of "bibliomaniac," though he possesses a comparably more modest number of volumes, while Wharton never once employs the word, though she owns more than twice as many. What this disparity furthermore suggests is how a certain kind of consciousness—an ethos of collecting, if you will—mediates relations between subject and object where collecting is concerned. Collections have a tendency to form under the banner of accrual, as opposed to *use,* in a way that would appear to differentiate the collector who merely collects from the more devoted *user,* or reader. Too, Wharton's privileged background may have served to soften and normalize her views toward book collecting, if not necessarily toward collecting in general. Wharton's stockpile of bound paper relics does not appear to give her pause, whereas Benjamin seems to register the oddness of his own actions. Like Macaulay, he is drawn by a compulsion to list, but not before inquiring. "Would it not be presumptuous of me," he asks, "if . . . I enumerated for you the main sections or prize pieces of [my] library?"[10] Here Benjamin's fears for presumption suggest that he may be likewise plagued by any number of related insecurities: Benjamin worries, throughout this essay, about how things will look to the audience who receives these impressions of his maniacal habits. He concedes that "every passion borders on the chaotic,"[11] and that the narrative he is therefore constructing—a narrative that is, at its heart, less about his library and more about himself—is therefore fated to appear similarly disordered, if not downright self-indulgent.

Neither Wharton's nor Benjamin's library collections would have been considered exorbitant or remarkable by early twentieth-century standards, though. This point is worth clarifying from the outset, because it helps to explain why Wharton's name, for one, has not previously surfaced amid the critical discourse surrounding print collecting or bibliomania. As previously mentioned, Wharton's own designated heir, William Royall Tyler, even, insisted that she was "not a bibliophile."[12] Yet she clearly loved books—loved them in a way that compares to Benjamin's definition of the ardent collector who, he argues, "studies and loves [the items in their collection] as the scene, the stage of their fate" and who seeks primarily to "lock[] individual items within a magic circle in which they are fixed as the final thrill, the thrill of acquisition, passes over them."[13] She did not distinguish herself as a collector, perhaps, but neither did Benjamin who, like her, was nonetheless practiced in the art of collecting and thus all too familiar with its "thrills." Too, Wharton's habit of featuring collectors as main characters in her fiction rather suggests that latent affinities toward collecting and collectors—affinities that were, first, nurtured and then, later, ripened as the result of her interactions with her own library—structured much of her thinking about objects and people, and about people whose lives are organized by their interactions with objects, most of all. In this way, Wharton's fiction models what an "emotional commitment to literature," in the words of Deidre Lynch, looked like during this era.[14]

It is therefore my project in this book to see Wharton and Wharton's library inserted within discussions of collecting, bibliophilia, and bibliomania, particularly as those discussions pertain to studies of readership, modes of literary distribution, and canonicity at the end of the nineteenth century and throughout the start of the twentieth. This task, which might look a bit straightforward from the outset, becomes all the more complex when we stop to consider how collecting, as a polite pastime, rubs up against a whole host of compulsive or pathologically situated modern behaviors and tendencies, including hoarding. Benjamin, for instance, is on track when he claims that the act of collecting requires navigating "the dialectical tension between the poles of disorder and order,"[15] and my interest in Wharton—both her writing and her personal library—forms in response to this observation: in Wharton's fiction, we witness the ebb and flow that results from conflicts between order and disorder, wrought in hypothetical fashion and filtered through the lens of modernity. This is also true of her library collection, which enumerates and adds material weight to those same tensions, at times making them uncomfortably explicit, as when price tags and discussions of monetary worth are brought to bear upon the amorphous and highly subjective compulsions and commitments of the collector. As such, her library forms a critical part of her archive. The books in it attest to her development as an author, to her righteous claims to self-fashioning and autodidacticism, and to her evolution as a producer not just of novels but of best-selling novels, with the phrase "best-selling" lending a kind of critical gravitas to her status as both a consumer and a producer of textual commodities.

Reading the Reader

Wharton's library has many important stories to tell, and my efforts in this volume hinge upon my desire to see them told. But it's important to note that only a small subset of those stories has anything to do directly with the person who was Edith Wharton. The others stem from the various bits and pieces—"dates, place names, formats, previous owners, bindings, and the like"—that combine and coalesce to form what Benjamin calls the "harmonious whole" that *is* the concept of the library, or the collection.[16] A library is, at its base, a polyphonic assemblage: it speaks to its various readers not as one "harmonious whole" but through a chaotic barrage of competing pitches and tones. This is why Friedrich Nietzsche, in his *Ecce Homo,* sees reading as governed by "the continual pressure of having to listen"—not just to other voices and to other periods of human history, but to "other selves." Indeed, my title for this book, *What a Library Means to a Woman,* offers a play on Nietzsche's comments in this section of his well-known treatise on his personal intellectual development. The "continual pressure of having to listen to other selves," Nietzsche proclaims—"that is after all what reading means."[17] I highlight this quotation for two reasons: first, because it captures the essence of my argument about Wharton's library—that it is, in fact, an archive that gives voice to Wharton's varied articulations of her "many selves." My second reason for drawing attention to it, though, has to do with the fact that Nietzsche held special significance for Wharton, as her much-marked, German-language editions of his complete works will attest.[18]

Indeed, as the ensuing chapters will make apparent, I have tried to take my cues *from* Wharton and to treat her library as a body of evidence. Doing that has required me, first, to follow the traces of Wharton's interactions with textual objects and, second, to align my own inspections of textual objects with hers. This has meant, sometimes, working with editions of texts that she herself knew and worked with, and seeing how those editions furnish clues about the material circumstances that defined her era and her world. This body of evidence becomes, at various points, better clarified but also deepened by the record of her physical interactions with her books. Reading, as Lynch observes, is "an activity that leaves few traces"[19] and thus presents many obstacles for study, but in Wharton's case underlinings and annotations help to light the way forward: they reveal the author as a reader and force us, as scholars, to complicate our understandings of the positions that authors occupy within the literary marketplace. As a writer, for instance, Wharton appears as a singular, productive node that lights up a map of literary interactions. As a reader, though, she loses the aura of omnipotence that so often appears to weigh upon discussions of literary production and creation. She gets revealed, in essence, for what she has been all along: a consumer as well as a producer, an agent of networked dispersal, and a purveyor as well as a patron of ideas about how human culture works.

A library means access—to history, to future realms, to spaces populated by other spaces and other people, to information and stores of knowledge, to tradition, to the dead. But a library, as Benjamin demonstrates repeatedly throughout his essay, also means inheritance: indeed, it often grants access only under conditions of inheritance, and thus it has a part to play in conveying and enforcing rules about ownership, property, and the bestowal of rights. A library may therefore mean different things to different people, depending on where systems of inheritance and ownership have positioned them and what kinds of rights have been duly extended as a consequence of that positioning. In the late nineteenth and early twentieth centuries—that is, during the era in which Wharton lived—one's gender dictated much of the conversation where both property and rights were concerned. As a woman, for instance, Wharton had no *right* to a formalized education; but she succeeded in becoming educated all the same. Likewise, she had no right to inherit her father's property, but she managed to do that as well.

In maneuvering between the various discourses of rights, then, Wharton developed an eye for diagnosing conflicts between "order and disorder," between what has traditionally been done and what one can, nonetheless, manage to get away with doing. Furthermore, she went on to create characters in her fiction that appear committed to testing the boundaries between those realms. Charity Royall in *Summer,* for example, tests the social sanctions that have been traditionally placed on women, only to find that most of them still apply; Lily Bart in *The House of Mirth* tests the limits of her own exchange value on the marriage market and suffers once they are realized; Halo Tarrant in *Hudson River Bracketed* and *The Gods Arrive* subjects her own economic privilege to a constant array of tests; and Lizzie Hazeldean in *New Year's Day* puts her social status and reputation to the test, risking both for the sake of her relationship with her husband. The fact that all of these characters—all of whom are female—fail, to greater or lesser degrees, the tests that they set up for themselves says something about the nature of the trials that they are nonetheless driven to undertake. But it also says something about Wharton's awareness of lurking, systemic imbalances where access and inheritance are concerned.

What a Library Means to a Woman is therefore not just a study of one woman and her library collection. It is a book about networked systems of social and cultural disparity, my investigation of which rests on discussions of a specific woman's initiation into a world of varied and unequal rules. Those rules, as I will show, function as appendages to the historicized discussions that we continue to have today about the meaning and worth of books, or of information. During Wharton's era, literary production, much like book ownership, was structured by mutable and fluctuating understandings about how information or knowledge became translated into *capital.* But as Karl Marx, via his interpretations of the British colonialist Edward Gibbon Wakefield, asserts, "capital is not a thing, but a social relation between persons that is mediated through things."[20] My objectives in this book marshal similar understandings of capital, and my aim in writing it is to show how Wharton's "things"—in this case, her library books—emblematize, reconstruct, or else mediate between networks of social relation that are, in and of themselves, productive.

This investigation has grown out of my long-term interactions with Wharton's library materials at The Mount. In the summer of 2014, I began work on a digitization project that has since granted me ongoing access to the collection and shown me that, beyond its relevance to Edith Wharton herself, the collection provides an evidentiary basis for the claim that a library is where one goes to read about others yet to discover the self. It offers us a snapshot of a historical reader's behaviors that, in turn, encourages us to ask questions of people and things that are not even remotely Edith Wharton. If Wharton, for instance, is "not a bibliophile," who is, or who *was* during this period? What did that term mean previously, and what does it mean now? How does bibliophilia—or its more extreme incarnation, bibliomania—mediate conversations about the worth and usefulness of collections of books, or of collections of objects more generally? I do not, in this book, make claims about what a library means in all contexts, to all people or to all book collectors—to all women, even. Rather, it is my objective to show how Edith Wharton's library collection meant something specific within the period in which it was created, and how and why it means something very different now.

Methods of the Material

Wharton's library provided a functionally stable antidote to a series of unstable, albeit consistently comfortable, modern living arrangements. In doing so, it became a kind of surrogate home, and Wharton went on to recreate that experience of library-as-home for many of her fictional characters. Lawrence Selden's home in *The House of Mirth*, as we shall see, is defined by his book collection, just as the specter of a dead husband's library presides over Lizzie Hazeldean's home in the novella *New Year's Day*. According to Benjamin, preoccupations regarding the space of the "home" survived and persisted in the early decades of the twentieth century as a kind of fallout from the nineteenth-century turn away from public space and toward the private interior. As Benjamin sees it, modernity's ongoing efforts to curtail public space at the end of the nineteenth century forced the new, urban-dwelling populace indoors. Left alone inside their individual residences, these atomized modern subjects became engrossed in the project of asserting control over the space that had come to define their existence. In other words, they became obsessed by the prospect of *dwelling*, and *to dwell*, as Benjamin asserts, "is a transitive verb—as in the notion of 'indwelt spaces.' . . . It has to do with fashioning a shell for ourselves."[21] Indeed, the idea of a library functioned as a kind of shell for Wharton, just as it does for so many of her characters; a library can be a protective device that, while not always attached to specific spaces or material enclosures, draws a reassuring mantle of material stability about the shoulders of its affiliates. It can offer, in other words, promises of containment. But it's important to remember that containers, in addition to granting protection, may also serve to imprison.

My commitment to assessing the library as *form,* and to understanding the breadth of its meanings and functions as such, links my study of Wharton's library to some recent scholarly work on the subject of conceptual containers. In *Forms,* her aptly titled work on the subject, Caroline Levine highlights the ways in which the discussion of forms—especially opposing or contentiously adjacent forms—results in a fruitful species of "collision" that "sometimes reroutes intention and ideology."[22] Indeed, my analyses of Wharton's library reveal not only the tensions that are inherent in *that* particular form but also the ways in which the library stands for (and so cannot help but refer to) a variety of other forms, or containers, or spaces. While the preceding discussion ought to have illuminated some of the ways in which Wharton's library asks to be read and understood as a *home,* such a reading does not, I feel, constitute an end in and of itself, nor does it invalidate other interpretations that might unfold at the level of form. It is, after all, important to remember that, for Wharton, any library was first and foremost a *school,* since her parents denied her participation in formal schooling. Wharton fancied herself an autodidact, in spite of the fact that she had plenty of help in the form of qualified governesses like Bahlmann. Her educational experiences thus mirror Benjamin's assertions about the link between study and collecting, as when he says that "collecting is a primal phenomenon of study: the student collects knowledge."[23] Education, as an intangible means of amassment and accrual, is often used to justify the hoarding of actual material objects as well. Wharton, due in large part to her self-identification as an autodidact, was driven to collect: her library speaks to her desire to amass, store, and retain the information and experiences that provided the basis for her intellectual growth. For Wharton, as for readers like her, the form of a library comes to functionally resemble the form of a school, which, in her special case, is simultaneously also formally a home. This is an example of the way that forms become "nested," according to Levine's thinking. The concept of nested or layered forms gains even more clarification via the work of the theorist Henri Lefebvre, whose particular interventions into the "ambiguous continuity" of social space shows how the "appearance of separation between spaces"—or the appearance of differences between forms—is, in fact, meant to disguise processes of "interpenetration" and "superimposition."[24] Spaces relate to and summon each other, Lefebvre argues, and this furthermore helps to explain how a single, conceptual space invokes a nested array of forms.

Levine transports her discussions of formal "collision" and deploys them within the arena of literary texts, a move that also underscores much of my thinking in this book. According to Levine, "The form that best captures the experiences of colliding forms is narrative,"[25] and I believe this is precisely the case where Wharton's fiction is concerned. Her stories and novels showcase the conflicts that result "when forms meet," in Levine's words,[26] but also how layers of meaning become sedimented and thus contained within forms themselves. As I already established, a library, as a form, means different things to different people. So while it might mean one thing for the likes of characters like Selden and Lizzie Hazeldean—characters that receive differing levels of succor and psychic nourishment from libraries—it is nevertheless still able to mean something different for characters like Charity Royall and Paulina Anson. These latter two figures appear in Wharton's novel *Summer* and in her short story "The Angel at the Grave," respectively, and they experience the form of the library in terms of confinement and even entombment. For them, a library is not a vehicle for accessing Lawrence Selden's coveted "Republic of the Spirit" but a forbidding means of enclosure designed to hold someone or something captive. The fact that some of Wharton's characters *suffer* as the result of their interactions with libraries, while others (like Selden, Lizzie, and Vance Weston in *Hudson River Bracketed*) mirror Wharton's own experiences of intellectual awakening, suggests that there is a dialectic at work in Wharton's fiction. On the one hand, Wharton credits the form of the library for starting her on her trajectory as a thinker and writer; on the other, though, Wharton acknowledges the specificity of her own experiences and shows how pernicious myths of universality can be. Some characters in Wharton's fiction, and Vance Weston is one of them, are "made" as the result of having positive, enriching experiences with libraries. But still other characters, like Charity and Paulina, suffer at the hands of those same experiences. What's more, these sufferings cut across disparities relating to economic privilege: Charity is more or less poor, whereas Paulina is more or less wealthy. Wharton therefore offers a spectrum of dialectically charged takes on the meaning of the library as a form that makes strict arguments about causality both difficult and impractical.

Levine, though, expresses dissatisfaction with dialectics. She purports to "unsettle the power" of the dialectic, which she believes is overused "as an explanatory form in literary and cultural studies."[27] And this is where my methods, though they have been inspired by *Forms,* depart from Levine's. When she argues, for instance, that the dialectic amounts to nothing more than a "binary opposition" that is, in fact, "just one of a number of powerfully organizing forms,"[28] she misrepresents both the process and the point of dialectical inquiry and overlooks its primary function, which involves the exposure of binary relationships as a necessary step on the path toward *synthesis.* Indeed, much of the work that has emerged under the banner of New Formalism (and under those of a number of related, recent critical movements) has helped to enhance the project that I have undertaken in this study. But the tendency of New Formalists to misconstrue and thus neglect the methods of historical materialism leaves me feeling all the more insistent about the latter's application to this project, and to object-oriented study more generally. Both New Formalism and historical materialism appeal to my desire to privilege readings of the material—that is, all the stuff of a networked, commoditized modern existence—but while New Formalism encourages critics to elevate their considerations of the material and to make them the centerpieces of their critique, historical materialism insists upon establishing avenues for networked contextualization and places the emphasis not just on *things* but on things as they exist *in circulation.* This allows us to see and to use the study of things as a staging ground for the consideration of wider networks of material exchange, and that ability is crucial to my task in *What a Library Means to a Woman.* Nathan K. Hensley, for example, in his elegant *Forms of Empire* (2016), notes how "cultural theories" that treat a political or social phenomenon, like imperialism, as "an ensemble of social forms, racial ideologies, and cultural attitudes" might be deepened by "materialist analyses [that] . . . presume instead the priority of economic and political factors, themselves complex and often self-contradictory."[29] Hensley's approach to disentangling the social phenomenon that is imperialism via a set of encounters with the material offers a model for my efforts to disentangle practices like collecting, hoarding, and stockpiling. These are practices that occur both at the individual level and at the larger, institutional or state levels, and they have the tendency to become more intense when they collide with modern economic anxieties, which act as an accelerant to our habits as consumers.

Wharton, for example, lived through the era that saw the rise of the public library as an American institution. The public library movement followed in the late nineteenth and early twentieth centuries upon the heels of an era that had seen steady growth of private membership libraries in the United States, and its stewards sought to extend some of the comforts and refinements of the private library experience to the tax-paying public. As Wayne A. Wiegand explains in his work *Part of Our Lives,* Andrew Carnegie, the father and economic force behind much of the public library movement, "issued a pamphlet containing six recommended designs" for public libraries in 1910 that "replicate[d] the programming capabilities of successful mid-nineteenth-century social libraries,"[30] demonstrating the ways in which the new public library movement was made to rest upon a foundation of historical, elite library usage. What's more, design schemes for public libraries built during this time drew inspiration from some of the great libraries owned by private citizens: "The atmosphere should be as gracious, kindly, and sympathetic as one's own home" was the way one public librarian in Minnesota put it in 1905, pointing to some of the additional links that existed between the private and the public realms where libraries were concerned.[31] As such, in the space that falls between the temporal brackets of Wharton's own lifetime, we see a triangulation forming between three versions of "the library": the private collector's library; the elite, subscription model; and the public, tax-supported model. Wharton, furthermore, had experience with all three of these forms in being at once a private collector, a member of a subscription library and, later, a public library benefactress.

But what Wharton's fiction and her library likewise show, as a result of being coerced into conversation with one another, is how competition and the fight for survival animated the various components of that triangle.

Private library owners, in the later decades of the nineteenth century, were spurred to collect by the thought of seeing their collections someday placed under institutional protection. That, and they stood to gain from selling their collections to prestigious university or public libraries, or else to membership associations. Similarly, research universities during this era went to great lengths to secure rare and valuable collections that might form the centerpieces of their library holdings and thus enhance the worth of their institution and, ideally, the reach of its scholarly brand. All of this scrambling to acquire rare and valuable books, of course, led to escalating prices, which heightened the stakes associated with private collecting. During the later decades of Wharton's own life, the growth of cost-effective printing technologies would make cheap, mass-market editions of popular books available to readers in the early twentieth century. The rise of *cheap and plentiful* on the one hand and *rare and valuable* on the other is, therefore, the history of a distinction between consumer and investor, between reader and collector. Mass-market paperbacks were good enough to read but not worthy of keeping or collecting, a fact that helped to make collectors—acting either independently or on behalf of institutions—more interested in the "good editions" of yore, with their emphasis on lavish custom bindings and luxury details and quality. In Wharton's fiction, accordingly, we encounter a number of different variations on the theme of this dialectic of the collector: Selden in *The House of Mirth* is a collector, but of the discerning, "good editions" variety, while Percy Gryce, who appears in the same novel, is a hoarder who keeps a miserly watch over his valued possessions while refusing to make use of them. In spite of their differences, though, these men collect the same things: books and women. Their actions therefore unite and tie them to a particular chapter of print culture history in a way that cannot be eroded by their apparent differences of character.

It is Wharton's consummate understanding of the field of libraries and book collecting that makes her work such an ideal venue—and her personal library such an ideal *site*—for the study of the triangulation between private collector, private institution, and public institution. And this book seeks to do precisely that: it offers an exploration of the many meanings of a library as a collection, and it reads a specific library collection through the dual methodological lenses of object-oriented methodologies and literary history. Its scope, however, is not limited to materialist analysis alone, as it additionally demonstrates what close reading of literary texts can reveal about historical developments *like* the American public library movement. Wharton's own activities as a collector were defined by their adjacency to the growth and development of institutional repositories like the public library, and her fiction furthermore permits us to contemplate the relationship between the practice of private collecting and the rise of the institutionalized hoard, as I call it. Viewing Wharton through the lens of her collection therefore invites one to consider the stakes of collecting more generally. It also requires one to situate the act of collecting in connection with early twentieth-century anxieties about the increasingly immaterial character of modern material culture. *What a Library Means to a Woman* thus surveys the ways in which a library collection succeeds in making and bestowing meaning, but it also acknowledges the ways in which a library collection may fail to transmit or to *speak* to later generations who are fated to inherit its messages.

Built into that acknowledgment is an argument about the instability of information that comes with the enlargement of the media landscape in the early part of the twentieth century. That very instability resulted in a new fanaticism regarding collecting in general and book collecting in particular: Colton Storm and Howard Peckham, two noted bibliophiles, would decades later characterize the period between the 1880s and 1910s as the "golden age" of American book collectors.[32] In Wharton's case, we see that she builds her anxieties about immateriality and instability directly into her fiction. *What a Library Means to a Woman* is grounded by a set of sustained, close readings that examine Wharton's efforts to translate her experiences and standards as a collector into her novels and stories. Chapter 1 reads Wharton's library at The Mount in terms of space. Wharton designed The Mount herself, in consultation with the architect Ogden Codman Jr., who also coauthored Wharton's first published work, *The Decoration of Houses*. This chapter assesses that text in connection with an analysis of the space that Wharton "authored" at The Mount. It then pivots from a discussion of private library space to a discussion of public libraries, focusing on Wharton's involvement with the Lenox Library, which she used as the basis for the fictionalized setting of her 1916 novel *Summer*.

Chapter 2 then goes on to examine the library as hoard, analyzing themes of obsessive collecting in Wharton's fiction. It places *The House of*

Mirth in conversation with an earlier, strikingly similar work of fiction, the novel *Eline Vere,* written by the Dutch writer Louis Couperus. Wharton's library "hoard" furnishes the substance of this connection, as Wharton owned copies of Couperus's novels. *Eline Vere* and *The House of Mirth* feature virtuous representations of the disciplined collector alongside less sympathetic misers who hoard their possessions without enjoying them. Both of these novels' protagonists die as the result of overdosing on prescription medicine, and this chapter accordingly concludes with a reading of the overdose as emblem of an overindulgent consumerism.

Chapter 3 focuses on an exploration of the library as social network. It reads Wharton's library collection at The Mount as a document of social interaction, charting patterns of affinity and affiliation. Working in large part from visualizations, charts, and graphs, this chapter constructs an image of Wharton's milieu, the members of which might be living or dead, and it uses this discussion of social milieus to bracket an assessment of Wharton's final novel, *The Gods Arrive,* the sequel to her earlier novel *Hudson River Bracketed* and the only work she wrote that ties directly to another. Wharton originally intended to call the first of these novels *Literature,* and this chapter argues in favor of viewing both of these works in terms of networks of literary production, distribution, and dissemination.

Chapter 4 builds on a thematic tension present throughout the preceding chapters: death. It is devoted to a study of the library as monument or tomb, and it takes its cues in part from Thomas Laqueur's *The Work of the Dead* but also from critics like Lynch, who note the ways in which "perverse" forms of emotional attachment (like that enacted between human subject and material object) can "collapse time and connect the living and the dead."[33] Wharton offers repeated comparisons between libraries and funereal architecture in her fiction, employing words like *vault, museum,* and *tomb* to describe certain libraries. This chapter examines the theme of memorialization on two fronts: within Wharton's fiction and within the space of Wharton's own library. It reinforces the connection between libraries and self-making that lies at the heart of this book, puzzling over the extent to which Wharton saw her library collection as her own "monument." Ultimately, this chapter reads the collection or hoard in terms of its purported functionality, arguing that the collection's chief purpose is to grant the collector a curatorial role in their own legacy and death. Two short fictional texts by Wharton, the short story "The Angel at the Grave" and the novella *New Year's Day,* ground my investigations of the library as tomb.

The conclusion documents the afterlives of Edith Wharton's library. It centers on the story of George Ramsden, the modern-day book dealer who was responsible for assembling Wharton's library collection in its present form. The story of Ramsden's prolonged involvement with the collection lends credence to Jean Baudrillard's comment that "withdrawal into an all-encompassing object system is synonymous with loneliness,"[34] as it sheds light, at various points, on an array of complex emotional attachments. This chapter also collects and aggregates the contents of my theoretical investigations into the subject of *worth* insofar as Wharton's library is concerned. Wharton's library went on to live many more lives, and to mean many different things, in the decades that followed her death in the 1930s, with the bulk of those meanings stemming from fraught negotiations about the worth or value of the individual items in it. Ramsden was a central actor and arbiter in those negotiations, and his story is a fitting coda to the larger narratives that grow from this book's analyses of the library itself.

More Than "A Middle Way"

Because of the way that it enfolds both *humans* and *things* into its discussions of the many meanings of the library, this book requires me to affirm methodological commitments to subject and object. Plainly put, I'm interested in things insofar as they prove capable of teaching me something about people. Indeed, I would argue that a reasoned insistence upon the primacy of the human subject must remain a responsible component of contemporary cultural studies scholarship, for the very reason that the work of people making things usually precedes the ability of things to make, or to influence, people. With regard to Edith Wharton's library, this means studying the ways that this particular collection or archive or trove has been *made by people* and, sometimes, doing some digging to find out who those people were and what roles they played in relation to its making. The people who therefore enter into all this talk about things include all manner of makers—from authors and readers (who make meaning from text in equal turn), to publishers, editors, bookbinders, booksellers, family members, friends, associates, teachers, preservationists, librarians, archivists, hobbyist collectors, appraisers, critics, students, and scholars. The full spectrum indicated by this list of different kinds of functionaries helps to show how textual artifacts are made, and how scholarship of the kind I am undertaking here requires an expansive and sympathetic understanding of the many varieties and means of production.

In order to ensure that kind of expansiveness, I have had to cobble together the pieces of a disparate methodological repertoire. My interest in fusing the methods of book history and media study with historical materialism, New Formalism, object-oriented ontology (or "new materialism"),[35] traditional close-reading strategies, feminist critique, and networked or vaguely "distant" reading practices, stems from my desire to achieve a more commanding view of the field that I have undertaken to study. Since my project privileges interactions between past and present—between old books and new readings, for example, or old archives and the people who labor and care for them today—it demands a kind of interfacing between new and old forms of critique, too. It should not, therefore, be mistaken as a contribution to the "pallid middle ground" that, according to critic Carolyn Lesjak, "tends to define 'reading' today," and which mirrors "conservative liberalism" in foregrounding a spirit of accommodation "to the given, to common sense, against the now discredited excesses of the theory years."[36] Lesjak convincingly characterizes the ongoing fight between New Historical–symptomatic reading strategies and "surface" or "distant" forms of reading as one of relational "extremes" that appear designed to "bring each other into crisis."[37] But she is too quick to locate the archive as a kind of middle (and, thus, depoliticized) ground in this fight, which she argues plays host to a brand of "middle reading" that is "neither new criticism nor Marxism."[38] The archive, like the library, cannot help but get swept up in larger political machinations by virtue of its status as a repository of capital. All capital, as Marx reminds us, is made by labor, and not by abstract conceptions of labor but the real labor of real human beings. An archive therefore must be viewed as a repository of labor, one that records a particular kind of history relating to processes of production and accrual. An archive is therefore not neutral but, rather, "human, all too human," to paraphrase Nietzsche, and exists only as a consequence, in many cases, of the combined work that has been done by generations of human laborers.

Given this formulation, I can't help but see Lesjak's arguments as doing disservice to both the archive and to the archival researcher. When she complains that the latter appears "middling and mousy," as devoid of a political consciousness, and as thus able to "adapt[] beautifully to the dictates of the neoliberal university,"[39] such mischaracterizations serve to devalue whole sectors of human investment and labor. And, even worse, they ignore the latent potential of the apolitical by casting it out of the larger political landscape altogether and by failing to acknowledge the role that it might already be playing therein. As an example, consider Benjamin's famous essays on the poet Charles Baudelaire, "a largely apolitical writer whose poetry we must nevertheless comprehend before we can formulate any responsible cultural politics of modernity," according to critic Michael Jennings.[40] Benjamin viewed Baudelaire as problematically apolitical, yes, but as nevertheless indispensable to our collective understandings of how life appeared within a crucial moment of world history. He was fascinated, for instance, by Baudelaire's treatment of crowds, which suggested, rather than mass politics and shared consciousness, alienation. "Baudelaire divorced himself from the crowd as a hero," Benjamin argues in his essay "The Paris of the Second Empire in Baudelaire."[41] Where writers like Victor Hugo celebrated the romantic potential of the crowd, Baudelaire sought to draw attention to the circumstances of his own detachment from it.

I have come to see Edith Wharton in much the same way, and this view has been reinforced by my interactions with her library. Like Benjamin in his analyses of Baudelaire, I acknowledge the political shortsightedness of much of Wharton's writing, and I take pains to draw attention to all the ways in which economic privilege might have caused her to overlook certain layers and segments of human reality. But also like Benjamin in his discussions of Baudelaire, I see Wharton as unavoidably connected to, though perhaps frustratingly sheltered from, some of the historical machinations of her era, particularly where modern discussions regarding the worth of learning, knowledge, reading, and information might be concerned. In Wharton, as in Baudelaire's poetry, such topics do not arise as the result of deep, "symptomatic" readings of the text, for in many cases they are overt, serving to organize and structure a given narrative, or else to distinguish characters and to lend moral weight to their actions. Such preoccupations appear telegraphed in Wharton's fiction because they likewise had a hand in structuring the world around her. Wharton gives us protagonists who are not "heroes" in the traditional sense but, rather, modern characters whose failures provide lessons in contrast. The various downfalls of characters like Lily Bart and Charity Royall thus connect to Benjamin's observation that "it takes a heroic constitution to live modernity."[42]

I employ a politics of contrast in my approach to reading Wharton's library as well as her work. There is nothing "middling and mousy" about that effort, though, nor is it the result of political negligence. Rather, my ongoing archival investigations, as I furthermore explain in the concluding section of this book, have been underscored and, at points, made more difficult by conditions of instability and by a certain flavor of neoliberal institutional precarity. The archive that I have been working with was barely an archive when I first encountered it as a graduate student, back during the summer of 2013: it was not organized or cataloged; it was not overseen by dedicated, full-time staff; it was in danger of being seized due to its parent institution's financial difficulties; it was underexamined and underexplored; and it was disintegrating—literally crumbling apart in my hands—after having been neglected and then improperly stored for decades. Indeed, my efforts in writing this book and my work on its sibling venture, the EdithWhartonsLibrary.org database,[43] have been animated by a spirit of preservation. I have been trying to help safeguard Edith Wharton's library to the same extent that I have been trying to figure out what it means, and only by interacting closely with its material components have I been able to arrive at an understanding of how to best go about doing either. While I take certain aspects of Lesjak's arguments to heart, then, I reject her characterization of the archive and the archivist as futilely occupying a sector of the political middle ground. It is my contention that the preservation of history matters, that preservationist efforts are not equally legitimized or supported by the state and its various financial appendages, and that what gets preserved is therefore nothing if not political.

My interactions with Wharton's library books have also served to rearrange my understandings of certain politicized hierarchies that relate to or else reflect some of our assumptions about literary prestige. When I first arrived on site at The Mount in the summer of 2013, I was constrained by feelings of awe for the subject I was researching—that is, for Wharton herself. But in working with this archive, I have come to know Wharton better as a human, and that has done much to soften and clarify my expectations of her. In learning more about her habits as a reader, for example, I have had to reckon with and to revise my understandings of her as a monolith and author. I have had to confront the specters of her stinginess and pearl-clutching (indicated, at points, by her placement of exclamation points in the margins of her books). And I've had to face certain unpleasant realities relating to her opinions and tastes, while learning to work through and interpret those realities based only on the evidence that has been made available to me through her archive. For instance, one might ask questions regarding Wharton's possession of an 1884 edition of Comte de Gobineau's *Essai sur l'Inégalité des Races Humaines,* an early work in the history of scientific racism, or eugenics. In that work, Gobineau famously "use[s] linguistic evidence to argue for racial differences," viewing race as the ultimate, explanatory component *of* human difference and claiming that "Aryans were not simply an ancient race, but the most 'masterly' and creative of races."[44] In her library at The Mount, Wharton retains volume one of what was originally a two-volume set edition of Gobineau's infamous treatise: it is custom-bound in marbled boards, with a morocco label affixed to its spine and one of Wharton's own bookplates (from the Sainte-Claire-du-Château, at Hyères) appearing on the pastedown. And it has been opened, though there is no evidence of markings having been added to the text. Did she read it? If so, to what end? The historian Daniel Pick points out that Gobineau's work was "little read" when it was first published in the 1850s, but that it was rediscovered at the end of the nineteenth century and "gave extreme expression to the view that historical degeneration was the effect of racial miscegenation, and the war was the moment where the weakness of the diluted race was exposed."[45] Wharton's personal outlook regarding the state of cultural "degeneration" that followed in the wake of World War I has been well documented:[46] we know that she regarded the Germans' aggressions as tantamount to a kind of cultural annihilation. Too, the inclusion of the Hyères bookplate (and the omission of a Land's End bookplate, which, if present, would indicate that she had owned the book for a long time)[47] suggests that Wharton may have acquired or else read this book in the years following the war. One cannot, therefore, help but wonder what her reaction to it was, then, given her status as a "social and philosophical conservative," in the words of Wharton scholar Alan Price.[48]

The inclusion of Gobineau's work therefore leaves a question mark hanging over aspects of Wharton's activities as a reader, as it does over other portions of her library. Part of my task, in working with her library collection, has been to decipher and to gain an impression of her habits as a reader, and this has meant coming to terms not just with her voracious and wide-ranging appetite for texts of all kinds but likewise with her limitations. Wharton was reading and buying books in the late nineteenth and early twentieth centuries—that is, during an era that saw the simultaneous rise of cheap print, on the one hand, thanks to more efficient technologies for producing wood-derived pulp paper, alongside the decline of linen paper and quality printing techniques. Being something of an aesthete, she favored quality bindings and linen paper editions, though I think it is clear that she did not collect for the sake of quality alone. As a consequence of those preferences, many of the books in her library permit easy access to her reading habits: we can tell if she read a book judging by whether or not its pages appear opened and have had their edges cut away from the adjoining, folded pages.[49] "Cutting" open a new novel was, after all, a hallmark of readership during this era, though the practice was on the wane. In *The House of Mirth* Lily Bart proceeds to "cut the pages of a novel" as she appears seated on a train in one of the book's opening scenes.[50] A prolonged inspection of these material aspects of Wharton's library helps us to see which books may actually have been read.

While Wharton's library offers up plenty of evidence of deep reading in the form of notes, marginalia, underlinings, and the like, so too does it point to more sporadic, less assiduous forms of interaction. For instance, in Wharton's copy of *The Discourses of Epictetus,* she has underlined a section of the text that appears on page 192 of the essay "Against the Quarrelsome and Fractious." The preceding sections of the essay, however, are unopened, with pages 189–92 appearing still laterally joined. What this suggests is that Wharton did not read the preceding material that formed the introductory parts of the essay, but that this nevertheless did not stop her from marking up a section on page 192 describing "counterfeit operations" in social discourse. It is not my intention to present this evidence as a smoking gun of any kind, but rather to draw attention to the variability of Wharton's behaviors as a reader and to argue, in connection with that variability, in favor of seeing her realistically as a consumer of texts. That realistic image is opposed to the way that many scholars and readers have tended to see her, as an austere paragon of self-education and self-discipline. But I have taken pains to show how the evidence is abundant regarding such realities: Wharton loved George Eliot, but her copies of both *Adam Bede* and *Romola* are unopened (though she may have owned others); ditto Flaubert, whose *Oeuvres de Jeunesse* contains many unopened sections, even though Wharton has added markings to his essay on Rabelais, which appears in the second volume; and in many cases it is possible to gauge the point at which Wharton abandoned a book, as with *The Ramayana,* which is unopened beyond page 185.

To this body of evidence, though, we must also consider all the ways in which Wharton's library speaks to histories of usage—by her, yes, but by others as well. Such histories may be ascertained not just with the help of marginalia and markings but via material additions and objects that appear "tipped in," to use parlance of the book-collecting trade, and inserted within individual volumes. Some of these additions appear throughout the ensuing chapters of *What a Library Means to a Woman,* but still others are so special and so idiosyncratic that they bear mentioning here. For instance, Wharton's books occasionally feature dried flowers that appear pressed inside the pages: one of my favorites is a four-leafed clover, desiccated and paper-thin but still intact after all of these years, that is incongruously stuck between the pages of John William Draper's *History of the Intellectual Development of Europe* (1899). Elsewhere, the title page of one work (Giacomo Liopardi's *Poesie* [1889]) appears tipped inside another (a volume from an 1813 edition of Swift's complete works), suggesting that it might have been used as a bookmark. A young Colin Clark, or possibly one of his siblings, has added blue crayon markings to several volumes. A fragment of pink ribbon has been laid inside the pages of Goethe's *Correspondence with a Child,* which is likewise heavily marked. A raffle ticket benefiting one of Wharton's wartime charities marks a page in a Tolstoy biography. Stamps, postcards, advertisements, and receipts spill forth from the random pages of random volumes (I found a charming advertisement for an 1899 Christmas sale at Brentano's Books in Washington, D.C., tucked inside a copy of *Don Quixote* that dates from the same year). And there is *hair*—some of it clearly human, some of it clearly not: for instance, in a copy of Lytton Strachey's *Queen Victoria,* a tuft of what can only be dog fur has become stuck to a place in the text where the spine has begun to separate and the adhesive binding is exposed. These objects comprise the subjective, animal detritus of Wharton's and others' interactions with this particular collection of books. Together they summon methods of understanding that go beyond textual interpretation and that call to mind, instead, modes of physical intimacy. And because they are sometimes created as the residue of human interaction—or else formed from parts of the human body, like hair—they do subjective work, acting as "dynamic agents of thoughts, speakers from the grave, commenting on their historical conditions of emergence and . . . exposing in advance the inadequacy of the models of reading we might use to explicate them."[51] Hensley's point here is that the reading of culture must not stop at the reading of text that appears printed on a page but must extend to encompass the reading of material and physical realities that surround and attend acts of textual production, too.

In the chapters that follow I have tried, in my reading of Edith Wharton's library, to convey a sense of two different realms of material reality: first, and foremost, the one in which Wharton herself lived, in the company of many, many other people at the turn of the century; second, the one that I have experienced throughout four summers of studying and interacting with her books, of spending my working hours in what was once her attic, kept company by the ghosts of the servants who, once upon a time, used to live up there. That second world appears like a photographic negative of the one that Wharton knew, with all its colors and shapes appearing inverted. And this situation is the result of a complex chain of events relating to processes of material preservation: The Mount, Wharton's historic estate, has undergone a series of continuous renovations over the past several decades, ever since it fell into the hands of the nonprofit Edith Wharton Restoration, who sought to reopen it as a historic site and museum in the 1980s. But these renovations have not yet extended to include the attic, since that area is off limits to the public, and it is there that the bulk of Wharton's remaining library books are stored. My experiences in the attic have thus been in keeping with Carolyn Steedman's claims about the nature of archival work, which, in her view, is all about dust, decay, isolation, and neglect. Steedman, taking her cues from the historian Richard Cobb, muses on the subject of the archivist as lonely, isolated flaneur, observing that "an extraordinary kind of aloneness emerg[es] in the Archive, when the Historian ponders on the historical subject who is most interesting to him."[52] During my summers at The Mount, that aloneness allowed me the time and space to get to know the archive and to become acquainted with the stories that, today, get told about it. These stories are the stuff of rumor and lore, but they are as much a part of Edith Wharton's library today as Edith Wharton was a hundred years ago.

Everyone who works at The Mount, for instance, has a ghost story. Two spaces in particular—the stable, which only recently underwent renovations, and the attic—seem to emerge as ready venues for these stories. This is likely because these spaces are, in comparison to the rest of the estate, alike in being rough, practical, informal, and out of the way. But what these locations also have in common are unglamorous histories of labor and usage: these are spaces where prestige and aesthetics break down and founder, and where we can glimpse holes and areas of oversight with regard to Wharton's detailed plans for her lavish estate. In the following chapter, I devote a fair amount of space and time to the formal, comparably more "public" space of the library, which Wharton also designed and which is situated in a sunny corner of The Mount's first floor, in an accessible location. But the fact remains that *my* interactions with Wharton's library—meaning her library *books,* and not the room—have largely taken place elsewhere, up in the attic. This is where the less savory parts of Wharton's library collection have come to rest and reside; this is where one discovers insects lurking inside archival boxes, damage wrought by "bookworms,"[53] and living mold colonies that lay nestled between pages. And the labor that I have undertaken there has, like that of the servants who lived there more than a hundred years ago, been largely invisible. It has been folded into the general operations of The Mount estate, and while it has not always been entirely solitary, it has been delectably lonely.

What often emerges from lonely forms of labor—and reading and writing are two preeminent examples—is an understanding of the contrasts and vicissitudes that govern human interaction. Edith Wharton's library survives as a record of human interaction that documents, among many things, varying degrees of kinship, intimacy, and love. We see that love, for example, in the caring inscriptions written by her father, her brothers, and yes, even by her mother, though Wharton has alleged that Lucretia Jones never encouraged her development as a writer; we see love in Wharton's copies of the books that were written by her friends and associates, too, people like Henry James, Howard Sturgis, Bernard Berenson, Violet Paget (and, of course, her lover Morton Fullerton); and we see the long arc of love and friendship represented through generations of successive ownership. Many of the books in Wharton's collection, for instance, feature her friend Walter Berry's "signature" custom binding (half-blue Morocco leather with marbled interior pages done by Stroobant's). And there are scores of books in her library that bear the marks of their previous owners—some of them still famous, some of them not, but all significant in their own right. I remember, for instance, when Julie Quain, who assisted me throughout successive summers on the EdithWhartonsLibrary.org project, opened The Mount's display copy of Wharton's *Italian Villas and Their Gardens* and discovered the bookplate of a deceased friend, the Wharton scholar Scott Marshall. When Julie held that book in her hands, I saw the essence of her relationship with its previous owner reflected in her physical treatment of it. In this way, and in many others, books in particular and libraries in general anthologize and curate the spectrum of our interactions with both the living and the dead. The meaning of Edith Wharton's library is thereby to be discovered only by means of varied and wide-ranging approaches to an understanding of what modern people mean to do, or to create, when they set about amassing hoards of physical objects. A hoard, whether it is the work of a single person or of an entire institution, represents an attempt to show how the stuff of human existence "adds up" to something.

1

....

The Library as Space
Self-Making and Social Endangerment
in The Decoration of Houses and Summer

> The meanings of places may be rooted in the physical setting and
> object and activities, but they are not a property of them—rather,
> they are a property of human intentions and experiences.
>
> —Edward Relph, *Place and Placelessness*

"INHERITANCE," WALTER BENJAMIN CONTENDS, "IS THE SOUNDEST way of acquiring a collection."[1] This proved true for Edith Wharton, whose father's modest "gentleman's library" furnished a basis for her own collection of books. George Frederic Jones died in 1882, when Wharton was just twenty years old, leaving behind a comfortable legacy for his three children.[2] Unfortunately for Wharton, though, this legacy was designated to be held in trust by Jones's male heirs—Wharton's brothers—the result being that Wharton herself saw very little of it. She succeeded, however, in wresting the bulk of her father's library away from her brothers, and this is no small feat when one considers that Wharton's brothers were both college-educated, whereas she never attended school in her life. Wharton varies in her descriptions of her father's collection, praising it, on the one hand, for granting her entry to the "wide expanse of the classics" and, on the other, naming it as the source of an educational "lacunae" on her part.[3] That "lacunae" was, as she saw it, shaped and defined by the dictates of a polite yet necessarily stolid brand of taste. Which is to say that Wharton's father's library was, like the other "gentleman's libraries" of his day, acquired with ownership and not utility primarily in mind.

Benjamin, in his touchstone essay on book collecting, exalts and sympathizes with the owner–collector, citing ownership as "the most intimate relationship that one can have to objects."[4] This is, in some ways, an odd point of logical culmination for Benjamin, as it gestures toward a collapsing of the subject–object dualism in a way that comes uncomfortably close to reification. But it's worth noting that Benjamin's concern lies not with the object or collection of objects per se but with relationship between object and owner. He explains this relationship via the rhetoric of inheritance and custodianship, stating, "A collector's attitude towards his possessions stems from an owner's feeling of responsibility towards his property. Thus it is, in the highest sense, the attitude of an heir, and the most distinguished trait of a collection will always be its transmissibility."[5] In other words, Benjamin is saying that the worth of a collection—most especially, a collection of *books*—may be measured by its ability to inspire custodial responsibility and concern in future generations. For Edith Wharton, the inheritance of her father's library signifies not only her willingness to assume responsibility for the items contained in that collection but also a form of validation. Wharton's own library grew from a collection of some two hundred-odd volumes bearing the inscription "G. F. Jones," and today those inscriptions salute and testify to a legacy of taste and cultural capital on her father's part. They speak, as Baudrillard tells us, in the tones of "an unconscious and triumphant discourse,"[6] with the "triumph" in question resulting from successful transmission and, by extension, prolonged existence. For what is inheritance but a plea for precisely this form of tribute?

It makes sense, then, to read Wharton's library collection through the lens of inheritance, and to consider the ways in which the collection might have been shaped by the particular concerns or standards of prior owners and prior generations. What's more, it makes sense to read Wharton's physical library at The Mount as an inherited space. This is in spite of the fact that Wharton designed the library herself, constructing it from the raw material *of* space. Wharton based her plans for her personal library at The Mount on two sources: her father's own library at her childhood home in New York City and "the best examples . . . found in France," as she explains in her 1897 work *The Decoration of Houses*.[7] But these two systems of influence, rather than competing for dominance within the space of the library, meld and intermingle in a way that can be summed up via Henri Lefebvre's concept of superimposition. According to Lefebvre, "Social spaces interpenetrate one another and/or superimpose themselves upon one another,"[8] which is to say that they speak to and summon associations with other spaces both past and present in a manner that compares to inheritance. These kinds of spaces, Lefebvre maintains, "are not *things*, which have limited boundaries and which collide because of their contours"; they are, instead, "social loci," wherein subjects and objects alike exist in "ambiguous continuity."[9] Lefebvre's arguments here descend from Michel Foucault's theorizing of spaces as "heterotopias" and from his point that, in the twentieth century, "space takes for us the form of relations among sites."[10] It is in this way that Edith Wharton's personal library at The Mount imagines a number of spaces like it, and a number of past and present libraries found in both public and private arenas. As a space, Wharton's library functions as a repository in that it protects and contains her father's books, but it also comprises a point of genesis in serving as the starting point for the procurement of her own collection.[11]

It's important to note, though, that Lefebvre's comments about superimposition refer specifically to "social space." Lefebvre labors in *The Production of Space* to define this particular quality of spatial relegation, which he attributes to those spaces that "contain[] a great diversity of objects, both natural and social, including the networks and pathways which facilitate the exchange of material things and information."[12] This description indicates that, for Lefebvre, the moniker "social" may apply to any space, be it natural or constructed, that has been transformed by social labor. Lefebvre later confirms this breadth of application, stating that, with very few exceptions, "any space implies, contains, and dissimulates social relationships" for the very reason that space "is not a thing but rather a set of relationships between things (objects and products)."[13] It would thus seem that a given space, regardless of its position either within the public sphere or within the confines of a private residence, is a *social* space so long as it "implies" and "produces," in Lefebvre's words, social relationships. Foucault, meanwhile, insists that it is in fact sets of legible social relations that become replicable and thus capable of being reenacted within superimposed space, rather than space itself. "We live inside a set of relations that delineates sites which are irreducible to one another and absolutely not superimposable on one another," Foucault asserts, drawing attention to the way that specific social requirements call for specific, and idiosyncratic, kinds of space. Yet this observation proves to be something of a straw man for Foucault, as he zeroes in on sites that stand "in relation with all the other sites, but in such a way as to suspect, neutralize, or invent the set of relations that they happen to designate, mirror, or reflect." Foucault labels these types of spaces "heterotopias" because, though real, they are governed by heterogeneous notions of the ideal—indeed, by fantasy.[14]

Wharton's private library at The Mount, I believe, is one such space. In fact, I want to argue that this particular library, this particular room, not only "implies" a rich history of social relationships enacted therein, but likewise continues to aggregate, stockpile, and accrue the evidence of social relationships still in the making. What's more, its ability to do this is unique; among the rooms at The Mount the library is, today, the only room that contains any of Wharton's personal belongings, making it the only room that retains the material residue not just of Wharton's public persona but of her actual person. Too, as I have already explained, it "implies, contains, and dissimulates" a wealth of information about the social substance of inheritance, since it offers material links between Wharton and her father (among other sources of inheritance). And, finally, though scholars have, in the past, primarily emphasized notions of privacy in Wharton's architectural and design schemes, viewing The Mount's library as yet another space designed by Wharton to "exclude" and to prevent the possibility of "interruption,"[15] it is clear that she likewise envisioned this space as catering to distinct social occasions and purposes.[16] Wharton designed her library with the intention of accommodating small groups of guests, regarding it as a quasi-public setting and a "background" to social discourse, much in the way that she viewed a properly decorated private library as a "background or setting to the books."[17] Her plans for it, in fact, rested on complex fantasies of communion and social intercourse, even more than seclusion.

It is for this reason that I approach Wharton's library in this chapter in light of these supposed binaries surrounding conceptions of public and private (or social and antisocial) space. I embark here upon a quest to "read the room," as per Gaston Bachelard,[18] and to expose the hidden social truths that saturate and define the space of Wharton's library. The process of uncovering those "hidden social truths" furthermore requires that I resist reducing the room to the level of mere metaphor. Rather, I pursue a kind of reading that aims to, in the words of Kate Marshall, "resituate[] . . . spaces and persons in the terms of communications and . . . attendant models of sociality."[19] Indeed, I want to argue that such a reading of this particular space yields a deeper and more socially aware understanding of Wharton's fiction and that we may, in fact, consider Wharton as an "author" of this space (and of the archive that it contains) to the same degree that we may consider her an "author" of her novels. I thus begin with Wharton's own musings on the authorship or creation of space—that is, with *The Decoration of Houses,* the design manual that she wrote in cooperation with the architect Ogden Codman Jr. (and also her first published work). I place my reading of the room in conversation with this text and also with a number of the private libraries that appear in Wharton's fiction. I then turn to Wharton's only discussion of the library as an established public space, focusing on her novel *Summer* (1917) and on her fictionalization of the Lenox Public Library as the initial setting for that work.

Wharton was an active member of the Lenox Public Library, which is still in operation today and located about a mile from The Mount. She served on its board, donated generously to it, oversaw the development of its catalog, and contributed books (including some of her own) for its circulating collection. Thus I conclude by offering an assessment of Wharton's relationship to the public library movement. In the early 1900s, thanks to wealthy individuals like Andrew Carnegie (whose summer estate, Shadowbrook, was located only a few miles farther down the road in Lenox), public libraries began to appear all over the United States, prompting both optimism and unease concerning the future of private library collections and the future of knowledge stewardship more generally. This unease animated much of Wharton's thinking about libraries, thinking that she channeled into two separate but correlated outlets—her book collecting and her fiction.

The Decoration of Houses and the Making of Space

Though she inherited the seed of her own library collection from her father, Wharton held the "self-made" library in high regard. To a great extent, even, she viewed the history of her own literacy and literariness in this light: in *A Backward Glance,* for example, she styles herself as an autodidact from the start, constructing a narrative of self-madeness that begins with her teaching herself to read.

> My father . . . managed to drum the alphabet into me; and one day I was found sitting under a table, absorbed in a volume which I did not appear to be using for improvisation. My immobility attracted attention, and when asked what I was doing, I replied: "Reading." This was received with incredulity; but on being call upon to read a few lines aloud I appear to have responded to the challenge.[20]

Irene Goldman-Price points out the "myth of self-making" that Wharton creates in this carefully manicured autobiography.[21] As Goldman-Price sees it, Wharton's correspondence with her long-standing governess, Anna Bahlmann, complicates this narrative of self-creation and puts pressure on Wharton's glib observation, "How I learned, no one ever knew."[22] The record of their correspondence shows how Bahlmann served as both a mentor and an intellectual companion to the young Wharton, overseeing her studies in both the German and English languages and in literature of all stripes. Why, then, all this insistence on self-madeness? Goldman-Price reasons that "Wharton's conviction about her intellectual and artistic isolation" likely "compelled her to deny her closeness to her teacher."[23] Furthermore, Goldman-Price reads Wharton's two published autobiographies *(A Backward Glance* and *Life and I)* as "deliberate attempt[s] to present herself as a literary orphan" on account of that fact that orphanhood itself "made for a better story."[24] Indeed, self-creation *does* make for a better story—particularly among American audiences, as Wharton demonstrates repeatedly throughout her fiction. Too, as the critic Andrew Piper reminds us, personal anecdotes surrounding a reader's intellectual development are often "shaded by a touch of hyperbole . . . Great readers have always read all the books."[25] From stories of "great reading," Wharton crafts an evidentiary basis, however thin, for her later triumphs as an author.

Accordingly, Wharton's novels offer up a successive retinue of self-made protagonists. These protagonists are often self-educated, or else they have been forced to develop an independent sense of appreciation for the education that was otherwise so readily handed to them. And, accordingly, they are often placed in the context of their (or others') private library collections. In *The Fruit of the Tree* (1907), for example, we meet John Amherst, whose job as assistant manager at the Westmore Mills aligns him with the working classes, and who lives in company lodgings, amid "poor monotonous houses, . . . trampled grass-banks, [and] lean dogs prowling in refuse-heaps" scattered along "the stagnant loop of the river."[26] In spite of its squalid surroundings, Amherst's house includes an ample library comprised of "crowded bookshelves": "There must be nearly a thousand of them," he tells his mother.[27] This is similar to Wharton's eponymous hero in *Ethan Frome,* who constructs a crude sort of library in the "small room behind the untenanted 'best parlor' . . . nail[ing] up shelves for his books . . . and a calendar with 'Thoughts from the Poets'" in an effort to mimic the study of a former educational mentor who, we learn, used to lend him books.[28] In Wharton's short novella *New Year's Day,* Lizzie Hazeldean marvels at her husband's private library, reflecting that "she had never before lived in a house with books in it."[29] After her husband dies, she inherits and maintains his library, even though she admits that the books, which she never learned to fully appreciate herself, have "lost their meaning . . . as most things have."[30] And in *Hudson River Bracketed,* Wharton gives us one final portrait of the self-made American literary aesthete: Vance Weston moves from Illinois to New York's Hudson Valley in pursuit of literary fame and there discovers the library of a deceased distant relative. Like Lizzie Hazeldean, Vance has "never been in a private library before; he hardly knew that collections of books existed as personal possessions, outside of colleges and other public institutions."[31] Yet this private library turns out to be the formative site of Vance's development as a writer.[32]

Throughout her fiction, Wharton rewards these aforementioned self-made characters—if not with actual success (for many of their stories end tragically), then at the very least with encoded forms of sympathy, esteem, and dignity. Wharton repeatedly pits these "good" and comparatively virtuous characters against a cast of shiftless dilettantes and philistines, all of whom either disdain books or reading or, worse, collect books in spite of their disdain for reading them. Percy Gryce in *The House of Mirth,* as I explain in greater detail in the next chapter, is an example of this kind of antagonist: he inherits his precious collection of "Americana" print materials rather than building it himself, and so earns his derisive treatment from Wharton. Likewise, in *The Fruit of the Tree* John Amherst's wife, after having been raised in a house that contained "a few morocco 'sets' imprisoned behind the brass trellisings of the library,"[33] cannot be persuaded by her husband's authentic love of poetry.[34] And in *Hudson River Bracketed,* the well-heeled Lorry Spear gauchely tells the bumpkinish Vance that books are made for collecting, not reading. "Personally I've never thought they were meant to be read. You can get all the talk you want—and too much—from live people; I never could see the point of dragging in the dead."[35] These characters are universally rich and, of course, universally hateable, and that is entirely the point for Wharton: she uses them to levy a critique against her own class background and milieu, separating and "orphaning"—to recall Goldman-Price's word for it—herself in order to affect the sort of distance that is so often a prerequisite to self-invention.

Wharton's 1897 *The Decoration of Houses* marks one of her earliest efforts at this kind of self-invention. She wrote the book with Ogden Codman Jr., a young architect who was just beginning his career but who would, years later, garner an impressive reputation among design enthusiasts. And though Wharton and Codman hoped the manual would serve as a guide for "those whose means permit of any experiment which their taste may suggest,"[36] they emphasize throughout *The Decoration of Houses* that money and good finances are not synonymous with good *taste.* This argument—which rises to the level of an incessant refrain in Wharton and Codman's writing—matches up with claims made by Edgar Allan Poe in an earlier essay entitled "The Philosophy of Furniture." In that work, Poe observes that all cultures and nationalities develop a shared sense of "taste" for which they are duly known but that Americans are unique in fostering a "preposterous" lack of taste. "How this happens, is not difficult to see. We have no aristocracy of blood," Poe explains, and so have fashioned for ourselves "an aristocracy of dollars." As a result, Poe argues, uncouth displays of wealth have supplanted the philosophical quest for taste: "we have been brought to merge in simple *show* our notions of taste itself."[37] What Poe is saying is that the American people, in lacking both extensive cultural history and the aristocratic ideals that are the perceived results of systems of hereditary transmission ("blood"), make do by spending as much money as they can—often in a vulgar, showy, and taste*less* manner.

Wharton and Codman similarly lament this state of affairs in *The Decoration of Houses,* taking pains to point out that taste cannot be bought. "According to the creed of the modern manufacturer, you have only to combine certain 'goods' to obtain a certain style."[38] But "style" itself, as the authors see it, is the endpoint of cultivated, restrained, and above all else proportionate taste. Taste and style alike cannot be bought because they are immaterial; they are not things in and of themselves but, rather, the products of perspective and cultivation made manifest via a system of habits. These habits can only be learned—from reading, from firsthand experience in the form of travel, and from studying the past. Throughout *The Decoration of Houses,* Wharton and Codman heap praise upon the practice of scrutinizing and understanding tradition, dismissing the tendencies of modernism that instructed architects to innovate and "make themselves anew rather than extend the long chain of the classical tradition," as John Barrington Bayley explains.[39] This disinclination toward independence and newness might seem at odds with Wharton's interest in self-creation and self-fashioning. But if Wharton believed in one's ability to educate and "make" oneself, she also believed that the best proscription for doing so included reading and entering into conversation with history and with tradition. The desire to make sense of tradition might have been, to some extent, prophylactic on Wharton's part, for she maintains a level of skepticism about tradition that runs throughout her fiction.[40]

In *The Decoration of Houses,* Wharton and Codman argue for a commonsense brand of adherence to tradition, observing that "to conform within rational limits to a given style is no more servile than to pay one's taxes or to write according to the rules of grammar."[41] And, even more interestingly, the two authors use labor and skill training—concerns that would appear to be beyond the purview of their class—to ground the claims that they make about tradition. In earlier ages, the authors point out, workmen "were trained in certain traditions instead of being called upon to carry out in each new house the vagaries of a different designer."[42] Wharton's sympathies might lie with the self-made "rugged" individual of American fantasy, but this does not prevent her from being a champion of programmatic forms of education and training. Indeed, one of her chief complaints against the modernist desire to "innovate" and "Make it new!" stems from the notion that innovation itself devalues labor and training.[43] As Bayley additionally points out, one of the most singular and lasting achievements of Wharton and Codman's interior design manual was its success in "kill[ing] off once and for all rooms in different styles in the same house,"[44] an American design trend that had, in the later decades of the nineteenth century, reigned supreme in connection with the credo of American "newness." The compulsion to innovate and experiment had, during this era, resulted in an American bourgeois fascination with stylistic eclecticism—gothic smoking rooms leading into chinoiserie parlors, and so on—which Wharton and Codman believed inhibited a decorator from practicing the "science of proportion" which is the "essence of great style."[45] Consistency, conformity, and proportion thus emerge as the moral of the story in *The Decoration of Houses*.

Wharton, accordingly, translated this abhorrent fear of architectural and stylistic irregularity into much of her fiction, most particularly in *Hudson River Bracketed*. Wharton takes her title for this, her second-to-last novel, from an architectural style[46] that was all the rage among the New York City elites who, in the late 1800s, erected summer residences up and down the Hudson Valley. For years, critics have drawn a straight line between Wharton's real aunt, Elizabeth Schermerhorn Jones, and The Willows, the fictional Hudson Valley estate that forms the initial setting of Vance's intellectual awakening in *Hudson River Bracketed*. Wharton's aunt owned a house in the Rhinebeck area of the Hudson Valley; Wharton visited it as a child and recounts her memories of its "intolerable ugliness" in *A Backward Glance*.[47] But while Wharton scholars have assumed otherwise,[48] it is nonetheless clear that the Schermerhorn Jones estate is not, in actuality, the basis for Wharton's The Willows. To begin with, Wharton's aunt's estate—called "Rhinecliff" originally and then "Wyndcliffe"—is built in the Norman style, with stone masonry and turrets, and so can't be classified as Hudson River Bracketed (also known as "Hudson River Gothic"). Rather, I believe Wharton's inspiration for The Willows (and, significantly, for the library at The Willows) came from an estate belonging to a neighbor of her aunt's. The Wilderstein estate, which lay adjacent to Jones's Rhinecliff, matches Wharton's description of The Willows

The Wilderstein estate near Rhinebeck, New York, which bordered Wharton's aunt's property and may have provided inspiration for The Willows in Wharton's novel *Hudson River Bracketed*. Photograph by the author.

in *Hudson River Bracketed* in featuring a "steep roof," a "jutting balcony," an "aspiring turret," an "ornate tower with a high shingled roof," exposed "wooden brackets," and "an arcaded verandah," with all of it "painted a dark brown."[49] Wilderstein, owned for generations by the Suckleys (who were kin to the Roosevelts), is likely what Wharton had in mind when she dreamed up The Willows.[50] Indeed, given that its own property bordered her aunt's, she would have likely seen Wilderstein when she was a young child in the 1860s, and then perhaps again in the 1890s, when she became reacquainted with the Berkshires and the nearby Hudson Valley through her purchase of The Mount.[51] This would have also been, significantly, the era in which Wharton was consulting with Codman in advance of writing *The Decoration of Houses*. Thus the Wilderstein estate, which epitomizes Wharton's complaints regarding architectural "irregularity," both within and without, may have surfaced as a case in point regarding how *not* to construct and decorate a house for modern living.

Regardless of whether Wharton ever managed to step inside of the house at Wilderstein, her architectural and design scruples would no doubt have told her what to expect therein. The Suckley family's private library at Wilderstein is, in many ways, representative of Wharton and Codman's comment that a "richly adorned room in which books are but a minor incident is, in fact, no library at all."[52] Inside the library at Wilderstein, one finds a dark, rigidly enclosed space that, thanks to some highly stylized stained-glass windows (complete with Gothic points at the top of their arches), affords very little natural light for reading.[53] A massive fireplace protrudes outward, imposing itself upon the small space, and the room's low ceiling (another one of Wharton and Codman's pet peeves) meets with highly ornamented walls, into which shoulder-high bookshelves have been set. The fact that the bookshelves do not extend all the way from the floor to the ceiling results not only in wasted wall space but in a surrounding perimeter of open shelves designed to hold not books but, rather, objects like photographs and knickknacks. On this point Wharton and Codman are very clear: "Nowhere is the modern litter of knick-knacks and photographs more inappropriate than in the library."[54] As Wharton and Codman see it, "knick-knacks," which are the American equivalent to the more worthy European objets d'art, essentially serve no purpose, since they are neither useful (as tools) nor beautiful (as art).[55] Elsewhere in *The Decoration of Houses,* the authors contend that "the simplicity and dignity of a good room are diminished by crowding it with useless trifles" (183) and that this very kind of "crowding" is itself the result of a failure to select and *choose.*[56] Taste is, at heart, nothing more than an informed and educated approach to the art of choosing, yet Americans, Wharton and Codman maintain, fail to choose and so are "apt to buy too many things."[57] I take this as a subtle yet perspicacious nod to the American tendency to hoard,[58] which Wharton and Codman label "the Western passion for multiplying effects."[59] Indeed, with regard to a space such as the Wilderstein library, Wharton and Codman would be quick to point out that an expanse of shelving is an invitation to hoard—that is, to accrue, accumulate, and over-crowd. But it's important to keep in mind that, when Wharton and Codman allude to a fear of hoarding in this way, that fear is itself the product of taste-based judgments. Which is to say, it is not the hoarding itself that is the problem but, rather, the way in which the space accommodates the hoarding of the *wrong* kinds of objects. There is, after all, little difference between a bookshelf and a knickknack shelf, save for the type of items that occupy each.

Discrepancies between well-ordered collections and anarchic hoards rest on the issue of premeditation. Plainly put, a bookshelf is a testament to intentionality, whereas a knickknack shelf is an appeal to accident and happenstance. Lydia Pyne, for instance, observes that "the bookshelf is how and where we create categories of knowledge and experience."[60] She suggests, in essence, that bookshelves invoke order because they are, in fact, designed with fantasies of order in mind. And with regard to taste and "choosing," as per the previous discussion of hoarding knickknacks, Pyne reminds us that "books, non-books, and everything present on book-shelves are there as the result of a series of choices."[61] Within the space of a library, be it public or private, bookshelves structure and convey a level of intentionality with regard to activity, use, and labor. At The Mount, Wharton put her bookshelves to work in defining and bracketing a space that was, in truth, designed for a very specific kind of activity: reading. To this end, Wharton's scheme for The Mount's library compares to Lefebvre's point that modern humans are induced to "fragment[] space and cut[] it up into pieces" in accordance with our assumptions about "the social division of labor."[62] The problem with this tendency, as Lefebvre sees it, is that it encourages us to see and treat space as *non*productive—"as space as such"[63]—rather than as a means of production. For space does more than simply reflect social relationships and hierarchies; it actively *produces* those relationships and hierarchies through practices of admission, exclusion, replication, and separation.

Wharton arrives at this same point in her 1925 treatise *The Writing of Fiction,* in which she argues that what was "novel" about the nineteenth-century realist novel was its ability to establish characters as the products of unique social arrangements and, yes, unique social spaces as well.

What was new in both Balzac and Stendhal was the fact of their viewing each character first of all as a product of particular material and social conditions, as being thus or thus because of the calling he pursued or the *house he lived in* (Balzac), or the society he wanted to get into (Stendhal), or the acre of ground he coveted.[64]

Here Wharton is making a Lefebvre-like connection between spatial parameters and social patterns, pointing out the ways in which these early realist writers sought to recreate the symbiotic relationship between "the house one lives in" and the life one lives inside one's house. Wharton intended for her library at The Mount to serve as a reading space in both a private and social capacity, but *not* as a writing or "work" space. Her décor and furniture choices furthermore proclaim and consecrate such distinctions between work and leisure. Before we can embark upon a reading of the objects existing within the space, though, we must first endeavor to read the space itself.

As a room, Wharton's library relies on the kind of "superimposition" previously described by Lefebvre in that it draws from and alludes to other spaces of its kind. The result of this superimposition is a kind of layering of elsewheres. The room invites one to imagine or else remember a multiplicity of additional spaces, to experience "a blend of memory and legend" that, in Bachelard's words, prevents us from "experience[ing] an image"—in this case, the actual room —"directly."[65] Indeed, even from the very start, Wharton imagined her library space via the lens of historical superimposition. She based her designs for The Mount on two other spaces: Raphael's plans for the Villa Madama, a masterpiece of Italian Renaissance architecture, and the English country estate Belton House (attributed, according to some sources, to Christopher Wren).[66] She avoided, as Fryer explains, both the "Villa in the Italian Style" that had formerly characterized Andrew Jackson Downing's work in the Hudson Valley as well as the "Hudson River Bracketed" (or hodgepodge Gothic) style that he would henceforth be known for.[67] But while Wharton praised Italian Renaissance architecture for its commodious affordances of space, light, and movement, The Mount's exterior ended up looking a lot more like Lincolnshire's Belton House than it did the Villa Madama, thanks to the addition of a cupola atop its roof. Too, Wharton copied the first-floor layout for The Mount directly from Belton House, which had, in the early 1800s, featured a library on the first floor, in the far northwest corner of the house.[68] Wharton chose to situate her library at The Mount in precisely this same corner, so that it might open out onto the surrounding terrace on two sides. The enfilade[69] arrangement of rooms on the first floor makes it so that two rooms—both Teddy Wharton's "den"[70] and the main drawing room—open into the library, making the space accessible and permeable on all four sides.

The permeability of the space, I believe, speaks to my earlier point about the room's inherent social qualities; though it was Wharton's intention that the library should be used for reading, she did not foresee that reading as being chiefly of the solitary sort. When Wharton gathered friends at The Mount—as she did often, inviting them in small groups— the library was often the center of activity, a background for conversations taking place with and about books, within a space that enabled discourse in the form of reading aloud. Henry James, for instance, observes as much in recording his experiences following a 1904 visit to The Mount. In *The American Scene,* James reflects upon the American inclination toward architectural permeability, remarking, "Thus we have the law fulfilled that every part of every house shall be . . . visible, visitable, penetrable, not only from every other part, but from as many parts of as many other houses as possible."[71] James is recording his own, intense reactions to the experience of superimposed space; he reads the rooms at The Mount not as enclosures but as designated points of access that enable a kind of allusory entrée to (and egress from) other spaces ("as many other houses as possible"). What's more, the rhythms of access and egress encourage, as James sees it, not only repose but also "conversation itself . . . the play of the social relation"; this combination of qualities prompts one to inspect the proscriptions and hierarchies of social discourse—the "dictates" of a given "social tone," as James puts it—that are necessarily at work in such a space.[72] This is another way of saying that these kinds of social spaces enable an inspection of the social means of production because social space is, after all, "a materialization of social being."[73]

As a case in point, let us consider a more recent example of how the space of Wharton's library at The Mount has been conceived and used. In August 2012 *Vogue* published an article about The Mount that sought to commemorate the hundredth anniversary of Wharton's novel *The Custom of the Country* via "recreated" scenes of habitation and leisure. An accompanying series of photographs, captured by the famed celebrity photographer Annie Leibovitz, featured actors posing as members of Wharton's milieu. Some of these "actors" were drawn from the literary world; the author Jeffrey Eugenides played Henry James and Junot Díaz played Wharton's lifelong associate Walter Berry. Other participants (Elijah Wood, Jack Huston, and Mamie Gummer) came from Hollywood, while the Russian supermodel Natalia Vodianova—a decidedly odd choice, given Wharton's own anxieties about her looks and her status as an author—played a limp and thoroughly lassitudinous Wharton, swathed from head to toe in lace and ruffles. In this and other respects, Leibovitz's photos get a lot wrong. They misinterpret life at The Mount as little more than a series of tea parties. Too, in most of the photographs the pale, waifish Vodianova appears dwarfed by her companions as celebrity stature and physical presence combine to push the fictional Wharton to the margins of each scene. Yet Leibovitz succeeds in getting one thing right: she imagines a scene that takes place inside Wharton's library as a *social occasion*.[74]

Leibovitz's photographs of the library showcase the dialectic of activity and indolence that James describes in *The American Scene*. Geoffrey Eugenides, playing Henry James, stands by the fireplace, reading aloud from Walt Whitman's *Leaves of Grass*,[75] while Vodianova, as Wharton, looks on and clutches a small papillon dog in her arms. Jack Huston, playing Wharton's irascible lover, Morton Fullerton (who, in real life, only visited The Mount once, and not while in James's company), lounges nearby in a velvet-upholstered chair. Leibovitz's insistence on natural light for this scene results in a dark composition, but that darkness is broken up by a diffuse, gray light that bleeds outward from its source, a set of French doors leading out onto the terrace. And even while the actors' expressions—including Huston's tilted glance, Vodianova's downcast eyes, and Eugenides's look of mild concentration—uniformly suggest *repose,* Leibovitz enacts a very busy scene in opting for a camera angle that is wide enough to take in the clutter of books, furniture, and assorted bric-a-brac. We see books scattered about the room, albeit in an orderly and respectful fashion (these are, after all, Wharton's own possessions, and Leibovitz does not force upon their arrangement a disingenuous air of carelessness or disarray). And though the scene is infested with the very kind of "knickknacks" that Wharton and Codman would have objected to, we see not one but multiple photographs on Wharton's desktop, as well as an ash tray, a cigar box, bundles of papers, and decorative lamps; the presence of these objects contributes to a sense of activity and visual commotion. The things in the scene combine to create what Lefebvre calls a "rhythm," in which "*things* matter little" yet succeed in both "divulging" and "concealing" "the production of repetitive time and space."[76] The space of the library appears to both permit and inhibit social intercourse, and Leibovitz herself amplifies this suggestion by positioning Wharton, Fullerton, and James (who, it is reported, was also attracted to Fullerton) within that space. The result of this triangulation and this mixing of idleness and activity is that we are forced to read the space itself as productive: something, the room tells us, is in the making here. The question is: What is it?

This nascent spirit of production is, I believe, consistent with the way in which Wharton viewed her library. She saw it as given to and destined for production, albeit production of a kind that she herself might not have been able to identify or name. This is because Wharton, when she began to dream up her plans for the library at The Mount, had only published one book, *The Decoration of Houses*; she had not yet begun to see herself, formally speaking, as a literary figure. That her plans for the space emphasize reading as production, however, point to the basis of an argument about the relationship between reading and writing, and between reading and *self*-production. To cite an example, in her later treatise on the craft of novel writing, *The Writing of Fiction,* Wharton links a programmatic commitment to style to both self-discipline and what she terms "self-consecration." "Style in this definition is discipline," she reasons, and the disciplined deployment of style is itself part of the act of self-fashioning.[77] Thus we can interpret Wharton's design choices for The Mount's library as a form of public proclamation: in adhering to a given style, and in designating the library as a sanctioned space for reading and social discourse alike, Wharton is both advertising and consecrating her habits as a reader and audodidact, and she is engaging in a process of self-authorship that is, in many ways, quintessentially American.

Indeed, the library is The Mount's most "American" room. In contrast to the rest of the mansion's interior, it highlights the use of domestic material: the walls are constructed from quartersawn American oak and the floor is parquet wood. This combination departs from the stucco walls and Italian marble floors that Wharton employs elsewhere inside the house. And while three of the four walls feature "plain shelves filled with good editions in good bindings,"[78] as per Wharton and Codman's directives in *The Decoration of Houses,* a fourth wall was, originally, covered with a Flemish tapestry. Wharton and Codman regard tapestries, alongside frescoes and quality paneling, as among the "three noblest forms of wall-decoration," since they are designed to function as part of (and not in addition to) the wall itself.[79] Wharton and Codman revere this level of intentionality in design because it speaks to permanence and imparts a necessary sense of history. It is, in fact, difficult to remove a fresco or a slice of paneling from its original context, as these forms were not designed with portability in mind. Thus, while Wharton's Flemish tapestry might not be American in origin, its presence in her library makes it so; the tapestry only exists in Massachusetts as the result of having been acquired and prized from its original, intentionally planned European moorings.[80] This kind of conquest and appropriation are furthermore entirely in keeping with the dominant narrative of the self-made American.

Themes of American self-madeness echo throughout the space of Wharton's library. The green marble fireplace, in particular, reinforces the relationship between self-making and conquest, with its carved fireback featuring Hercules in the act of slaying the fabled Lion of Nemea. Wharton and Codman reject the English practice (inherited by Americans, and employed in the library at Wilderstein) of allowing the mantel and chimneypiece to extend outward into the room, for the very reason that such a design results in excess shelving, and shelving, as we already know, leads to knickknacks and to hoarding.[81] The American "craving for knick-knacks," as the authors explain, "spread from the tables to the mantel" and "the use of the mantel as a bric-a-brac shelf led in time to the lengthening and widening of this shelf, and in consequence to the enlargement of the whole chimney piece."[82] Here the authors are in effect charging the American compulsion to hoard and accumulate with having destroyed, via imposition, the architectural integrity of a given space. They argue that such imposing fireplaces are not appropriately scaled to the spaces in which they are so often found, and so end up dominating the space and calling out for "the accumulation of superfluous knick-knacks."[83] The result is an endless chain of collecting and accrual wherein an American finds himself sealed away within the prison of his own collection.

Collecting is, furthermore, a profoundly antisocial act; through collecting, an array of objects is erected to stand between the collector and the rest of society, first replacing and then, eventually, nullifying opportunities for social discourse. This happens because, as Baudrillard points out, objects do not, in actuality, "speak." "This is why withdrawal into any all-encompassing object system is synonymous with loneliness," Baudrillard says—because "the discourse voiced through [the] collection can never rise above a certain level of indigence and infantilism."[84] Wharton, in essence, envisions and constructs a library space that discourages the collecting of objects in favor of the collecting of human *relationships*. She does this by insisting upon a space that is structured by only two forms of spatial arrangement: shelves for the accommodation of books and furniture for the accommodation of people. In the years to come, even as she developed into an understanding of herself as a professional author, Wharton would continue to limit her writing activities to only the most intimate space in the house: her bedroom.

In *The Decoration of Houses,* Wharton and Codman emphasize that the quasi-public environs of a private library have, in fact, come to be "regarded as a necessity of every gentleman's establishment" and every cultivated person's home.[85] That Wharton understood private libraries to be spaces of *privilege,* though, is nonetheless evident. In *The House of Mirth,* which Wharton wrote while living at The Mount, her protagonist, Lily Bart, views Laurence Selden's library in light of gendered privilege specifically, remarking, "How delicious to have a place like this all to one's self! What a miserable thing it is to be a woman."[86] The novelist Paul Bourget, a close friend of Wharton, would later characterize her as an "intellectual tomboy" who he saw as bent on transcending the dictates of gender privilege via self-education and intelligence.[87] Thus it's clear that Wharton perceived certain forms of privilege and "inheritance," to recall Benjamin, as being part of the equation where acts of self-making might be concerned. Not every American, certainly, could hope to lay their hands on these sources of privilege.[88]

It was with this insight in mind that Wharton, in the early 1900s, became active with the public library in Lenox, Massachusetts. She gave generously to it, and it gave to her in turn, inspiring the opening scenes of her 1917 novel *Summer*. In that novel, Wharton positions the public (or quasi-public, privately endowed) library[89] as a complex site of civic interaction, wherein social ties are negotiated through the lens of cultural capital. Yet her understanding of the public library as a site of social exchange was most likely informed—at least indirectly—by the experience of gendered exclusion. Prior to the rise of free public library movement in the late 1800s, private subscription libraries flourished throughout New England. These establishments, which charged fees in exchange for membership, often disallowed the admission of female borrowers.[90] What's more, subscription libraries were, as Richard Wendorf notes, a uniquely American invention. They were designed to combat the popularity of American circulating libraries, which were "often criticized for the shallowness and moral laxity of their book stock and customers" and which appeared to "cater[] to the frivolous and to the less educated."[91]

In opening pages of *Summer*, we glimpse Charity Royall within the space of the Hatchard Memorial Library. Charity does not own any books, and yet she has access to them. But access alone, as Wharton reveals in this novel, is not enough to surmount deficiencies of privilege. One must have or else must procure the cultural capital that is necessary to make use of a library's resources. Vance Weston, in *Hudson River Bracketed,* succeeds in doing this; Charity Royall does not. In both cases, Wharton suggests, the decisive factor has to do not with personal ability but with the support that comes from an existing social context or milieu. As such, we see that *Summer* reinforces the same kinds of claims that Wharton's private library at The Mount makes about discourse and social exchange.

Social and Spatial Dependence in *Summer*

The tragedy of *Summer* begins simply enough: Charity Royall exits the house of her guardian, "lawyer Royall," and proceeds down North Dormer's main street on her way to the Hatchard Memorial Library, where she is employed as librarian. But while the extent of Charity's ill-fated bildungsroman is slow to unfold in this novel, her tragic circumstances are clear from the start. Charity is an orphan, having been rescued at birth from conditions of dire poverty and "saved" by Mr. Royall, "who brought [her] down from the Mountain" and removed her from the community of backwoods "mountain squatters" into which she had been born.[92] Charity's status as an orphan is the first thing that sets her apart from the rest of her small-town community in North Dormer. The next is her occupation. As Wharton describes, "At three o'clock on a June afternoon," North Dormer's "few able-bodied men are off in the fields or woods" while the women are positioned "indoors, engaged in a languid household drudgery."[93] But Charity is not among the latter, just as Lucius Harney, the "stranger" whom she glimpses on the main street, is not among the former. Wharton thus begins her novel with the introduction of two social outsiders: an orphan and a stranger. Neither of these characters "belong" in North Dormer, and this lack of belonging forms the basis of their attachment to each other. Unlike Harney, though, Charity is fated to remain within the spatial confines of the North Dormer community, regardless of whether or not she "belongs" to it. The great tragedy of *Summer* is that she does not realize this—that is, not until it is too late.

Charity's naiveté results from a lack of education, social exposure, and training. Wharton imparts a biting and ironic tone to her characterization of Charity, who toils all day at the Hatchard Memorial Library in the company of books yet cannot be bothered to read or learn from any of them. This is because Charity has no conception of the "value" of books; she has not been taught to appreciate them, or to view the reading of them as worthwhile. Charity's view of culture includes "railway travel," "shops with plate-glass fronts," "cocoanut pie," the "theatre," and a ration of associations and images gleaned from a single outing to the nearby (but much larger) town of Nettleton. By contrast, she complains that North Dormer appears "abandoned by men" and "left apart . . . [by] all the forces that link life to life in modern communities" since it has "no shops, no theatres, no lectures, no 'business block.'"[94] Likewise, she dismisses the town's only cultural asset, the Hatchard Memorial Library, as being "a library for which no new books had been bought for twenty years, and where the old ones mouldered undisturbed on the damp shelves."[95] From this it's clear that "culture" is synonymous with newness in Charity's eyes, for the very reason that she has not been schooled in the art of tradition for tradition's sake, or in the "ideologies of tradition," as John Guillory calls them. And insofar as "a given tradition is much more revealing about the immediate context in which that tradition is defined than it is about the works retroactively so organized,"[96] we may furthermore read Charity's indifference toward books and reading as illustrative of Wharton's anxieties about the overall stability of these practices in the early part of the twentieth century.

Charity, in fact, rather embodies Bourdieu's account of the blithely desirous mondaine who enjoys culture without understanding it.[97] She recounts, for example, her attendance at a lecture in Nettleton where she "listened to a gentleman saying unintelligible things before pictures that she would have enjoyed looking at if his explanations had not prevented her from understanding them."[98] Understanding is, for Charity, an impediment to appreciation, while the dictates of cultural capital suggest that it ought to be the other way around. In contrast to Charity, Lucius Harney, the "stranger" on the street who is visiting a family relation in North Dormer (and who will, eventually, father Charity's bastard child), represents Bourdieu's conception of the "pedant who understands without feeling."[99] Charity reflects that Harney looks at her "as if he knew lots of things she had never dreamed of," and she jealously speculates about "vague metropolises, shining super-Nettletons, where girls in better clothes . . . talked fluently of architecture to young men with hands like Lucius Harney."[100]

Unlike Charity, Harney professes a deep and abiding interest in old things—architecture most especially, but books as well. Charity senses that these interests are "authentic," though she struggles to comprehend the meaning or purpose of that authenticity: "Charity had seen the letter from a New York publisher commissioning him to make a study of the eighteenth-century houses in the less familiar districts of New England." Charity, though she acts as Harney's tour guide on this venture, is subsequently puzzled by the whole "incomprehensible" business and cannot "understand why he paused enchanted before certain neglected and paintless houses, while others, refurbished and 'improved' by the local builder, did not arrest a glance."[101] Because Charity has been taught to value newness in lieu of tradition, she cannot fathom Harney's interest in the decrepit ruins of her native region. For Harney, these ruins act as repositories of tradition, as "places where the past, with its destinies and transformations, has been gathered together into an instant of the aesthetically perceptible present," in the words of Georg Simmel.[102] But to Charity, who dreams of "shining super-Nettletons," they are merely old.

This attitudinal clash forms the substance of an ever-deepening conflict in *Summer*—one that begins, significantly, within the space of the Hatchard Memorial Library. It is there that Charity and Harney meet for the first time, though, at first, Harney is so busy inspecting "the rows of rusty bindings" that he doesn't even notice Charity. He eventually does, though, and inquires as to whether or not the library keeps a card catalog. Charity's baffled reply ("A *what?*")[103] is a summation of the state of affairs at the Hatchard Memorial Library: the Dewey Decimal System, which debuted in 1876, would have been forty years old at this point.[104] Wharton herself would have grasped the indispensability of cataloging systems, too, since she herself had helped to oversee cataloging at the Lenox Library only a decade previous. But Harney is, tellingly enough, unperturbed by the Hatchard Library's lack of adherence to a modern sense of order; indeed, he's charmed by it, and tells Charity that "it's so much pleasanter, in a small town library like this, to poke about by one's self—with the help of the librarian."[105] As Harney sees it, order and utility ought not to be imposed at the expense of charm and quaintness. He is, however, troubled by the state of the library's books, which suffer from "worms . . . getting at them," from damp, and from neglect, though Charity maintains that this is not her fault nor her concern, even though she is the librarian. "Nobody ever looks at them," she reasons, so there is little sense in maintaining them.[106] She cannot comprehend the library's worth—not through the vulgar terms of exchange value,[107] via the logic of utility, or in the context of cultural capital.

All forms of value are, in fact, uniformly alien to Charity because she has little direct experience with the subject. Even when she enters into an arrangement with Harney, receiving payment in exchange for acting as his tour guide and pointing out old houses in the region, the money she earns is remitted directly to her guardian, Mr. Royall, on account of the fact that it is Royall's "property" (his horse and buggy) that Harney is renting. Harney is, of course, also purchasing Charity's time and labor power, yet she does not understand this, either; rather, she views it as an act of "unexpected" generosity when Mr. Royall "toss[es] a ten-dollar bill into [her] lap"—a ten-dollar bill that she has earned by working for Harney—and commands her to "go get [her]self a Sunday bonnet that'll make all the other girls mad."[108] In this scene, Wharton offers us a whiff of the circumstances of exploitation that bracket Charity's social existence and induce her to embrace what she terms "the sweetness of dependence."[109] Wharton's Charity is the very antithesis of the self-made, autodidactic, book-loving American. She has been conditioned to crave dependence, rather than to seek out the ingredients of independence through books and learning. Her name, even, is a testament to this sad state of dependence: Mr. Royall christens her "Charity" in order to "keep alive in her a becoming sense of her dependence"—that is, to remind her of *his* beneficence.[110]

Wharton's Charity, in appearing so thoroughly helpless a figure, is representative of a type: she is the very sort of person who may stand to benefit from public philanthropy and cultural enrichment—the kind offered by public libraries, say. But she is also a realization of Wharton's fears regarding the modern American culture's insistence on newness and its resulting impatience with tradition and with history. Such anxieties also appear on display in Wharton's own library, where the underlinings she has added to her copy of William Hazlitt's essay "On Reading Old Books," for example, additionally illuminate the modern individual's fraught relationship with tradition. Wharton places multiple marks alongside Hazlitt's comments that old books "bind together the different scattered lengths of our personal identity" and serve as "landmarks and guides in our journey through life."[111] Elsewhere, she also scores Hazlitt's arguments linking an appreciation for "old books" to a worthy human existence (a life lived "not . . . quite in vain").[112] When viewed in light of these selections from her archive, Wharton's philanthropic investment in the Lenox Library appears animated by a desire to save others—particularly the residents of rural regions like the Berkshires—from the "vanity" of a life lived in a state of intellectual, emotional, and educational dependence.

Undercurrents of noblesse oblige therefore help to explain Wharton's interest in the library, but she also had familial attachment to it. In 1871 the Lenox Library, already twenty years old, had received a new home, thanks to the generous support of Adeline Schermerhorn, wife of Peter A. Schermerhorn (the brother of Elizabeth Schermerhorn Jones, Wharton's aunt and the owner of the Rhinecliff estate).[113] Adeline Schermerhorn had purchased the building that had formerly served as the Berkshire County courthouse, and the Lenox Library Association was thus installed at 18 Main Street.[114] As a consequence of railway expansion, wealthy elites from Boston and New York City had "discovered" the Lenox area in the middle of the nineteenth century and established summer residences throughout the region. Adeline Schermerhorn was an early representative of that tribe, and her philanthropic doings with the Lenox Library preceded the Berkshires "building boom" of the 1880s that would draw thousands more to the region during the summer months. Wharton, along with her husband Teddy, purchased the land that would become The Mount in 1901, and the couple moved into the completed house in the summer of 1902, becoming part of the population boom that transformed Lenox from a town of 104 residents to more than 3,000 in the space of just a few years.[115] Wharton, like some of the region's other wealthy "cottagers" (which included Westinghouses, Vanderbilts, and Morgans), sought to inoculate the town of Lenox against the sort of cultural myopia that haunts the North Dormer community in *Summer*. She desired a well-funded and well-apportioned library, not for the benefit of the rich summer residents (they had their own libraries, after all), but for the rural poor who lived in and around Lenox and supplied labor for the likes of the Lenox Iron Works, the Crane Paper Mills in Dalton, the factories in Lee, and the cotton and wool mills located in Adams. Wharton was fascinated by the contrasts between rich and poor in the Berkshires. She built this fascination directly into *The Fruit of the Tree* and also into both of her short Berkshires novels, *Ethan Frome* and *Summer,* focusing exclusively on the lives of the working classes in both of these latter works. What these novels indicate, though, is Wharton's awareness of the lack of suitability of endowed, small-town public resources to the communities they are designed to serve.

No one in *Summer* uses the Hatchard Memorial Library, with the exception of Lucius Harney, who hails from New York City and so, clearly,

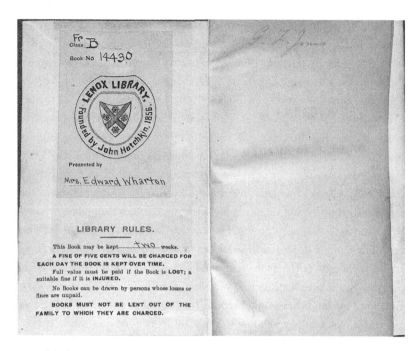

One of the books that Wharton donated to the Lenox Library, a copy of *The Letters of Madame de Sévigné,* in French. Wharton's father's signature appears in pencil on the fly, indicating that this book came from her own collection. EdithWhartonsLibrary.org. Courtesy of The Mount.

does not truly require access to its modest resources. If the locals do use the library, Charity tells Harney, it is not for its intended purposes. "Do you suppose anybody ever comes here for books?" she asks. "What they'd like to come for is to meet the fellows they're going with—if I'd let 'em." And though Charity concedes that she is unskilled as a librarian, admitting, "I don't know about books all I ought to," she is well versed in the social habits of the North Dormer community. That knowledge has inspired her to preserve the library's sanctity as a space, if not necessarily its contents.[116] Charity's tirade in this scene, in fact, suggests that what is truly lacking in North Dormer is consecrated *social* space. Public access to books and learning is well and good, but the North Dormer community, it is clear, suffers from a fundamental lack of healthy social discourse as a result of the paucity of public space. Charity enjoys access to only two spaces: Mr. Royall's house and the Hatchard Memorial Library. Her occupation of both of these spaces, though, is tenuous, dependent on labor and liable to be revoked. She earns her access to the space of Mr. Royall's home by working as his (unpaid) housekeeper, yet this labor affords her neither privacy nor protection.[117] Her situation at the Hatchard Library is actually quite similar: there she sits alone in her "vault"-like surroundings (where she is at least paid), as the result of having refused to cede the library space to inappropriate forms of social activity.

For Wharton, unused space of any kind—private or public—constitutes a sin against the principles of design. In *The Decoration of Houses,* Wharton and Codman insist on seeing space as subordinate to purpose in this way and proclaim, "A building, for whatever purpose erected, must be built in strict accordance with the requirements of that purpose."[118] Other early twentieth-century library enthusiasts agreed. Wayne A. Wiegand explains that "the commitment to providing community space" was a hallmark of the Carnegie free public library movement as well, and that a 1910 pamphlet outlining the six recommended designs for Carnegie libraries uniformly included plans for "a lecture or community room that many then used as an auditorium."[119] The trouble, as many saw it, with libraries like Wharton's fictional Hatchard Memorial Library was that they placed too much emphasis on books and not enough emphasis on *readers* as people occupying and using the space. Arthur E. Bostwick, in his 1910 treatise *The American Public Library,* laments this state of affairs in his introduction to that work, explaining that, whereas old libraries are too often seen as "storehouses," "the modern public library believes that it should find a reader for every book on the shelf" and that "this emphasis on reader as well as book . . . may be described as a process of socialization."[120] The Lenox Library, like other libraries during this era, was thus accordingly outfitted with large meeting rooms designed to accommodate public lectures, performances, and gatherings.[121]

What's interesting, though, is the way in which Charity's comments about the misappropriation of the Hatchard Library space subtly establish the average library "user" as *female.* The "they" of Charity's accusations refers to the young women who would come to the library "to meet the fellows they're going with." This is because it is women, particularly, who suffer in being denied the right to occupy space in North Dormer.

Throughout *Summer*, we see that Charity is constantly forced to commandeer space for herself, either out of doors (as when she lies on the ground with the "warm currents of the grass running through her") or in abandoned, out-of-the way places (as in the old farmhouse that serves as the site of her encounters with Harney, and of her eventual impregnation). These are the only spaces that are available to her without the complement of public scrutiny and surveillance. For Charity is in all other instances "instinctively aware that few things concerning her escaped the eyes of the silent man under whose roof she lived." This instinct summons a sinister premonition: Charity senses that, if she is seen as being too flagrant in her interactions with Harney, "Mr. Royall might . . . make her 'pay for it.' How, she did not know; and her fear was the greater because it was indefinable."[122] Here Wharton is offering a harsh indictment of the manner in which life for the female residents of North Dormer, as for so many women during this era, is organized and arranged by the dictates of the male gaze.

This is why all of the "users" of the Hatchard Memorial Library (including characters like Charity and Miss Hatchard, but also Orma Fry, Ida Targatt, and "the youngest Targatt girl")[123] are, in this novel, unvaryingly female: these women are fleeing surveillance. They might not be using the library for its intended purposes, but their presence in it is nonetheless consistent with a modern trend that, in the early 1900s, saw female borrowers as constituting the bulk of public library patrons. As Wiegand points out, women overwhelmingly frequented public libraries more than men, though this was often assumed to be the result of the public libraries' unwillingness to cater to men's particular tastes.[124] Whereas the subscription and membership libraries of yesteryear had operated more or less like men's social clubs, public libraries had, by the turn of the century, become female-dominated spaces. Consequently, when Wharton joined the Associate Board of Managers of the Lenox Library in 1902, she found herself on an all-female oversight committee for a library that employed a staff of entirely female librarians.[125] Wharton became a prominent supporter of the library during this time, donating an average of $40 (equivalent to approximately $1,100 today) per year to the library as well as "new carpets and books" and "furnishing a clubroom for French-speaking residents of

The Lenox Library in Lenox, Masschusetts, the basis for the Hatchard Memorial Library in Wharton's *Summer*. Wharton's description of the building's "temple-like" attributes reflects the Greek revival style of its architecture. Photograph by the author.

Lenox."[126] Her descriptions of the Hatchard Library in *Summer* additionally reveal that she based her conception of it on the Lenox Library's real edifice.

In Wharton's version, the library appears as a "queer little brick temple with white wooden columns supporting a pediment on which was inscribed in tarnished gold letters: 'The Honorious Hatchard Memorial Library, 1832.'"[127] Once inside it, Charity hangs her hat on a plaster bust of Minerva and proceeds to open the shutters. But Wharton mounts a subtle critique in *Summer* of the building (which, as I previously mentioned, was not designed to house a library in the first place). The Hatchard Library's interior, we learn, is a singularly depressing space; Charity calls it a "prisonhouse," yet Harney reasons that the place's faint, mausoleum-like vibe results from poor maintenance and a lackadaisical interior design scheme, and not from a fault in the architect's original plans for the space. Harney takes in the "melancholy penumbra of the long narrow room," which includes "blotched walls," "discoloured rows of books," and "stern rosewood desks," and at length he tells Charity that the library need not be as depressing as it seems. "Of course it's a bad job to do anything with a building jammed against a hill like this ridiculous mausoleum; you couldn't get a draught through it without blowing a hole in the mountain. But it can be ventilated after a fashion, and the sun can be let in."[128] Harney is ventriloquizing Wharton and Codman's arguments about the importance of interior, not just exterior, planning when it comes to shaping a space with a desired function or purpose in mind. Harney is supposed to be an architect, yet the recommendations that he makes to Miss Hatchard on behalf of the library apply entirely to interior design and concern, for the most part, simple modifications to window treatments, ventilation, and lighting. Wharton is suggesting, in effect, that the community's disinterest in using the library space for *reading* is related to a series of interior design choices that have, collectively, conspired against this very application or activity.

This is no doubt why so much of Wharton's involvement with the Lenox Library centered on modifications to its interior space (carpets, furniture, etc.). Though Wharton also collaborated with library staff to oversee the library's catalog project during the summer of 1902, it is nonetheless evident that she believed that a useful public resource like a library must begin with a usable public space. Wharton continues to develop this point in *Summer,* suggesting that, if Charity had only been granted access to usable space of this kind—in particular, to a space designed to accommodate social discourse in addition to reading and individual contemplation—she might have, in turn, developed an appreciation for the intellectual pursuit of reading, and things might have turned out differently for her. For instance, Charity might have been prompted to take down Thomas Hardy's *Tess of the D'Urbervilles* from the shelves of the Hatchard Library, and instead of spending her time crocheting a "half-yard of narrow lace which she kept wound about the buckram back of a disintegrated copy of 'The Lamplighter,'"[129] she might have opted to read Hardy's novel. Therein, she might have gained useful exposure to a story that reads very much like her own—a story of a young, impoverished woman who is deceived by a wealthy rake and then saddled with the consequences of their sexual union. For indeed, Wharton admired Hardy's *Tess* and grafted some of its narrative onto her own in *Summer.*[130] Had Charity managed to read it, she might have thought twice about trusting Lucius Harney. But as a space the Hatchard Library works against this impulse and brings us back to Lefebvre, who argues that space "speaks" in terms of "dos and don'ts" and that, "above all, it prohibits."[131] As a space, the Hatchard Memorial Library, as we have seen, in fact prohibits both social interaction and intelligent introspection: it does this primarily by "speaking" to Charity through the language of deadness, disuse, and neglect. As the building is neglected so are the books inside it neglected, with the result being that proper use of the space is, in turn, neglected even while alternative uses are prohibited.

All of this amounts, for Charity, to feelings of entrenched futility, for, as she puts it, "It's no use trying to be anything in this place."[132] In fact, Wharton suggests from the very start in *Summer* that Charity's journey is to be a cyclical one and, for that matter, a failed one, too. At the beginning of her novel, we see Charity exiting Mr. Royall's house, proclaiming that she "hate[s] everything!" about her life in North Dormer, and at the end of the novel Wharton returns us to this very scene, with Charity and Royall entering Royall's "red house" underneath "cold autumn moonlight" as man and wife.[133] It is a depressing conclusion, but it is not, Wharton argues, an inevitable one. Rather, it is one that can be obviated by means of education and exposure, particularly where women are concerned. Libraries, Wharton contends, can become spaces of social transformation and "self-making" for women, but only if they are designed with these potentialities in mind.

Endangered Futures: Public and Private Libraries in Early Twentieth-Century America

I began this chapter with Benjamin and with his assertion that inheritance is the most secure route of acquisition where a library is concerned. Benjamin formed this and the rest of the statements found in his essay "Unpacking My Library" in the early 1930s. During that time, he was also working on *The Arcades Project,* his experimental and genre-defying collection of observations aimed at dissecting modern living and modern life. The link between Wharton and Benjamin might appear, at first glance, like an unconventional one, and yet it is clear to me that these two writers were similarly preoccupied with the storage, housing, function, and care of libraries, and with the future of print-based information more generally. In the 1930s Wharton, by then in her seventies, reunited with her old friend Ogden Codman Jr. Though a major fight had stymied relations between them a few decades earlier (while they were both overseeing construction at The Mount), they succeeded in patching up their relationship and, in 1936, embarked on a project to update, edit, and re-release *The Decoration of Houses.* Wharton, it seems, had returned full circle and was revisiting her schematics for design and decoration even while, an ocean away, the United States was in the midst of a depression that would see the fields of art and design modernized, rationalized, and "stripped of their sheaths." One wonders what kinds of "updates" Wharton and Codman might have made had their revisions not fallen short of their conclusion: Wharton suffered a heart attack in 1937, while staying as a guest at Codman's country estate in France, and she died a few months later.

The link between Wharton and Benjamin, though, is strengthened if we situate their anxieties about libraries and print knowledge within this joint temporal context. Both, it is clear, wanted to study the past and to examine the social, cultural, and actual "architecture" that, previously, shaped the spaces of history. And both, I believe, were prompted to do this because they viewed those spaces as increasingly under threat. Benjamin ruminates on this very subject in *The Arcades Project* when he considers the "connection between the shrinking of residential space and the elaborate furnishing of the interior." For help on the subject he turns to Balzac, who he quotes as saying, "Small pictures alone are in demand because large ones can no longer be hung. Soon it will be a formidable problem to house one's library."[134] The correlation, of course, between large portraits and the storage of books has to do with wall space, and in the modern century Benjamin saw wall space located within the private home as having been tragically truncated. Benjamin's observations on this subject link up with Wharton and Codman's observation that "the housing of a great private library is one of the most interesting problems of interior architecture." Instead of corroborating what Wharton and Codman prophesize in *The Decoration of Houses*—that the "great private library" is, in America, "still so much of a thing of the future"[135]—Benjamin's statements confirm that the private library is, to a very great extent, already a thing of the past by the start of the 1930s.

Indeed, one could argue that private library spaces were, at least in America, already endangered when Wharton and Codman published *The Decoration of Houses* in 1897. Design historians, for example, attach the name of Elsie de Wolfe (who, according to *The New Yorker*, "invented" the profession of interior design)[136] to Wharton and Codman. De Wolfe's very popular tract on modern interior design, *The House in Good Taste*, appeared in 1913, a full fifteen years after *The Decoration of Houses*. But while *The Decoration of Houses* purportedly inspired *The House in Good Taste*, there are marked differences between the two works. Notable among them is the fact that de Wolfe's "house" does not contain a library. Instead, de Wolfe treats books as she might any other household item. And rather than preserving the "separation of labor" and the specific functions of specific rooms, de Wolfe encourages readers to combine and merge spaces. "Why not make [the dining room] a dining- and book-room, using the big table for reading, between meals, and having your bookshelves so built that they will be in harmony with your china shelves?"[137] It is a suggestion that seems engineered to draw shudders from the Wharton and Codman camp, for it strips books of their special status as useful objects and demotes them to the level of that most abhorrent of household items, the knickknack.[138]

The dwindling concern for private library spaces is demonstrative, of course, of the dwindling demand for private libraries more generally. At

the turn of the century, Pyne points out, Americans' interests were shifting in favor of institutionalized library collections over the enhancement
and growth of one's personal hoard of books. So great was the institutional investment in accruing wealthy individuals' private collections that
"libraries—particularly institutional libraries like the Library of Congress,
New York Public Library, or any university library—were acquiring books
and materials at a rate that some librarians considered unsustainable."[139]
By the time de Wolfe's *The House in Good Taste* was published in 1913, the
private, home library, if it was valued at all, was valued not as a possession
but, chiefly, as a commodity. Book collecting as a sport rose in popularity for a time as well-endowed collectors scrambled to pick up rare and
first editions in the hopes of later selling off their collections to university
libraries for profit, or else bequeathing them for posterity. But what this
moment of institutional fervor additionally suggests is that by 1913 the
age of the well-loved, well-used, and thoughtfully curated home library—
the library for the library's sake, as it were—was closer to its end than its
beginning.

In spite of their enthusiasm for the expansion of institutional library
systems, then, both Wharton and Benjamin register levels of anxiety
concerning the death of the private collector's library. Benjamin, for one,
names this anxiety outright, stipulating that "the phenomenon of collecting loses its meaning as it loses its personal character. Even though public
[library] collections may be . . . more useful academically than private collections, the objects get their due only in the latter."[140] Benjamin is mourning the loss of a particular kind of closeness and pining for the experience
of controlled intimacy between a person and their possessions—that is, between subject and object. A personal library, as Benjamin sees it, stands as a
record of one's mental development, character, and habits, and while public
libraries may grant their patrons access to reading material and educational
advancement, they cannot grant them such experiences of intimacy, introspection, and "responsibility," to recall Benjamin's earlier point about
ownership. What's more, Benjamin discerns a direct connection between
the expansion of public libraries and the diminishment of that personal
responsibility, so far as books are concerned: as institutionalized collections
grow, the impetus to collect and to take responsibility for one's own collecting appears to shrink. The result is that Benjamin, as a devoted bibliophile,

is conscious of feeling "behind the times" and, possibly, faced with the moment of his own extinction. He credits this feeling of personal endangerment, though, with allowing him to see himself and his habits all the more clearly, arguing that only in extinction is the collector comprehended."[141] This statement is illustrative of Benjamin's willingness to conflate collector and collection, and also of his anxiety regarding the fate of both subject and object: only when faced with extinction is he, as a collector, able to comprehend himself and his desire to collect; only through extinction will he, as subject, be made legible to the world via this collection of objects. This is because the modern world is, according to Benjamin, increasingly a universe of things, not people; modern living makes the concerns and experiences of people subordinate to the housing of things.[142] Where the private collection once stood for and signified a person, its owner, the public collection stands for and signifies only itself as repository, hoard, or stockpile. Just as the bank houses and controls one's wages, separating the alienated laborer from the products of his or her work, the institutionalized library houses and controls records of human thought and creation, granting temporary access to them but prohibiting intimacy and sustained discourse *with* them.

This is how Benjamin sees it, at least. But Baudrillard speaks to this subject–object rivalry, too, warning that the collector, in allowing the collection to stand "for" and signify himself, is doomed to disappointment, alienation, and loneliness from the start. "It is because he feels himself alienated or lost within a social discourse," Baudrillard says, "that the collector is driven to construct an alternative discourse that is for him entirely amenable."[143] The collector's relationship with his collection thus comes to define him, in Baudrillard's view, the result being that the collector who speaks of his collection speaks merely of himself. Yet the level of discourse that the collector imposes upon the collection (in an effort to make it "speak" *to* his loneliness) is marked by a kind of infantilism—that is to say, it is based on immature standards of emotional attachment, including base sentiment, jealousy, and a childish quest for control.[144] It is with these limitations in mind that Baudrillard asks, "Can objects ever institute themselves as a viable language? Can they ever be fashioned into a discourse oriented otherwise than towards oneself?"[145] He stops just short of furnishing answers to go along with these questions, but one might go looking for them within the discourse of what Benjamin himself has labeled inheritance and "transmissibility."

One might question, for example, why Edith Wharton, who had no children and so lacked "heirs" in the traditional sense, didn't simply will her library to an academic institution, or to the Lenox Library, for that matter. Was it because she was trying to bequeath the experience of being a "real collector" and the blessings of "ownership," to paraphrase Benjamin, on members of a future generation? Or was it because she feared that her collection would, if added to the ranks of the Lenox Library's materials, end up resembling the Hatchard Memorial Library in *Summer* and languishing in disuse? In fact, I would argue that, if we defer to Baudrillard and view the collection as a form of "speech," then concerns for audience and for the intended recipients of that "speech" are necessarily forthcoming: in order to speak at all, the collection must speak to someone. As such, we can see Wharton's decision to will the two halves of her library to two young, distantly related male heirs as heavily influenced by assumptions about audience. Both William Royall Tyler and Colin Clark were born to wealth and prestige, but, even more than that, their fathers were notable collectors: William Tyler's father, Royall,[146] was a famed collector and connoisseur who had developed a renowned eye for quality and detail—an eye that he put to use in helping Mildred and Robert Woods Bliss establish their now-famous collection of pre-Columbian art at Dumbarton Oaks. Likewise, Colin Clark's father, Kenneth Clark, the famed British art historian and television personality, was described upon his death as being "a critic of immense intelligence and of unfailing discrimination" and as occupying a "role in the modern world [that] was comparable to that of Ruskin in the nineteenth century."[147] Thus, it stands to reason that neither William Tyler nor Colin Clark, given their fathers' reputations and vast resources, really *needed* the books that Wharton willed to them. Rather, I think it's clear that Wharton needed Tyler and Clark to serve as her audience, to hear and receive the messages conveyed by her collection. Wharton needed them to serve as the joint stewards of her collection because, in an age of waning interest in private library collections, she saw these boys as having inherited a rare and somewhat outmoded appreciation for the art of collecting.

But Wharton and Benjamin's shared anxieties about the future of book collecting turned out to be, to a very great extent, legitimate. For instance, as I previously explained in the book's introduction, William Tyler neglected his half of the collection, depositing it in a storage unit in London in September 1938, shortly after acquiring it. In November 1940 the warehouse containing the collection was destroyed by enemy fire during the London Blitz. Tyler went on to claim compensation in exchange for the destroyed collection, receiving "between £800 and £900."[148] But one can't help but notice that, prior to its being destroyed, the collection sat neglected in a warehouse for more than two years. Too, Tyler explains that, during that interim, he did not have time to catalog the collection properly and so did not know what was in it and could not provide an accurate assessment of its value when submitting his insurance claim some years later. And according to George Ramsden, Clark's portion of the collection also suffered—in this case, from inattention. Some of Clark's books were destroyed by fire while others fell prey to "dampstain," the result of having been stored at the family's rural estate, Saltwood Castle.[149] While these circumstances might not amount to wholesale disinterest on the part of Wharton's heirs, they do indicate a certain level of heedlessness.

That heedlessness was not personal, though, and it was not limited to the likes of Tyler and Clark. Rather, I think we can view it as a sign of the times. When these two men were born (Tyler in 1910, Clark in 1932), the age of mass-market print was already well underway, a circumstance that likely contributed to the cavalier attitudes with which they—and, in Clark's case, their families[150]—viewed the objects of their inheritance. The steady development of more cost-effective printing technologies, along with the expansion of paperback ("unbound") books, meant that early-twentieth-century readers were not often prompted to take protective measures concerning their books; they no longer felt compelled to invest in custom bindings or appropriate means of housing their collections, despite the fact that those same cost-effective technologies had hastened what Thomas R. Adams and Nicolas Barker term a "decline in durability." Indeed, cheaply produced books, where the "cover often costs as much as the text within it,"[151] had become the norm by the 1930s, with the result being that Tyler and Clark didn't see their inherited collections as particularly *valuable,* or as requiring any kind of specific care. Tyler, as previously noted, argues in his 1985 letter to Ramsden that Wharton "was not a bibliophile" for the very reason that her collection did not appear to be worth very much, suggesting that the true test of bibliophilia comes not from utility and care but, rather, from resale value. This is, however, entirely at odds with Jacques Bonnet's description of the bibliophile who, ever aware that books are "expensive to buy and worth very little if you try to sell them," collects anyway, compelled by a kind of obsessive love for the objects themselves and a blatant disregard for the logic of value.[152]

What unites Wharton and Benjamin, then, is their shared status as members of a disappearing class of devoted collectors. From their writing, it is apparent that both Wharton and Benjamin dwell among and through their books, viewing their library collections not only as extensions of their selves but as ambulatory homes or vessels for the housing of the self. Wharton declined the opportunity to name an institution as the inheritor of her library collection because she was banking on the hope of remaining "legible" to the world—to use Benjamin's word for it—through the eyes of a new generation of bibliophiles. But what the fate of her library collection makes painfully clear is that that new generation failed to fully materialize. Indeed, the threat of "extinction" that both Wharton and Benjamin perceived in the 1930s continued to grow throughout the twentieth century, and it is still with us today (even if bibliophiles are, proportionately speaking, not). Bonnet's 2006 *Phantoms on the Bookshelves,* for example, reads like a eulogy for the practice of bibliophilia, in its death throes now for almost a century. "A tide is coming in and the kingdom of books, with their white pages and endpapers, their promise of solitude and discovery, is in danger . . . of being washed away," James Salter opines in his introduction to Bonnet's book.[153] Likewise, Bonnet warns that such "unwieldy personal collections of a few tens of thousands of books are likely to disappear, taking their phantoms with them. *[Phantoms on the Bookshelf]* is being written from a continent which is about to be lost forever."[154] In both cases—that is, in Benjamin and Wharton's moment of public libraries and institutional expansion, and in Bonnet's post-2000s world of digital texts and apathetic readers—what these authors fear most is the loss of the library as a home for the housing of the self, as opposed to an impersonal site for the housing of information and content.

In Benjamin's *The Arcades Project,* he offers an extended rumination on the meaning of the verb "to dwell," the very conception of which, he argues, was a nineteenth-century invention. "The original form of all dwelling is existence not in the house but in the shell. The shell bears the impression of its occupant. . . . The nineteenth century, like no other century, was addicted to dwelling, [to conceiving] the residence as a receptacle for the person."[155] Benjamin and Wharton, both born in the nineteenth century, can be viewed jointly as reacting to the distress of living through the changes that modernity wrought to the experience of dwelling within space. Wharton's first response to that trauma was an attempt to consecrate and bolster the logic of nineteenth-century, indwelt space: both *The Decoration of Houses* and her designs for The Mount are, in their own ways, monuments to inherited spatial traditions. Next she turned to fiction, devising her novels with a clear sense of architectural form (the "house" in *The House of Mirth* and the references to architecture in *Hudson River Bracketed* being two clear examples). But for Wharton, as for Benjamin, space in the twentieth century proved traumatic, not just in its diminishment and its curtailment but, even more significantly, through the fact of its instability. Both Wharton and Benjamin lived through the era of the First World War, wherein the boundaries marking national space were dramatically redefined and contested; what's more, they both became exiles, with Wharton, in 1911, moving to France in order, in part, to secure more leverage in her divorce from Teddy Wharton[156] and Benjamin emigrating from Germany to France and, later, Spain in the aftermath of Hitler's rise to power.

Both Wharton and Benjamin thus experienced, on a personal level, the weight of Benjamin's observation that "the world of the shell" was, in the early twentieth century, "unsettled in a radical way," with dwelling itself becoming "diminished"—"for the living, through hotel rooms; for the dead, through crematoriums." Benjamin continues to develop this point in *The Arcades Project,* defining the process of dwelling as "ha[ving] to do with fashioning a shell for ourselves."[157] For Benjamin, such a shell affords not only separation and protection but also conforms and grows around the self, furnishing a material reminder of one's indisputable materiality. This is what Wharton was trying to achieve when she built her library at The Mount: she was trying forge the material proof of her own existence. The tragedy is that, in the end, it proved impermanent. Wharton's husband arranged the sale of the property in 1911, while she was away in France (though this result constitutes, in many ways, the best possible outcome;

Bookplates found in Edith Wharton's books at The Mount that correspond to three of her private residences: Land's End, Pavillon Colombe, and Saint-Claire-du-Château. Photographs by the author. Courtesy of The Mount.

she would have lost it anyway in the ensuing divorce). In fact, throughout the three decades following her departure from the estate, Wharton's library *books* seem to have been, if not the only, then certainly a primary source of consistency and material stability for her.

Today the books in Wharton's library offer up a mobile record of her movements, proclaiming each of her addresses in turn via a system of custom bookplates. Wharton's bookplates track her journey from Land's End, the first home that she shared with Teddy Wharton in Newport, Rhode Island, to Pavillon Colombe, her home in the Parisian suburbs, to Sainte-Claire-du-Château, the former medieval convent that became her house on the French Riviera. Her collection does not include a bookplate for the library at The Mount, though: she never had one made, a fact that constitutes, in my view, a telling omission. Wharton never designed a bookplate to identify her books at The Mount because she likely never imagined that she would leave that residence, or that her books would depart the space that she had so conscientiously designed for them. Wharton, in other words, believed that she, like her library, had come "home" to The Mount when she laid out her designs for it. That she so assiduously adopted the practice of adding bookplates to her volumes after she left The Mount is a testament to the shock of impermanence that she must have registered upon her exodus from Massachusetts (and, indeed, from the United States more generally) in 1911. Henceforth, understanding both modern space and modern "dwelling" as impermanent and thus highly volatile, Wharton, like Benjamin, came to see her books and personal library as not only an origin of the self, to recall the previous conversation about "self-making" that appeared at the start of this chapter, but likewise as a uniquely malleable and portable location for the continued maintenance of the self in defiance of the transitory nature of modern space.

It has been my project in this chapter to sketch the terms of Wharton's investment in the act of acquiring a personal library, and to triangulate Wharton's efforts to construct a library collection and a library space alongside a narrative of self-making. In all, Wharton inhabited the space that she created at The Mount for less than a decade, and the time that she actually spent within the walls of the Lenox Library was, to a similar degree, likely negligible. Yet Wharton went on to envision these and other, similar library spaces within her fiction, resituating fantasies of inherited space in novels like *Hudson River Bracketed* and recasting her memories of the Lenox Library in *Summer.* Her insistence on resuscitating the library as both theme and setting in her fiction rather suggests that, for Wharton, writing and reading alike are characterized by the same kind of production that results in the production of material space—that is, that they contribute to the "materialization of a 'social being,'" as Lefebvre calls it, or the replication of the social relationships and social conflicts that inform, shape, and define space as such.[158] Wharton's optimism about the "great private library" in America being still "so much a thing of the future," much like her late-life return to *The Decoration of Houses* (her first "home" as writer), is indicative of a desire to forge a lasting and permanent version of space in an increasingly impermanent and immaterial modern world. Lefebvre, in a similar fashion, points out that all space but, most especially, that space which we dream to call *our* space "unleashes desire. It presents desire with a 'transparency' which encourages it to surge forth in an attempt to lay claim to an apparently clear field." Our fantasies of personal space, in other words, lend shape to our desires, which might otherwise be without "object," encountering "nothing desirable."[159] It is an effort to locate the finite boundaries and contours of desire, I think, that lies at the heart of Wharton's investment in libraries as spaces, be they public or private, material or imagined.

2

· · · · · · · · · · · · · · · · ·

The Library as Hoard

Collecting and Canonicity
in The House of Mirth *and* Eline Vere

Own all the books you can.

—F. B. Perkins, *The Best Reading*

A MONG A HANDFUL OF FAMOUS SCENES FROM EDITH WHARTON'S *The House of Mirth* is the "tableaux vivants." In it, Wharton's protagonist appears alongside "a dozen fashionable women," members of New York high society who have been "induced . . . to exhibit themselves in a series of pictures"—that is, in silent, motionless, staged displays designed to mimic famous paintings, sculptures, or historical scenes.[1] The tableaux include ensemble renderings of Botticelli's *Spring,* for instance, in addition to paintings by Goya and Titian. But when Lily Bart at last appears in this scene, she does so alone, and this positioning is strategic on Wharton's part: Lily has by this point already begun her precipitous fall from social grace, as indicated by her solitary appearance onstage as "Mrs. Lloyd," after the painting by Joshua Reynolds. Wharton explains that "the participators [in the tableaux] had been cleverly fitted with characters suited to their types," though Lily's "type" is conveyed here not through artistic allusion but through the act of performance.[2] Lily, we see, is of the beautiful but solitary "type"; she is desirable yet somehow undesired, at once both the subject of envy and of contempt. And for this reason her "type" is also destined for tragic ends.

Tableaux vivants, literally translated as "living pictures," were a popular form of semi-erotic entertainment during the nineteenth century. Tableaux preceded the rise of photography, and the titillation factor lay in their ability to marry the live qualities of theatrical performance with the kind of voyeuristic permissibility granted to viewers of paintings. Wharton, certainly, gives us one of fiction's more memorable tableaux vivants, but she was not the first novelist to mention the art form. Sixteen years before the publication of *The House of Mirth,* the Dutch writer Louis Couperus featured a very similar scene in his novel *Eline Vere* (1889). Couperus is not well known in the United States but is, to this day, still viewed by many of his countrymen as the "greatest Dutch novelist of his time."[3] *Eline Vere,* the first of many best-sellers for Couperus, played a part in launching what the *New York Times* hailed as a "'literary revolution' in Holland" that, in the 1890s, saw "fresh hands . . . plowing up the heavy Dutch soil . . . the crop [of which] is to be a new order of fiction."[4] Three years after its initial publication, *Eline Vere* was translated into English and released in the United States as the first in Appleton's widely advertised Holland Fiction Series, indicating that the publishers, at least, foresaw an American audience for Couperus and his contemporaries in the 1890s. Wharton numbered among that audience as she purchased multiple works by Couperus, a fact that may help to explain why Couperus's opening tableau vivant scene compares in many ways to the version that she enacts in *The House of Mirth.*

In Couperus's tableaux, we find the same character names as we do in Wharton's. There is a managing artiste named Paul, and also a young female participant named Lili.[5] The subjects of the tableaux prove likewise similar. Wharton's Lily Bart is tempted by an "impulse to show herself in a splendid setting—she had thought for a moment of representing Tiepolo's Cleopatra."[6] But while Lily opts for Mrs. Lloyd over Cleopatra, Couperus's Lili, Frédérique, and Marie enact Hans Makart's painting *La Mort de Cléopâtre* (1875). Couperus narrates: "In the white glow of the Bengal light, ancient Egypt came to life . . . while on a couch borne by sphinxes reclined a waning Cleopatra with cascading tresses."[7] True, Lily is a conspicuously placed object in Wharton's version of the tableau while Couperus's eponymous heroine is conspicuously absent from his tableau scene. Yet both novels connect the staging of tableaux vivants to nascent themes of tragedy. Couperus, in titling his novel after his protagonist, encourages us to read for Eline Vere's absence in this scene, prompting readers to gauge the significance of her nonappearance in the context of an unfolding tragedy. His peripheral characters reinforce this connection, too, as when Madame Verstraeten strategically remarks, "Such a shame that Eline is not here," and then asks, "What is wrong with her?"[8] For something *is* wrong with Eline Vere. Is it the same something that is wrong with Wharton's Lily Bart?

The tableaux vivants scene in *Eline Vere* forms a bridge between that work and *The House of Mirth,* but it is by no means the only point of connection between these two novels. Many scenes in *The House of Mirth* echo those that we see in *Eline Vere,* situating Couperus's novel as a likely progenitor to Wharton's own. Progeneration, though, is not the focus of my argument. Rather, my aim in this chapter is to sketch the terms of a relationship that does not privilege claims of influence or antecedence. I'm interested in placing these two works in conversation with each other for the very reason that, despite their similarities, no one else has.[9] For more than a century, critics have kept busy pointing out the myriad systems of influence at work in *The House of Mirth,* hitting on the French,[10] English,[11] and American[12] literary traditions. But resituating *The House of Mirth* within the context of Dutch literature—and in proximity to a novel that, though largely unread in America, bears more than a little resemblance to what is, arguably, Wharton's *most* famous novel—sheds light on the kinds of long-standing assumptions that underpin contemporary notions of canonicity. For Wharton's own library collection, even, encourages such a comparison: today one can find translated versions of Couperus's novels on her library shelves at The Mount.[13]

We know from Appleton's 1892 launch of the Holland Fiction Series that there must have been an English-speaking market for these works sizable enough to warrant the labor of translation.[14] Pascale Casanova reminds us that translation is, like criticism, a "process of establishing value" and therefore also a "weapon[] in the struggle by and for literary capital."[15] To this end, the translation history surrounding Couperus's *Eline Vere* may, in part, hold a key to the mystery of its canonical neglect. Appleton's release of its Holland Fiction Series coincided with the first English-language version of *Eline Vere*; J. T. Grein translated the text for the British publishers Chapman and Hall, who published Couperus's novel out of London earlier that same year. But if Grein's translation establishes the "value" of this novel to late nineteenth-century audiences, the persistence of Grein's translation nevertheless suggests a process of devaluation occurring over the course of the ensuing century. For more than a hundred years, Grein's translation was the only version available to English-language readers, and from this we can surmise that *Eline Vere* fell out of favor with Anglo audiences somewhere in the middle of the twentieth century.[16] An updated, English-language translation of *Eline Vere* did not appear until recently in 2010, indicating the limits of the novel's claims to "continued life," as Benjamin would call it,[17] or "cultural capital," as Bourdieu might call it, throughout much of the twentieth century.

Ina Rilke's 2010 English translation of *Eline Vere* has succeeded in clearing a modest place for Couperus in contemporary criticism. Rilke's new translation fits with Simon During's claim that the contemporary market for global literature is, in fact, tied to the overall expansion of globalized capital. "The interest in world literature obviously follows the recent rapid extension of cross-border flows of tourists and cultural goods around the world, including literary fiction," During argues, attaching the post-2000s popularity of world literature to a Bourdieusian decline occurring within the field.[18] According to During's (and Bourdieu's) logic, a new translation of *Eline Vere* becomes possible in 2010 because literature matters less now, enabling world literature to matter more. Contemporary reviews of Couperus's novel appear similarly bent on establishing its value with respect to established canonical heavyweights. Rilke's updated text has earned praise from the likes of the *New York Times,* the *Wall Street Journal,* and the *New York Review of Books,* with the bulk of this press emphasizing firm links between Couperus's novel and the French naturalist tradition.

Considering the similarities between them, then—and considering that Wharton's *The House of Mirth* has, for a hundred years, also been read in light of its ties to French naturalism—an analysis of the correspondences between these two works seems not just timely but, in fact, quite overdue. I aim to show that, though both novels have been appraised with deference to French naturalism, *Eline Vere* and *The House of Mirth* actually have a lot more in common with each other than they do with the

French naturalist oeuvre. Neither of these novels, for instance, focuses on the working classes, the traditional subject of French naturalism; instead, they feature precariously construed representatives of a descendent upper class and, in a related way, highlight these characters' complicated pre-occupations with material culture. The twin tableaux scenes convey the transference of people into *things,* and both Eline and Lily suffer in these novels when their desires for material advantages and things clash with their desires for independence. Both *Eline Vere* and *The House of Mirth,* I argue, center on discourses of paranoid accumulation wherein characters exhibit anxiety about the fluctuating nature of *value* and so seek refuge in fantasies of material consumption and, to a certain degree, in the hoarding of objects.

Eline and Lily are both converts to the ideology of material accrual, but they are also both victims of it. In this chapter, I analyze themes of collecting and material accumulation in *Eline Vere* and *The House of Mirth* in order to solidify the relationship between these two works. I locate both of these novels within a framework of fin de siècle anxieties about mate-rial consumption, maintaining that the expression of these anxieties forms a significant (and understudied) link between Couperus's and Wharton's work. I begin with *Eline Vere,* surveying the ways in which Couperus af-fects a contrast between his protagonist's relationships with objects and her relationships with other people. I then turn to *The House of Mirth* and to Wharton's particular fascination with one form of collecting: bibliophilia. I conclude by way of a return to the subject of this introduction, canonicity, in order to establish the extent to which a library, at any given moment in time, means a canon. A library, after all, comprises a particular selection of titles and texts that makes legible one's assumptions about their cultural, historical, and nationalistic priorities.[19] In this sense, a personal library em-bodies, on the surface, its owner's investment in canonical structures of worth. But, as I think the connection between Couperus's *Eline Vere* and Wharton's *The House of Mirth* makes plain, a library can likewise mean the very opposite of canonical consecration, pointing to changing interpreta-tions of cultural capital and highly idiosyncratic understandings of value, taste, and cultural prestige. Thus I argue that reading Wharton's novel in concert with Couperus's reveals a wider sphere of relation (if not necessar-ily straightforward influence) than may have previously been assumed with regard to Wharton's work—a wider sphere, certainly, than can be imagined via the strict discourse of canonicity.

Eline Vere as Collector

Eline Vere is, as Couperus's subtitle informs us, "a Novel of The Hague." But Eline Vere and Lily Bart are creatures cut from the same pattern, despite their geographic and cultural differences. Eline thinks and acts like Lily; she is plagued by some of the same romantic quandaries as Lily; she even dresses like Lily;[20] and eventually she will die just like Lily, via an overdose of sleeping medication. In the meantime, though, Eline is, like Lily, preoccupied with the subject of her own beauty. That preoccupation is less about vanity than it is about anxiety, for Eline senses that her beauty is her only asset, the only thing that can grant her the luxury and aesthetic plenitude that she craves, and the only thing that can save her from "dinginess," which is Wharton's word for poverty. As with Lily, this fear is in part the residue of a remembered trauma: Eline's parents died when she was young, and this event forced Eline and her sister, Betsy, to live under the guardianship of a widowed aunt.

Characters like Aunt Vere serve to deepen the connections between the two works. Eline's Aunt Vere is the spitting image of Mrs. Peniston, Lily's aunt in *The House of Mirth*. Like Mrs. Peniston, Aunt Vere represents the tragedy (as Lily and Eline both see it) of a wealth that has been tarnished by stinginess.

> Aunt Vere spent her days in her spacious front room amid the gently stultifying trappings of her wealth, invariably clad in sweet-smelling, velvety garments, with a thick Deventer rug underfoot, a flaming log in the grate and by the door a Japanese screen of yellow silk embellished with scarlet peonies and storks on the wing.[21]

Aunt Vere's taste is, as we see, genteel, but also "stultifying," stuffy, and restrictive in a vulgarly bourgeois way. This stultification prompts Eline (who, like Lily, lays claim to an artistic temperament) to seek refuge in individualistic methods of consumption and accrual. Eline is driven by a desire to *possess* beauty, and this desire inspires her belief in possession as an antidote to change and impermanence. Her own beauty, she knows, will alter and fade, but beautiful things may be beautiful forever. In this way Eline learns the ideology of accrual, seeing a hoard of beautiful objects as a defense against the "dinginess" that she so fears.

After Betsy marries, Eline moves in with her sister and brother-in-law, Henk, but here, too, she resents the constraints of her economic dependency. She responds by consuming "with modest means yet refined taste," and her bedroom becomes a monument to her fantasies of independence wherein "refined taste" becomes a substitute for the kind of sovereignty that she actually desires.

> She had succeeded in creating an impression of luxury with artistic overtones. . . . A small writing table was littered with precious bibelots, while sculptures, paintings, feathers, and palms filled every nook. . . . To the side stood her dressing table, abundantly flounced with tulle and lace, which she had touched up here and there with satin bows left over from ball bouquets.[22]

We see here that Eline seeks solace in a hoard of objects and possessions that appear to speak to her uniqueness and individuality. This outlook corresponds to what Diana Fuss identifies as a nineteenth-century "modern fantasy" built on the belief "that the domestic interior and all its furnishings illuminate the inner personality of its inhabitants."[23] And Eline is not the only one who exhibits behavior consistent with such a fantasy; in *The House of Mirth* Lily also longs for "subtle elegance" and reacts to her miserly Aunt Peniston's "charmless" accommodations by adding "a few frivolous touches, in the shape of a lace-decked toilet table and a little painted desk surrounded by photographs."[24]

Draping one's dressing table in tulle might look like an insignificant gesture, but for both of these characters it is an act of feeble agency, the significance of which stems from there being a limited array of available recourses. Both Eline and Lily are, like the vast majority of women during this era, financially dependent; the money they spend is not their own. They both perceive, however, a connection between economic self-sufficiency and speech under the modern capitalist paradigm, and so they both learn to "speak" (and to protest) via the language of material self-expression. The problem, though, lies in the incompatibility of their methods and their goals. Both women imagine success as a kind of winning of one's individuality, but both struggle in imagining a version of individuality that is not defined by consumer practice and by the accruing of material goods. For this reason, both persist in ignoring the irony that is inherent in such an outlook—namely, that the path to that kind of independence is paved in codependence.

Lily and Eline both require husbands in order to become the versions of themselves that they desire to be, but neither of them actually wants to be married. They want, in other words, the things that will make them people, but they do not want the people that come with the things. Eline, for instance, takes refuge in material culture and in the collecting of things, but she neglects to consider the ways in which things are, in the words of Bruno Latour, "full of people."[25] This neglect forms the substance of Eline's undoing in Couperus's novel. When we meet Eline, she is of marrying age and has, like Lily, already passed up a couple of opportunities. While visiting the opera one night, she develops an infatuation with a dashing young baritone named Théo Fabrice. She nurtures this infatuation through two activities: purchasing collectible portraits of Fabrice and a little light stalking. Eline takes secret pride in her ever-growing stash of collectible portraits, which she purchases

> over a period of time with much discretion and nervousness, now in
> one shop, then in another, never returning to the same one in case
> the shopkeeper might guess what was on her mind. On one occasion,
> when she was in Amsterdam for the day . . . she had been particularly
> daring: she had swept into a bookshop with an air of haughty indiffer-
> ence and had bought seven at once. No one there knew who she was,
> anyway, and she vowed never to set foot in that shop again for as long
> as she lived.[26]

Clearly, Eline experiences a kind of shame in connection with these purchases. As with her daily walks, which she rearranges in deference to Fabrice's commute to and from the opera house, she is modifying her actions and practices in order to escape notice and to offset those feelings of shame. But why should Eline be ashamed?

The answer lies not in the act itself (the purchasing of fan memorabilia), but in the intensity of Eline's feelings for the objects that she collects. Eline is exhibiting what Scott Herring labels "deviant object relations," which stem from one's anxieties concerning their attachments to "the stuff of normal life."[27] But Couperus's novel troubles Herring's claim that such relations "developed in the twentieth century."[28] Indeed, Couperus's *Eline Vere* points to a prehistory of deviant object relations, locating, in the late nineteenth century, nascent feelings of shame experienced in connection with "abnormal" approaches to material consumption. Eline is ashamed of purchasing the Fabrice portraits because she is aware of doing so abnormally; she senses that there is something wrong with her motivations for owning them,[29] and that wrongness may have to do with her growing preference for these and other objects over the companionship of actual people.

Eline's obsessive interest in collecting Fabrice's portraits is, in many ways, prophetic in that it announces her priorities in this novel and presages the complications that arise when she chooses things over people (or, similarly, when she chooses people *because* of things). Later in the novel, Eline arranges her Fabrice portraits in an album. She is inspired to do so when she sees Madame Verstraeten's album of family portraits, and here Couperus does not attempt to conceal the irony of his character's motivations: for Madame Verstraeten, the photo album is a thing that signifies her relationships with people, while for Eline the album is a thing that supplants the necessity for relationships with people. Couperus describes how "Eline's thoughts flew to Fabrice as her eye fell on the album. . . . Yes, she would buy an album for her own private use, in which to keep portraits of Fabrice; it would be a little shrine to her love, before which she could lose herself in the contemplation of her idol."[30] Here Eline begins by thinking of Fabrice but these thoughts are quickly replaced by her interest in the actual thing. Alone in her room, she kisses Fabrice's portraits[31] and experiences "a passion that replenished her mind with [] bliss," and this sensation is so strong that she vows "to make any sacrifice that might be demanded of her"—that is, for the sake of the sensation itself and not for its supposed author, Fabrice.[32] Eline expresses loyalty to a feeling that she experiences and not to the person who is supposed to inspire it, and her desire to collect and accrue similarly arises from a preference for things that is, at root, really a preference for herself.

Eline's problem, in other words, stems from an unrestrained and undisguised form of selfishness. Couperus's other characters observe that "Eline cares about no one but herself . . . she's incapable of making the slightest sacrifice for anyone" and that her thoughts and actions are ruled by "egotism, sheer egotism."[33] Eline's tragic decline in this novel is, to a great extent, the result of her inability to understand the roots of her own selfishness. Yet Eline is no Emma Bovary; her selfishness does not manifest itself as cruelty to others. Rather, Couperus creates in his protagonist a model of sympathetic self-indulgence that at once appears to both represent and validate the turn-of-the-century compulsion to collect and accrue. Lori Merish, for example, has established the ways in which practices of "sentimental ownership," or accruing and owning for the sake of a perceived emotional payoff, developed in nineteenth-century America, comprising "a form of national pedagogy."[34] Couperus's *Eline Vere* severs the nationalistic angle from Merish's argument, showing that Dutch consumers, too, during this era, sought emotional gratification via the corroboration of individual "taste" and the purchasing of mass-produced goods, and that such sentimental motives are symptomatic of modern capitalism in general (and only of nationalism in specific).[35]

Such universality is, in fact, precisely what Marx and Engels observe when they argue in *The Communist Manifesto* that, under capitalism, "in place of the old local and national seclusion and self-sufficiency, we have intercourse in every direction, universal interdependence of nations. And as in material, so also in intellectual production."[36] The affiliations that I am observing between Wharton and Couperus are, in essence, affiliations of class that yield comparable forms of class-based consumption and accrual, with the similarities between Wharton's and Couperus's novels bolstering Marx and Engels's contention that "intellectual creations of individual nations become common property . . . and from the numerous national and local literatures, there arises a world literature."[37] Eline's selfishness is descendent from a superstructural insistence on "new wants," as Marx and Engels call them. This array of "new wants"—in part the result of the expansion of global markets—define and drive the bourgeois compulsion to consume under the auspices of modern capitalism.

These "new wants" clutter and crowd Couperus's novel, prompting some reviewers in the 1880s to complain of its "minuteness of detail" and also of its length.[38] The impression we get in *Eline Vere* is of Couperus—described universally by critics as a "dandy"[39]—reveling in the glory of a self-indulgent modern materialism. Couperus's fondness for detail transforms his novel, at points, into a rather ponderous inventory of material possessions, but it also fuels Couperus's compassionate treatment of Eline's selfishness. Eline compels, if not our esteem, at the very least our pity; we sense that she is fated for misery as the result of her having just enough privilege to be able to make the wrong choices about what to do with it. Her selfishness causes her to turn her back on marriage proposals and family affiliations, as she rejects anything that looks like an imposition on her independence, chiefly because she has no conception of or experience with the idea of independence.

Consider, for example, her rejection of Fabrice, her idol. Eline passes Fabrice every day on the street, yet she makes no attempt to speak to him. Eline fears what would happen if she did and, in doing so, exhibits a general mistrust of people that is predicated by her fears of change and instability. At one point, Eline appeals to God, childishly begging "please . . . make everything stay the same it as now! I'll die if anything changes."[40] But humans are naturally variable and inconstant, and this means that objects end up looking like a comparatively more solid bet for Eline. She would rather interact with a collection of Fabrice's photographs than speak to him on the street because, where the photographs are concerned, those interactions can be counted on to produce predictable outcomes (an experience of "passion" and "bliss"). By contrast, her interaction with the real Fabrice is liable to produce a range of outcomes that may or may not include rejection since "ordinary human relationships," as Baudrillard points out, "are the site of the unique and the conflictual."[41] And so Eline comes to prefer her relationships with objects to her relationships with people, a preference that proves disastrous by the conclusion of Couperus's novel.

After worshiping her stockpile of Fabrice portraits for many months, Eline is eventually forced to reckon with the reality of his person. Couperus describes the event in question in a curious way, with Eline positioned in front of her bedroom looking glass, contemplating her own reflection while "reliving the moment" of her tragic disillusionment. Here as elsewhere in *Eline Vere,* Couperus lavishes attention on material specifics: Eline wears "her pink rep silk [] with the aigrette of pink plumes in her upswept hair, the very ensemble she had worn when she first set eyes on Fabrice."[42] From this, we get a sense of ritualistic reenactment as we see Eline standing before the mirror, dressed for a date with her own memory rather than for one with the real living Fabrice. Eline has just returned from seeing Fabrice perform once again, though this time in closer proximity. But that closeness has destroyed her fantasies about him. "He looked common and overweight, with a disagreeable, sullen expression about the bearded mouth. . . . She had felt as if she were seeing him for the first time," she recalls.[43] Indeed, she has seen Fabrice for the first time insofar as this is the first time that she has allowed herself to come close enough to study him in detail. The shock of the experience sends Eline into a rage in which she destroys "the shrine of her love, the temple of her passion, the secret place where she worshipped her idol"—that is, the photo album, which here transcends its status as mere thing in functioning also as a location (shrine, temple, place).[44] Eline has, in effect, constructed the photo album as a location for the housing of her fantasies about herself. Her destruction of it in this scene thus speaks to its status as a "bundle of qualities," in the words of Levi R. Bryant;[45] the photo album signifies Eline's apparent attachment to the real Fabrice, but more than that it signifies her attachment to herself, to her dreams of ownership and selfish accrual, and to her anxieties about living independently. For what Couperus chiefly describes in this scene is not a "crush" that has soured but rather a crisis of self that sees Eline wrestling with feelings of "ridicule" and "disgrace, the stain of which would cling to her forever, haunting her like a spectre of mockery."[46] Yet these feelings are the result not of social censure but of self-critique: Eline has told no one of her "crush"; there is no one to mock her, save herself. Thus Eline's destruction of the album (she lingers over each individual photograph, feeding them individually into the fire) is a prelude to larger, more significant acts of self-destruction. Eline ends up hurting herself, even, in the process of destroying it, "scorching her fingers" and "breaking a fingernail."[47] These small injuries are, I believe, indicative of a culminating crisis, and Eline has already started the process of dying for the sake of her own selfish fantasies.

Eline eventually gets engaged, to a soft-spoken man about whom she feels decidedly ambivalent, and all because of a fan. We learn more about the fan than we ever do about Otto, the man who gives it to her. "On a grey-velvet pillow lay a fan of exquisitely carved mother of pearl . . . 'Bucchi,' she murmured, peering at the signature along the edge. 'Bucchi . . .' It was indeed a fan painted by the famous Italian artist; a fantasy of roses and fairies on ivory satin."[48] Eline's brand consciousness in this scene (it is not just any fan, it's a *Bucchi* fan) resonates with Richard Ohmann's observation that marketers were "discovering" the value of brands beginning in the 1880s, a process that would culminate in "an advertising revolution in the 1890s" and in the expansion of the public's investment in branded goods.[49] This brand-name fan prompts Eline's decision to marry Otto, a decision she later retracts due to anxieties about her own worthiness combined with an inkling that she is marrying for the wrong reasons. And it is a Lawrence Selden–like character, an itinerant member of the "republic of the spirit,"[50] who develops those inklings and spurs her toward her rejection of Otto.

Like Selden in *The House of Mirth,* Eline's cousin Vincent has the effect of "cheapening her aspirations, of throwing her whole world out of focus."[51] This "cheapening" is due in part to Vincent's apparent disregard for material wealth and his placid acceptance of a very minor kind of poverty. Couperus describes Vincent's apartment in a manner that suggests both thrift by requirement and refinement by design:

> The antique sideboard bearing the silver jug and few oriental objects looked sorely out of place beside the shabby armchairs upholstered in Utrecht velveteen, just as the antique prints on the wall struck a jarringly aristocratic note among the cheap engraving and common chromolithographs.[52]

By comparison, Selden's apartment in *The House of Mirth,* with its "old prints," "letters and notes heaped on the table among his gloves and sticks," "walls of books," and "faded Turkey rug," speaks to a similar aesthetic.[53] Like Selden, Vincent tries to coach Eline, encouraging her to think through the roots of her desires for material opulence since those desires, in his view, necessitate a degrading dependence on others. Vincent lectures to Eline on the subject of free will and Eline makes the logical connection to her arrangement with Otto. "You believe, for instance, that if I marry Otto all I'm doing is following a preordained path?" Eline asks, with "preordained" in this instance referring to bourgeois expectations of behavior that match up with her understandings of her class status. Vincent's response to this is noncommittal, but it is enough to nurture the germ of self-doubt in Eline's brain.[54] Otto, Eline recognizes, will never be the Bucchi fan; he will never be "exquisite" and her life with him will never be the stuff of "fantasy." Objects, she reasons, are safer than people, but is the attainment of object-based independence worth the commitment to person-based codependence?

Eline continues to mull the connections between objects and people as she descends from the heights of material privilege. Her rejection of Otto renders her a persona non grata in the eyes of society, and she is bereft when Vincent, with whom she has decided she is in love, leaves The Hague, exercising the kind of free will that is both the subject of his lectures to Eline and his privilege as a man. Eline then spurns the company of her sister and brother-in-law and, like Lily, winds up residing with some working-class friends, the Ferelijns. She appears on their doorstep in the middle of the night, crying, "Please, please, forgive me. . . . There I was, out in the dark street, in the wind and the rain! . . . But you must understand, I simply had to leave" in a manner that recalls Lily's appeal to Gerty Farrish in *The House of Mirth*.[55] Eline eventually picks herself up and, like Lily, seeks work, but her health continues to wane and she lands once again at her sister's house, where the scene of her morphine overdose eventually occurs. True to her word, Eline has made "sacrifices" for the sake of her fantasies of material advantage and stability, the last of which is to be herself. She chooses to die in lieu of living a life that has been "cheapened" by material disadvantage, dinginess, and base codependence. In fact, though, she is dying of selfishness, surrounded by the company of things and not the company of people.

Couperus's treatment of Eline's death builds to a thematic conclusion: Eline is possessed by her possessions. In her final scene, we see Eline, back in her old bedroom at Betsy's house, surrounded by the hoard of objects symbolizing her fantasies of selfhood. Couperus's positioning of Eline within this space compares to Adorno's observation (via Kierkegaard) that in the nineteenth century "the self is overwhelmed in its own domain by commodities and their historical essence."[56] Everything in Eline's room, from the figures of Cupid and Psyche on the mantelpiece to the flower bouquets[57] that are her trophies from balls of yore, appears weighted with history. In the presence of these objects, Eline is reminded of the choices that have brought her to this point of impasse: just before she dies, she pries Otto's photograph from the locket that she wears about her neck and, as with the album of Fabrice portraits, she makes to destroy it, compelled by humiliation and rage. Her strength, however, is failing, and so she puts the photograph into her mouth instead, resolving to "swallow it, since she no longer had the strength to tear it up or destroy it in any other way . . . and she began to chew the rejected proof of Otto's portrait."[58] Here Couperus has Eline ingest a beloved object out of self-disgust and anger; we see her funnel her rejection of Otto into a rejection of herself that is likewise reflected in the object (it is a "rejected" photographic proof—something that Otto previously threw away). Jane Bennett notes the ways in which material objects signal forms of human agency and gesture toward the human "ability to make things happen, to produce effects."[59] But in this scene, Eline's relationship to the object in question—a rejected portrait of her rejected suitor—announces the power of objects to remind us of our inactions and failures to "make things happen." Eline chews the portrait of Otto with the cognizance that he was her best bet and with the self-hatred that comes from knowing that she is the architect of her own misery. Eline's final act of material consumption is thus—like all those that preceded it—also one of self-destruction: she eats Otto's photograph as she dies, the result of having overdosed on prescription morphine.

Her "overdose" is, in this case, emblematic of Eline's tendency to overconsume. She is entirely aware of the fact that she is overdoing it and going beyond what is both normal and advised, even as she appears to ponder the consequences of her overindulgence. "What if she took a few more drops than the dose prescribed by that physician in Brussels?" she wonders. "How many more drops would it be safe for her to take? The same amount again? No, that would be too much."[60] But Eline, drawn as always to excess, does it anyway. Her last thoughts are in this way littered with the language of surplus: phrases like "a few more," "many more," and "too much" proliferate in Rilke's translation. And though Couperus lets a question mark linger over the scene of Eline's death (was it an accident, or suicide?), Eline's intentions are couched in patterns of repeated behavior. We know that she is prone to overindulgence and temptation; we know that she can't help but consume more than what is acceptable or wise—more than what is good for her.

Lily Bart as Collectible

While the similarities between them abound, *Eline Vere* differs in many ways from Wharton's *The House of Mirth*. Chief among these differences is the fact that <u>Eline Vere is a collector while Lily Bart is a collectible</u>. This much is clear given Wharton's take on the tableaux scene: in it, Wharton places Lily squarely in the spotlight of public scrutiny and, in so doing, converts Lily into a piece of "superfine human merchandise."[61] Lawrence Selden (who, given a different set of circumstances, would be her most ideal romantic match) foresees Lily's tragic denouement when he glimpses her onstage in the tableau: "In the long moment before the curtain fell, he had time to feel the whole tragedy of [Lily's] life."[62] It is for the sake of men like Selden that Lily places herself on display in this scene, yet Selden does not see it this way. Rather, Selden prefers to see himself as distinct from the members of his and Lily's social milieu and so resists—initially, at least—interpreting Lily's performance in a way that would compromise that distinction. Selden observes other men observing Lily's "dryad-like curves," and he responds, in turn, with "indignant contempt," reflecting, "This was the world *she* lived in, these were the standards by which *she* was fated to be measured!"[63] What Selden fails to grasp here is not only his own inclusion in that world but also the extent of his responsibilities as an engineer of it.

Cynthia Griffin Wolff reasons that such failure results from Selden's persistence in seeing Lily as an object akin to a work of art. "Lily has been formed to accept a definition of femininity of which men like Selden are the supreme evaluators," Wolff explains. "Lily comes closest to Selden's expectations for her in [this scene]. . . . Her choice of costume reveals her increased understanding of Selden's visionary demands of her."[64] Wolff situates Lily as an objet d'art in Selden's eyes, but she stops just short of laying her hand on the subtending ideological motivations that often structure our interactions with desirable objects—namely, the ideology of collecting.[65] Wolff touches on the subject of collecting briefly in her discussion of Lily's second-best suitor, Percy Gryce. "Gryce's vanity is of a simple order: he collects Americana; he would add [Lily] to that collection."[66] Here, though, Wolff commits the same mistake as Selden: she sets him apart from the behaviors of his milieu, making him appear distinct from Gryce in a way that excuses both his arrogance and his treatment of Lily. Selden is, like Gryce, a "collector," but of a slightly different sort. For instance, he repeatedly employs the rhetoric of appraisal and evaluation when discussing Lily, viewing her as an object of value but also as a risky investment. "He had a confused sense that she must have cost a great deal to make, that a great many dull and ugly people must . . . have been sacrificed to produce her,"[67] Selden reflects early in *The House of Mirth*. His ruminations on the subject of "cost" establish him as a kind of collector, though not, perhaps, in the ordinary sense. He explains to Lily that he is not interested in an object's value or price, and he does not collect simply in order to add to a preexisting stockpile of objects. Rather, Selden craves, as he puts it, "good editions"—that is, high-quality versions of the things of which he is already "fond." Here again we see Selden's attempts to distinguish himself from his peers: Selden views himself as a discerning aesthete in contrast to the average collector, who, he tells Lily, "values a thing for its rarity."[68] But this is Wharton's way of laying the groundwork for a conflict that is rooted in self-deception. In time the roots of Selden's hypocrisy rise to the surface. His inflated sense of self-worth prevents him from sympathizing with Lily, whom he initially views as a "good edition" worth pursuing, but only if the price is right.

More than anything else, Selden's personal library collection speaks the truth about his hypocrisy and hubris. In the opening scenes of *The House of Mirth*, Wharton encodes her feelings for her male romantic lead via the language of bibliophilia. Selden's initial meeting with Lily occurs in his library, which takes up the majority of his apartment. Once inside, Lily begins to roam about the room,

> examining the book-shelves between the puffs of her cigarette-smoke. Some of the volumes had the ripe tints of good tooling and old morocco, and her eyes lingered on them caressingly, not with the appreciation of an expert, but with the pleasure in agreeable tones and textures that was one of her inmost susceptibilities . . . she turned to Selden with a question. "You collect, don't you?"[69]

Here Wharton offers a study in contrasts: on the one hand, we have expertise, albeit of a somewhat deluded variety; on the other, we have a form of inexpert but nevertheless sincere appreciation. Lily admires Selden's library books but she does not purport to do so from the vantage point of an aficionado. She is, for her all her faults, both too sincere and too self-aware to pretend to be anything that she is not. Selden, meanwhile, prides himself on his expertise and on his perceived ability to recognize and apprehend quality when he sees it.[70] He imagines that his interest in quality is both superior to, and thus distinct from, an interest in worth, but he is wrong in this regard, and it is Lily who will suffer the consequences of his self-deception.

The conversation about books in this scene then quickly becomes a conversation about marriage. Lily offers a sly critique of Selden's fascination with quality, noting that the ability to choose based on quality is predicated on one's ability to choose in the first place. So far as marrying is concerned, she tells Selden, "A girl must, a man may if he chooses."[71] The subtext of this comment is nonetheless clear: Selden, as a collector, waits to choose while Lily, as a collectible, waits to be chosen.[72] But this is not to say that an object that is chosen may not act. An object acts, according to Latour, through processes of translation, attraction, and refraction in which the object is not "the source of an action but the moving target of a vast array of entities swarming towards it."[73] Lily is, to a very similar degree, defined in this novel not by her actions but by her tendency to attract (and, in some cases, refract) action. Selden even admits that this is part of what he likes best about her when he tells Lily that "you're such a wonderful spectacle. I always like to see what you are doing."[74] Yet the truth is that Lily, as a *jeune fille à marier,* succeeds in doing very little. Her actions are banal by requirement and curtailed at every turn by the threat of social censure. Rather, her interactions matter most, since Lily's value is, like Marx's vision of the commodity, only realizable through exchange and circulation.[75]

In this way we see that Lily's interactions with Selden's library in the first few pages of *The House of Mirth* encapsulate a variety of developing conflicts. These interactions reveal Wharton's thematic interest in the kinds of conflict that result from competing estimations of worth. As Lily continues to question Selden about his habits of collecting in this scene, she keeps one eye on the collection itself, "lift[ing] now one book and then another from the shelves, fluttering the pages between her fingers." Wharton names only one of these books in particular, "his first edition of La Bruyère."[76] Lily holds this book in her hands for a while without appearing to apprehend its worth, her inability to fathom its value being representative of her inability to fathom or recognize Selden's motives more generally. Lily doesn't know it, but she is holding the evidence of Selden's hypocrisy and lies in the form of a very rare first edition text by the French author Jean de la Bruyère. Wharton, certainly, was acquainted with the value of this text, for she also owned a first edition of it.

Wharton's volume of La Bruyère's *Les Caractères des Théophraste* is dated 1688 and marked "Edition originale," most likely by a bookseller who came by it after her death. It is bound in full red morocco leather and bears the bookbinders' stamp ("Chambolle–Duru"),[77] in addition to elaborately gilt-tooled panels, a triple-ruled gilt border, and gilt-edged pages. What these material details add up to is evidence of an investment; a first edition of La Bruyère's *Caractères* would have already been 217 years old in 1905 and thus quite rare. The quality of the binding speaks to a previous owner's investment in the object itself; while Wharton owned multiple works bearing the Chambolle–Duru mark, it is unlikely that she had any of them personally bound. Rather, as is indicated by Wharton's placing of her own bookplate over another's, a previous owner probably ordered the custom binding some time during the late 1800s, no doubt as a means of protecting the investment, given the age of the text.

The morocco leather and Chambolle–Duru custom flourishes make this text a "good edition," but they are merely cosmetic: they augment but are not chiefly responsible for creating the value of this already valuable object. I would argue that Wharton's placement of the La Bruyère text in this scene is meant to expose Selden's dishonesty from the outset and to warn readers against trusting him. For Selden *is* lying—to Lily and to himself. He maintains, for instance, that he is not a collector but rather a lucky aficionado who succeeds, every now and then, in "pick[ing] up something in the rubbish heap."[78] But his finding a first edition of La Bruyère in such a location is highly implausible, given the text's value during this, the "golden age" of American book-collecting.[79] Thus, for all of Selden's professed interests in "good editions," it's clear that he wants what every other man like him wants: not an article from the rubbish heap but a "good edition" of something that has already been established as valuable. Howard Horne, in his *The Binding of Books* (1894), quotes from Goethe while discussing how the book-binding trade in the late nineteenth century flourished in contrast to the rise of cheaply printed books. "Productions are now possible . . . which, without being bad, have no value. They have no value because they contain nothing; and they are not bad, because a general form of good workmanship is present to the author's mind."[80] In her own copy of Horne's book, Wharton has placed an "x" next to these comments from Goethe—suggesting, at least, that the subject caught her attention. The

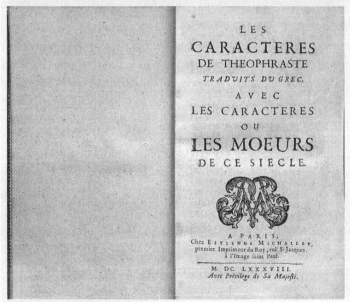

Wharton's first-edition volume of La Bruyère's *Les Caractères de Théophraste*, 1688. EdithWhartonsLibrary.org. Courtesy of The Mount.

quotation rather captures Selden's outlook, though, as he seeks to define himself through the acquisition of "good editions" in contrast to the type of value-ridden, cheaply produced objects that Goethe describes in this passage.

Selden's library is the first of three that appear in the opening sections of *The House of Mirth*. Wharton places Selden's shabby furnishings and "good editions" in contrast to the kinds of libraries owned by the Trenors or Percy Gryce. The Trenors' library is "never used for reading," while Percy Gryce is a renowned book collector whose collection, Lily has heard, is "the finest in the world," making it too valuable to be handled or read.[81] Having benefited from a providential inheritance, Gryce's collection is "already noted among bibliophiles."[82] Wharton laces her description of Gryce's management of the collection, however, with tinges of mockery:

> He subscribed to all the reviews dealing with book-collecting in general, and American history in particular, and as allusions to his library abounded in the pages of these journals, which formed his only reading, he came to regard himself as figuring prominently in the public eye, and to enjoy the thought of the interest which would be excited if the persons he met in the street or sat among in traveling were suddenly to be told that he was the possessor of the Gryce Americana.[83]

Gryce is interested in books because he is interested in himself and in the perpetuation of his family name. He is of the vainglorious brand of collector—the kind driven by a compulsion to stockpile, hoard, and accrue. To Gryce, who does not read the books that he collects, books are a form of currency, which he treats just as he would money: he deposits his books "in a fire-proof annex that looked like a mausoleum" just as he deposits his money in accounts that he oversees "with becoming reverence into every detail of the art of accumulation."[84]

Gryce embodies what Colton Storm and Howard Peckham identify as a "cruder sort" of book collector. "It must be candidly admitted," the authors note, "that some collectors buy rarities for show or profit. They are found most frequently in large cities, where people care what their friends suspect they do."[85] The last sentence of this quotation speaks, in particular, to the "public" character of Gryce's collection, and to his motivations for collecting it as well.[86] Wharton thus offers us a set of contrasts: Selden appears to be a bibliophile (he *loves* books) while Gryce is a bibliomaniac (he collects compulsively, rather than lovingly);[87] Selden uses and interacts with his collection while Gryce embalms his own. Wharton is suggesting that, for men like Gryce, use and wear have the effect of devaluing a stockpile of treasured goods. And since value is the endpoint of this particular mode of accrual, use must be formally discouraged and prevented. Gryce, in fact, ends up dismissing Lily as a marital candidate on similar grounds. Bertha Dorset gossips to Gryce about Lily's outstanding string of former paramours, and Gryce subsequently comes to see Lily as used and, thereby, devalued. Selden, by comparison, lets Lily touch his books when they are alone together in his apartment, and he seems to value them as usable objects. Yet Selden and Gryce are, in truth, similarly motivated to hunt for that which is rare and worthy.

Gryce's pursuit of his treasured Americana compares to Selden's pursuit of Lily, in fact. He relies, for example, on the rhetoric of the hunt, as when he succeeds in catching Lily "in a moment of disarray." Selden rejoices in the "poignancy" of their meeting and reflects, *"That is how she looks when she is alone."*[88] He is happy to have caught Lily in this way—alone, defenseless, and without the customary façade of social artifice. Wharton defers once more to this kind of language of pursuit in the tableaux scene, wherein Selden senses "the touch of poetry in [Lily's] beauty that [he] always felt in her presence, yet lost the sense of when he was not with her"; here, Selden imagines that he sees Lily "divested of the trivialities of her little world" and exults in "catching for a moment a note of that eternal harmony of which her beauty was a part."[89] Selden cherishes moments like this because he believes that he alone is privy to them. He imagines, in these scenes, that he has achieved a rare glimpse of Lily's true nature or essence. And from this it is clear that Selden places a great deal of value in the concept of authenticity, a rarified quality that is made all the more precious and valuable given Selden's inclusion in a circle of New York high-society elites, who depend on superficiality and artifice in their interactions with each other.

Indeed, Selden seeks constant exposure to authentic emotional experience, and this yearning mirrors Percy Gryce's interest in the kinds of "authentic" textual artifacts known as "Americana." As Carl L. Cannon explains in his *American Book Collectors and Collecting*, Americana was, in the late part of the nineteenth century, "undoubtedly the point of highest interest to the modern [American] collector" and likewise "recognized as one of the most important fields open to an ambitious and intelligent student."[90] The collecting of Americana became a popular pastime for the well-monied amateur scholar during this era. In part, this was due to the fact that, in the early part of the twentieth century, libraries and academic institutions were just beginning to develop the abilities to invest and procure such collections. Lydia Pyne explains that during this era "libraries—particularly institutional libraries like the Library of Congress, New York Public Library, or any university library—were acquiring books and materials at a rate that some librarians considered unsustainable."[91] The addition of new institutional players to the arena of an old gentleman's pursuit enhanced the stakes of the game, driving up prices on individual volumes and causing some collectors to speculate on the wealth of their individual collections. The collecting of Americana, in particular, became a high-stakes pastime for the well-monied gentleman: the term refers to a finite array of ephemeral documents and materials, the bulk of which were manufactured before the rise of formal printing operations and large-scale presses during the colonial era.

But Selden does not collect Americana; he collects "classics." And what is a classic? The poet James Russell Lowell, in his 1870 ode to bibliophilia, defines a classic as

> properly a book which maintains itself by virtue of that happy coalescence of matter and style, that innate and exquisite sympathy between the thought that gives life and the form which consents to every mood of grace and dignity, which can be simple without being vulgar, elevated without being distant, and which is something neither ancient nor modern, always new, and incapable of growing old.[92]

Lowell's definition of the term "classic" emphasizes both timelessness and grace; a classic is, in Lowell's eyes, "neither ancient nor modern" but is, rather, seen as an object of value throughout the ages.[93] A classic lays claim to persistent and lasting value by modeling the standards of aesthetic "dignity." Like Lowell, Lawrence Selden ascribes a level of dignity to his habit of collecting. Instead of "rubbishy old books" (the phrase that Judy Trenor uses to describe Percy Gryce's collection of Americana), Selden favors "good editions" of classic works of European literature. For Selden, the label of "classic" affords both dignity and economic protection, since classics are less susceptible to market fluctuation and thus less likely to see their value depreciate over time. What this means is that Lily Bart, if she wants to be "purchased" by Selden, needs to convey both quality (a "good edition") and a dignified resemblance to other, vetted forms of investment (a "classic"). That is to say, Lily needs to appear as a desirable version of a commodity that has stood the test of time.

Lily's appearance in the tableaux vivants scene, however, compromises Selden's understandings of her worth and quality. Wharton gives us the sense that the performance of the tableaux teeters just at the edge of social respectability. Carry Fisher, a double divorcée with a less than stellar reputation, supervises the performance, which takes place in the mansion of the Wellington Brys, a nouveau riche family desperate to prove themselves and gain entrance to elite society. There is, in fact, an air of sordidness about the entire scene, an air reflected in Ned Van Alstyne's crass comments about Lily's body[94] and likewise in the larger history of tableaux as an art form. Tableaux, as previously mentioned, were a somewhat racy form of entertainment, since they enabled a level of unseemly public ogling. In Wharton's tableaux scene, we see that Selden enjoys looking at Lily but also that he chafes at the knowledge that he is not the only one doing the looking. Selden becomes flustered when he recognizes that he is, in fact, behaving just like other men. His first resort is competition; he tells Lily that he loves her immediately following the tableaux because he is eager to beat someone else to the opportunity. His feelings are inspired by antagonism, though, and not by true appreciation. When Selden overhears the comments issued by Ned and the rest of the peanut gallery, he becomes all at once aware of Lily's exchange value in the context of a desiring market. He then senses that he must reject Lily in order to avoid being seen—by his social milieu and by himself—as part *of* that market. His individuality and his "republic of the spirit" are at stake.

Selden's concerns for his own self-worth thus trump his interests in marrying Lily Bart and likewise his concerns for her well-being. From the crass banter of his male peers, he gleans an understanding of Lily's worth as a commodity, and Wharton ends the tableaux scene not with Selden's declaration of love but with his inclusion in a vulgar, locker-room style of conversation. Throughout it, we see Lily's exchange value first assessed and then gutted. "Talk of jewels," Ned Van Alstyne says, "what's a woman want with jewels when she's got herself to show? . . . I never knew till tonight what an outline Lily has."[95] This comment plays on interpretations of Lily's worth as an art object; her body, Van Alstyne concludes, is "worth" just as much as her jewelry. But Selden, though he has previously entertained similar interpretations of Lily's worth (recall his reflecting that "she cost a great deal to make"), is banking on Lily's value as a "good edition" and a "classic"—that is, as a singular object of worth, as opposed to a mere commodity.[96] Selden is reacting to an environment of gross commoditization and threats to authenticity; he views jewelry and the conspicuous display of wealth to be beneath his notions of "personal success" and "independence,"[97] and like Vincent in *Eline Vere*, he has previously tried to persuade Lily to see the merits of such a mindset, preaching the values of prudence and thrift. But what the tableaux scene makes obvious to Selden is that Lily *is* a commoditized object and is thus incapable of existing outside the commodity relations that define her. What's more, Selden understands that, as a commodity, Lily is subject to and defined by processes of exchange. Through the haze of cigar smoke, Wharton's male characters handle Lily in this scene as though she is a book in Selden's library, passing her around and leaving their metaphorical fingerprints all over her person. As a result, Selden is, like Gryce, forced to confront estimations of her use and wear.

Where Lily might have once been a "good edition" and a "classic" that appeared to be worth the purchase price, Selden now sees her as used, worn, and effectively worthless. Recall that, previously, Selden bragged about "pick[ing] up []things in the rubbish heap." We now know that, so far as the La Bruyère was concerned, this was a lie. What Wharton furthermore shows us, though, is that lies and hubris have structured Selden's interactions with Lily from the very beginning. Selden ends up rejecting Lily, turning his back on her when she needs him most, because he grasps the pernicious fluidity of commodity exchange and senses that Lily is (apropos of Marx's description of the commodity form) "a born leveler and cynic . . . always ready to exchange not only soul, but body, with each and every other commodity."[98] This is another way of saying that the commodity is chimerical and devoid of allegiance and so cannot help but betray its supposed "owner." Thus, Selden's reasons for rejecting Lily are, in fact, identical to Percy Gryce's: both men are experienced collectors, and both view Lily as a bad investment.

Wharton reinforces Selden's role as collector–investor when she returns us, in the final pages of *The House of Mirth,* to the scene of his library. Lily meets to speak with Selden one last time and finds his library "as she had pictured it . . . She recognized the row of shelves from which he had taken down his La Bruyère and the worn arm of the chair he had leaned against while she examined the precious volume."[99] But this passage contains two very telling inconsistencies. To start, it was Lily, not Selden, who took down the La Bruyère on that previous occasion, with Selden remaining content to "sit there looking up at her."[100] Wharton's phrasing in this earlier scene establishes Lily as the confirmed object of Selden's spectatorial gaze in a manner that presupposes the events of the tableaux. Yet here, in the moment of their final and conclusive tête-à-tête, Wharton misconstrues (or else intentionally confuses) the specifics of that earlier scene. Lily remembers Selden as the active agent in that former encounter, "taking down" the La Bruyère, offering it to her, and furthermore "leaning" against the arm of the easy chair from a standing position. This is the first inconsistency; the second has to do with the word "precious." Previously, Lily appeared ignorant of the La Bruyère volume's worth; in this scene, though, she describes it as "precious." The question is, why? What has changed and enabled Lily to discover the value of this particular object?

The answer is, nothing whatsoever. In fact, I believe that these sins against narrative continuity are indicative of Wharton's feelings toward her manqué male protagonist, Lawrence Selden. Wharton, certainly, knows the value of a La Bruyère first edition; so does Selden. Nothing has happened in the interim to clue Lily in and make her similarly aware of the book's value, but something has happened to make her understand the depths of Selden's vanity and deception. To put it simply, Lily now knows Selden for what he is, a liar, and this knowledge permits her to make assumptions about the worth of the La Bruyère in turn.[101] In the context of his bibliophilic hoard she encounters Selden for the last time, surrounded by his "good editions." She then leaves his apartment with the knowledge that Selden has chosen, for once and for all, to rest rather than to invest. Wai Chee Dimock, in her reading of Selden's motivations, defers to the language of risk and investment, describing Selden's metaphorical "portfolio" as rich with "spiritual stocks." "Selden has been saving and hoarding for so long that he is afraid there might be 'a chance of his having to pay up,'" Dimock explains.[102] Selden is a hoarder, but not in the contemporary sense of "cluttered entryways, domiciles overstuffed with knickknacks," and the piles of useless objects that today summon anxieties of deplorable excess.[103] Rather, Selden's hoarding reflects the etymological evolution of the term "hoarding," which Herring says begins as "a sign of immoral greed" and then becomes, in the late twentieth century, "an accepted psychopathological diagnosis."[104] Like Couperus's Eline Vere, Selden chooses things over people—in this case his hoard of "good editions" and his bachelor's "portfolio" of licentious carryings-on with already wedded women over a marriage with Lily Bart. Selden professes a desire for quality, but he is, at heart, a shrewd investor. He wants to "own all the books he can," to recall the quotation from F. B. Perkins that forms the epigraph to this chapter. He is "loath to part with his assets,"[105] and he knows that, if he settles down and "buys" Lily, this will prevent him from acquiring additional assets (or purchasing additional books) in the future.

It is thus Selden who, like Eline Vere, appears entombed within the confines of his hoard in the last pages of *The House of Mirth*. Wharton effects a contrast between Selden's apartment—which is crammed full of books and furniture and includes a fire burning in the grate—and Lily's cold, empty apartment, a space that is almost bereft of objects save for a few items of clothing. Among them, significantly, is the dress that she wore as "Mrs. Lloyd" in the tableau. "It had been impossible for her to give it away, but she had never seen it since that night, and the long flexible folds, as she shook them out, gave forth an odour of violets."[106] Much like Eline Vere with her dried flower mementos from festive balls, Lily reminisces in the company of objects, remembering "the flower-edged fountain where she had stood with Lawrence Selden and disowned her fate."[107] Unlike Eline, though, she has very few objects to choose from, and Wharton's use of the word "disowned" here is significant: it suggests that Lily's prized possession has always been herself. Lily is conscious, however, of having "given away" her fate where, once, she might have sold it to the highest bidder. She has managed her assets poorly, and like Couperus's Eline she feels she has only herself to blame for her resultant suffering and disappointment.

Lily's tragic flaw lies in her inability to distinguish between value and cost. She understands that the life that she desires has a price—that is to say, it costs money—but she does not perceive the full array of informal costs, social and otherwise, that come along with it. This is what causes her to enter blunderingly into a business arrangement with Gus Trenor; her narrow and decidedly vulgar view of economics prevents her from seeing the "costs" that are expected of her in that particular situation. She is no more cognizant of her value as a market commodity than she is of the value of Selden's La Bruyère. She views Selden as different from the likes of Percy Gryce, and herself as different from the likes of her female competitors, but she is wrong in both regards. While their collections might appear dissimilar, Selden and Percy have the act of collecting in common. And as a commodity Lily is valuable only if she remains in constant circulation. The moment of her purchase is therefore fated to coincide with the moment of her death.

The Collectible Literary Canon

In placing a common and concerted emphasis on themes of collecting, both *Eline Vere* and *The House of Mirth* highlight discourses of paranoid accumulation, as I have called them. The "paranoid" aspect of such discourse stems from anxieties surrounding the concepts of value, worth, use, and wear, and from the drive to accumulate and collect that is, I believe, an outgrowth of mounting fears concerning "the stuff of normal life," to recall Herring, at the turn of the twentieth century. Many scholars (including, most notably, Richard Ohmann) have described the ways in which the maturation of consumer capitalism and the attendant explosion of mass-produced goods during this era enhanced both the viability and the reach of so-called mass culture. Ohmann, in his *Selling Culture,* interprets the spread of mass culture with relevance to the growth and appeal of hegemonic structures, noting the ways in which not just goods but "cultural experiences" became available for purchase during this time and so were able to be "bought and sold in markets" under the auspices of enforced hegemonic "consent."[108] In both *Eline Vere* and *The House of Mirth*, we see the ways in which this kind of commoditized experience begets, in turn, a paranoid quest for its opposite: *authentic* experience. Both Couperus's and Wharton's protagonists are afraid—afraid to live materially disadvantaged lives, yes, but also afraid to commit to the conditions of material advantage that might nullify the possibility of living "authentically." Eline and Lily fear that a commitment to material advantage will have the effect of compromising their claims to authentic individuality. Selden, likewise, fears that investing in and marrying Lily will put a halt to the very processes of exchange that make her a worthwhile investment (and an authentic possession for an aspiring collector like himself) in the first place. And within these fears lie deep-seated anxieties concerning the perceived collapse of subject–object dualism during this time. Diana Fuss, for instance, explains that "the rise of capitalist production and the spread of commodity culture led to the naturalization and personification of the material object on the one hand and the mechanization and objectification of the human subject on the other hand."[109] In other words, early twentieth-century subjects (people) feared for their reification as objects and so sought to master, control, and "own" all the objects they could as a means of reinforcing the feelings of authenticity that they viewed as sacred to their identity as human subjects. What Couperus's and Wharton's characters collectively fail to comprehend, though, is that all these anxieties, which are really anxieties about the fluctuating nature of value and worth, cannot be offset by the acts of collecting and accrual (indeed, they are often made worse by them). So Eline, Selden, and Lily continue to collect and to accrue, naïvely imagining that the source of their suffering and misery—*stuff*—will someday transform into the source of their salvation.

Edith Wharton's library, as I argued in the Introduction to this book, similarly sketches a history of anxiety concerning the link between authenticity and accrual. Wharton is forever placing her characters in the context of books, and often these descriptions of personal libraries come with overt nods to canonical "standards." In *A Backward Glance,* for example, Wharton describes a "background of books" as being "an essential part of the old New York household. In my grandparents' day, every gentleman had what was called a 'gentleman's library.'" Wharton then goes on to name the authors that formed the basis of this kind of collection, explaining that "Macaulay, Prescott, Motley, Sainte-Beuve, Augustin Thierry, Victor Hugo, the Brontës, Mrs. Gaskell, Ruskin, Coleridge had been added to the French and English classics." Such authors, she observes, "represented a standard," connecting to estimations of "good breeding" and class prestige.[110] Yet note how many of the authors she lists are French. Though Wharton's ethnic background excludes overt claims to French ancestry,[111] French language and literature clearly formed the bedrock of her canonical understanding, even from a young age. This is because, as Casanova explains, France (and, in particular, Paris) had functioned for centuries as "the capital of . . . a kingdom of literature set up in opposition to the ordinary laws of states, a transnational realm whose sole imperatives are those of art and literature: the universal republic of letters."[112] For Wharton and her milieu, French literature meant both value and worth; indeed, it means the same thing to Selden in *The House of Mirth,* and it has continued to mean this for much of the Western world throughout the twentieth century.

The ability of French literature to bestow this kind of instantaneous canonical prestige explains, in part, the persistent links between Wharton's name and the French naturalist tradition. In her *The World Republic of Letters,* for example, Casanova describes a metaphorical line that compares to the prime meridian and

> makes it possible to estimate the relative aesthetic distance from the center of the world of letters of all those who belong to it. . . . The aesthetic distance of a work or corpus of works from the center may thus be measured by their temporal remove from the canons that, at the precise moment of estimation, define the literary present.[113]

That "line," Casanova furthermore explains, stands for Paris and for the periodic resurgence of a revolutionary spirit that characterized French culture throughout the nineteenth century (following the revolutions of 1789, 1830, 1848, 1870–71, and so on). Locating Wharton's work close to this "line" makes her novels worth more; it lends canonical esteem to her writing and situates her characters within a long trajectory of revolutionary artistic production. Wharton, for her own part, would not have resisted such an association. Indeed, her library collection shows that she was thoroughly invested in the European canon and in French literary traditions, a subject that I will explore in chapter 3.

Another reason that France continues to claim such canonical prestige, Casanova points out, has to do with its relationship to notions of fashion and to actual modernity. Casanova, like Walter Benjamin, calls Paris the "capital of modernity," explaining that "it was where fashion—

the outstanding expression of modernity—was made."[114] This means that, for literary producers to be seen as modern at the start of the twentieth century, they had to establish the relevance of their literary products to a specifically French brand of modernity. This is because we tend to see age as a prerequisite for the realization of modernity: "It is necessary to be old in order to have any chance of being modern or of decreeing what is modern," Casanova argues.[115] It is an observation that, to my mind, bears a lot of resemblance to Theodor Adorno's point in his work *Minima Moralia* that "one must have tradition in oneself, to hate it properly."[116] Modernity, certainly, registered as a kind of "hatred" of tradition in the early part of the twentieth century, or at the very least as an attempted usurpation of tradition. This is what Adorno is getting at when he says that "snobs show more aptitude than proletarians for avant-garde movements in art" and links a willingness for experimentation with a hatred not just of tradition but of one's *own* traditions, in particular.[117]

But if Paris is the "capital of modernity," is that to say that modernity is uniquely Parisian, or French? Eric Hayot puts pressure on this suggestion, arguing that "modernity is a specific historical and social formation that does in fact arise in Europe (and through Europe's relationship to the world)," but that a narrowing of the canon of world literature results as consequence of acknowledging such a Eurocentric outlook.[118] Hayot claims that modernity is *not* a uniquely European phenomenon but that it has its roots and origins in European culture and so effects a stranglehold on scholars' attempts to read and assess "other modernities . . . in places outside Europe."[119] What matters to my consideration here is that, for both Couperus and Wharton, France clearly was the center of fashion, modernity, and, yes, literary production in the late nineteenth and early twentieth centuries. Lily's inspection of Selden's copy of La Bruyère compares to the way that Couperus's Lili "settle[s] back in her favorite armchair" with a copy of Hugo's *Notre Dame de Paris*, "bound in red calf with gilt edges."[120] In both of these scenes Wharton and Couperus defer to France and to the automatic quality of the cultural capital contained therein.

Wharton and Couperus, then, have France in common. But this observation is not a groundbreaking one: indeed, any writer who hoped to be taken seriously during this era would have been well advised to highlight the commonalities between their work and the likes of Balzac, Flaubert, and Zola. As such, the fact that Wharton and Couperus have France in common is less interesting than the fact that they have *each other* in common. Throughout this chapter I have highlighted the correspondences between *Eline Vere* and *The House of Mirth* in an effort to point out a critical gap that has resulted, as I see it, from an overdependence on—perhaps, even, an *overdetermination* of—discourses of canonicity. It makes sense to see Couperus's *Eline Vere* as a source text for Wharton's *The House of Mirth*; the similarities between the two rather speak for themselves. But what's more, reading Wharton's *The House of Mirth* in concert with a novel that is, in the United States, less read and less appreciated today helps to historicize and refine the contemporary parameters that tend to structure the debate about canonicity. Analyzing the connection between Wharton and Couperus shows us that the canon wasn't always thus, and that literary value has always been (and therefore very much continues to be) subject to negotiation and revision.[121] Wharton, it seems, "valued" Couperus's work enough to read, own, and derive inspiration from it. But Couperus, for his own part, has gone unmentioned throughout the history of Wharton scholarship for the very reason that *his* name lacks canonical value. To put it another way, because Couperus could not "add" to the value of Wharton's name and oeuvre, he has merited little attention, despite the clear and compelling influence of his work on her own.

The problem of Couperus's worth (or lack thereof) is really a problem of national allegiance. As I mentioned in the introduction to this chapter, Couperus's language and nationality lack certain forms of "prestige" in the eyes of the World Republic of Letters. But in an effort to solidify the connections that I have outlined here between Couperus and Wharton, I want to offer one final, argumentative point: *Eline Vere* is as much "a novel of The Hague" as *The House of Mirth* is a novel of New York City. Which is to say, it isn't. What these two novels communally expose is, I believe, the permeability of national and cultural borders, given the pervasive reach of world markets at the turn of the century. These novels exhibit and are also framed by discourses of paranoid accumulation, as previously mentioned, but what matters is that they furthermore succeed in repackaging those discourses and deploying them within two distinct national arenas. This is why Couperus is able to subtitle *Eline Vere* "A Novel of The Hague" and why early reviewers of *The House of Mirth* saw it as "document" of

New York City society that would "surely be treasured by historians as testimony."[122] Both of these novels suggest that mass production has made the fin de siècle world a smaller and frighteningly inauthentic place. The impulse to hoard and to collect the fast-disappearing relics of an authentic world—be they "good editions" or hand-painted Bucchi fans—becomes thereby understandable. But such an impulse transcends national boundaries. Indeed, it defies the parameters of civic participation, implying that, under industrial capitalism, we are all citizens of capital.

The impulse to collect books in particular—which in its more innocuous form amounts to the bibliophilia of Lawrence Selden and, in its more pernicious form, to the bibliomania of Percy Gryce—also makes sense given these complicated yearnings for authentic engagement. Books encode lived experience, thought, and sensation, but even more than that they monumentalize national feeling in offering up a record of a language that is unique to the moment of its creation. Wharton comments on the relationship between national literature and national language in *A Backward Glance* when she notes that the foreign language "classics" in her father's "gentleman's library" were probably not often read but remained on the shelves in order to "fight[] for the protection of the languages they had illustrated."[123] For Wharton (and for Wharton's characters), book collecting amounts to a perceived investment in the precapitalist world of cultural specificity and authenticity, a world that predates Marx and Engels's description of "intercourse in every direction" and the "universal interdependence of nations." Wharton never lived in such a world, but she dreamed of accessing it through her library, coerced by fantasies of authenticity.

3

· · · · · · · · · · · · · · · · ·

The Library as Network
Affinity, Exchange, and the Makings of Authorship

WHARTON'S OEUVRE OFFERS A CHRONICLE OF SOCIAL EXCHANGE. Soured friendships, ugly divorces, asymmetrical attachments, disastrous risks undertaken for the sake of stability or social advantage— these entanglements form the narrative backbone of her novels and stories. Wharton's preoccupation with social networks, in fact, extends all the way from her earliest works to her latest, with her final two completed novels, *Hudson River Bracketed* (1929) and the sequel *The Gods Arrive* (1932), offering a double dose of her thoughts on the subject. In both of these works, not just individuals but, likewise, artistic careers are forged as the result of networked interactions. It is the study of networks, then, and of the detritus that results from sprawling patterns of social affiliation, that thus defines Wharton's oeuvre. Friendships, marriages, and sexual liaisons may come and go, these works collectively argue, but they leave identifying marks on a person, branding them for their future travels about the spheres of networked human intimacy. Wharton's method of exposing those webbed intricacies serves to remind readers of the ways in which they, in the words of Antonio Gramsci, are "products of the historical process to date, which has deposited in you an infinity of traces, without leaving an inventory."[1] Indeed, the underlying project that unites all of Wharton's fiction, I argue, amounts to an inventory of modern forms of social engagement.

But while Wharton's fascination with social networks remains consistent throughout her fiction, her conclusions about the meaning of a networked life differ. In some of her earliest works, Wharton emphasizes the restrictive and dangerous qualities of social networks: Lily Bart in *The House of Mirth* moves through and occupies a number of positions within her elite New York society, but never for long, and her frenetic travels between various nodes or points make her an easy target for elimination.[2] Lily tries, but fails repeatedly, to gain access to the network's core and is thrust ever further from the center as a consequence of those efforts. When she dies at the end of the novel, she is far away—both in terms of social status and in terms of location—from where she started out at the beginning of it. She has gone from being an object of attention and exchange, circulating somewhere close to the network's central hub, to being an outlier consigned to its margins. Whereas we meet her on page 1 standing in the midst of Grand Central Station (a symbolic as a well as a functional "hub"), we find her occupying a lonely attic apartment at the close of *The House of Mirth*. But Lily is still *there,* she is still part of the network: it cannot use her but neither can it shed her completely,[3] a situation that mirrors Selden's feelings toward her and so justifies his appearance at her bedside, where he confronts the results of her fatal overdose.

Many of Wharton's early short stories present a similar, cautionary view of the hazards that tend to accompany modern, networked existence. Among such examples is the well-anthologized story "The Other Two," published in 1904 as part of Wharton's collection *The Descent of Man.* Wharton's name for her protagonist in this story, Mr. Waythorn, rings like an unsubtle riff on her own, and the story focuses on how networked webs of social exchange threaten intimacy. Waythorn's new wife, Alice, delights him with her "unperturbed gaiety,"[4] but she has already been married twice before, and, in time, murky legacies of attachment begin to weigh on the couple's relationship. Alice has a child from her first marriage, which means that her first husband, Haskett, is legally fated to remain a fixture in their lives. In time, it becomes clear that Alice is a social climber who, like many a Wharton heroine, has used marriage as a "passport to the set whose recognition she coveted."[5] She has, in other words, been continually engaged in a process of "trading up," a fact that requires her to shield aspects of her own social past, including those parts that remain—either legally or biologically speaking—necessarily extant. With regard to her first husband, Waythorn reflects, "nothing was known. [Haskett] was vaguely supposed to have remained in the outer darkness from which his wife had been rescued."[6] Here Wharton is commenting on the way that social networks serve to illuminate a person, revealing lines of attachment and, even, their movements throughout time and space. Alice's social origins, which appear shrouded and mysterious at first (Waythorn credits her second husband for "unearthing" her from somewhere—"Was it in Pittsburg or Utica?"), soon become discernible thanks to Haskett, whom Waythorn calls a "brute."[7] To make matters worse, Waythorn is subsequently forced into doing business with Alice's second husband, Varick, and at this point in the story multiple kinds of networks—domestic, social, and professional—begin to collide. "He had known when he married that his wife's former husbands were both living, and that amid the multiplied contacts of modern existence there were a thousand chances to one that he would run against one or the other," Waythorn reflects.[8] By the end of the story all three husbands wind up together, sitting down to tea in the company of Alice, who acts as a central hub filtering and mediating the men's networked interactions.

Throughout "The Other Two," networked collisions of this kind strike Waythorn as being unlikely and therefore "ironic." He does not see them coming, even while he anticipates the possibility of their happening. This is why the word "irony" surfaces twice during his brief initial encounters with Varick.[9] He meets Varick on a commuter train heading into New York City and then, on that very same day, in a busy New York restaurant. In both instances, he goes to great lengths to avoid Varick, observing that "there was an irony in their renewed nearness."[10] Seated in the restaurant, he eats his lunch alone while, across the room, Varick does the same, with Waythorn watching and itemizing every part of his rival's meal. Then he leaves, "taking a circuitous way out to escape the placid irony of Varick's nod."[11] Thus we have two uses of the word "irony" in the space of a single page, prompting us to view these encounters through the lens of serendipity and happenstance. Waythorn is aware of the ways in which modern life depends on networked social attachments, but he has not fully accepted this knowledge and so is not ready to acquiesce to its demands. He is tormented by thoughts of the role that his wife has played in managing such networks: her function as a metaphorical hub is, after all, suggestive of penetration, violation, and unsavory forms of use, and the child that she retains from her first marriage serves as a living testament to that kind of use. But Waythorn also reflects that Alice has learned to be a better wife and partner as a consequence of all that use, by virtue of the "traces it had left on her nature."[12] He therefore concedes, at the last, that a networked life might just have its own "ironic" merits.

There is a sense, in stories like "The Other Two," of newness and of confusion. Waythorn resents the ways in which his private, domestic affairs are made to overlap with more public sectors of social engagement, including business (Varick) and the law (Haskett). That response, though, gets coded as a process of adjustment: Wharton is showing us how life in the modern world now depends on the successful navigation of complex social networks and how that navigation requires flexibility and a certain degree of compliance. While this was certainly the case for people living in the nineteenth century, the stakes surrounding such navigation and compliance rose in the twentieth, in part because of the way that new technologies and modern conveniences served to enlarge the terrain of social contact. Caroline Levine, for instance, argues that the nineteenth-century novel is particularly successful "at analyzing the complexity and power of networked social experience."[13] Levine centers her discussion of networks on a reading of Charles Dickens's *Bleak House*, "a novel that casts social relations as a complex heaping of networks that not only stretch across space but also unfold over time," according to her thinking.[14] If *Bleak House* shows us the emergence of social networks in the nineteenth century, though, I would argue that Wharton's fiction shows us how they become entrenched and thus regularized in the twentieth.

Whereas stories like "The Other Two" highlight the surprising consequences and ruinous limitations of this new, networked existence, later works like *The Gods Arrive* present networks as inevitable features of modern social life. Gone is the sense of alarm and confusion when, in these novels written only a few decades later, characters who knew each other in rural Midwestern environs meet up in Paris or Monte Carlo or London; gone, too, is the "irony" that Wharton once used to describe two occupants of the same city meeting by chance on a train traveling toward that city. The power of social networks gets crystallized over the course of Wharton's oeuvre, up until the point where everyone and everything appears, if not known, at least know*able*. This process furthermore mirrors the ways in which information and knowledge began, during this era, to be disseminated through the expansion of publishing networks. As Michael Winship attests, "Between 1880 and 1916" (that is, during the years that saw Wharton's rise as an author) "a distinctive national book trade system emerged" alongside the "rapid growth" and "modernization" of the United States publishing industry.[15] Libraries, bookstores, subscription services, new forms of advertising, and new printing technologies were combining to exponentially grow the various networks surrounding print distribution and consumption. Wharton's library, in fact, provides a body of evidence that both speaks to and complicates our understandings of this particular moment in the history of print. As such, it is crucial that we take the time to *read* Wharton's library—not simply in detail via its relationship to representative examples from her writing, as this study has largely done up to this point, but as a whole.

This chapter reads Wharton's library as a composite whole, or corpus, a process that sometimes defies detail-oriented forms of critique and so calls for larger, macroanalytic methods. It rests on the observation that the library collection itself is both a product and an agent of networked social existence at the dawn of the twentieth century; Wharton's books speak to interwoven processes of inheritance and association, but so too do they illuminate the person that was Wharton by revealing the various extents of her social interactions. For this reason, I begin this chapter with a reading of the human network—that is, the milieu—that subtended and supported Wharton's development as a thinker, writer, and author. I forge connections between human subjects and print objects in order to show how Wharton's library survives as a document of not just material but social interaction as well. This discussion of social networks transitions into a discussion of numbers, wherein the primary focus falls on the networked dispersal of text and information. I parse the corpus that is Wharton's library according to editions and dates, according to content and subject matter, and according to individual languages and volumes that appear in translation. What all these data add up to is more than just a portrait of Wharton; indeed, it offers us a window onto a wider landscape that, much like a Thomas Cole painting, shows individual subjects *like* Wharton being dwarfed by their surroundings.

That scene, in turn, is made all the more legible through a discussion of networks. Eugene Thacker, in his foreword to Alexander Galloway's *Protocol,* a foundational text on the subject of networks, asserts that in an abstract sense, a network constitutes "any relation between discrete entities."[16] But Thacker continues by showing how Galloway's use of the term "network" encompasses not just abstraction and metaphor but also materiality, and that this very combination suggests a kind of "incipience." When viewed in terms of abstraction, a network speaks to the possibility of something that is on the verge of being brought into being, or "about to enact itself."[17] Networks function as realms of possibility for both Thacker and Galloway—as sites of nascent becoming, wherein the abstract might just signal the beginning of something material. In a similar way, this discussion toggles between abstraction and materiality: Wharton's library books allude to and describe networks that once had their basis in material reality—living human beings, say. But time has erased much of that materiality, and those people have long since died. The books in her library survive and exist, though, furnishing the material residue of what has since been reduced to abstraction.

Mapping Wharton's Milieu

Reading Wharton's library first requires us to expand the breadth of the questions that we would ask of it. In lieu of a question such as "What can Wharton's library tell us about Edith Wharton?," large-scale forms of reading and analysis encourage broader forms of thinking that redirect our attention and point us toward questions like "What can Wharton's library tell us about reading and print consumption at the turn of the twentieth century?" One of the more immediate, more apparent answers that arises in response to such a question has to do with social networks. For Wharton, and for many readers like her during this era, reading constituted a social act. A survey of the social actors who contributed to Wharton's reading and who served as points of exchange and conveyance makes that idea all the more clear, and it supports Richard Ohmann's observations about how reading is often "embedded in and reinforced by social relations."[18]

Let's start with a graphic that places Wharton at the center of a social network that includes more than a hundred people. All of the disparate figures in this group are linked by a single criterion: they all possessed, at various points throughout history, one or more of the books that can be found today on the shelves of Wharton's library at The Mount. Some of these people were Wharton's own family members and had close ties to her; others were dead by the time she was born and so retain only remote links to her, forged by processes of material exchange and circulation. In this graphic, nodes represent individual people, with thicker lines and larger nodes correlating to the number of books that passed from this person's hands into Wharton's own. The closer the node is located to the central hub (which represents Wharton), the tighter the social affiliation or connection is to her. The larger nodes that appear clustered around Wharton (for example, appearing above and slightly to the right of the center) represent members of her own family. The most prominent of these nodes marks Wharton's father, George Frederic Jones, from whom we can directly trace at least 170 volumes in Wharton's library: Jones gifted many of these books to his young daughter, while other books in the collection formed part of his original property and estate and thus were willed to Wharton's brothers. These visualizations were drafted from a sample of 2,200 books in Wharton's library, and the resulting data indicate that George Frederic Jones is responsible for roughly 7.75 percent of Wharton's total library collection. Indeed, he is the largest single contributor to it, aside from Wharton herself, whose individual purchases and acquisitions account for a much larger share of the collection.

These findings corroborate much of the existing story about Wharton's library. We know that she revered her father's "gentleman's library," which consisted mostly of uniformly bound sets of classics, even as she grew to see its shortcomings: it was only a "second son's collection," as Lee points out, and by all indications Jones wasn't much of a reader anyway.[19] While Lee credits Jones for giving Wharton "her first serious form of education through his 'gentleman's library,'"[20] this point elides some of the other forms of giving that were surely taking place in the Jones household. For instance, there are the books that Jones gave to his daughter and that differ sharply from the kind that would have been included in his own library, such as the ten-volume set of Maria Edgeworth novels, the first of which bears the inscription "Edith Newbold Jones—from Papa—Xmas 1874." Too, there are the many books that Wharton received from other

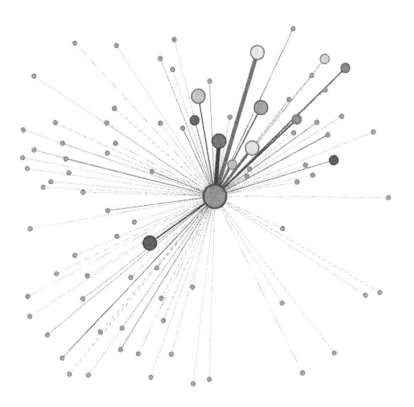

Edith Wharton's social network as represented by the books in her library. Nodes indicate people who previously owned books in her library or who gave them to her.

family members.[21] These include volumes given by her mother, who Wharton dismisses as being "so little a reader" in *A Backward Glance*,[22] yet who presented her daughter with a four-volume set of the works of John Keats, among others, handsomely bound in red morocco leather. Wharton also received books from her brothers, and in some cases she appears to have stolen them outright, which is why her library retains her brother's copy of Emerson's *Essays*: it is dated 1865 and features Frederic Jones's signature in addition to handwritten listings for his New York addresses. The younger Jones later went into business as a bookbinder, so it is unlikely that he would have parted with his own books willingly, suggesting that Wharton may have acquired them by more indirect means.

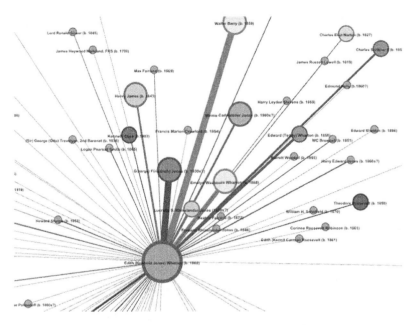

Detail of Wharton's social network as represented by the books in her library.

Family might seem like the most likely of stories where such a library is concerned, but Wharton goes to great lengths in her autobiographies and elsewhere to argue otherwise. Her father's library, she insists, was modest; her mother wasn't a reader; her brothers, though they were college educated, were not much interested in books. Such disavowals are vital, if not necessarily to the person that Wharton is or was then to the person that she was intent on making herself *into*. We may therefore see Wharton's familial network as proof of the kind of material incipience described by Thacker and Galloway—that is, as an abstract network that is nevertheless based on material forms of networked relation (biological, legal, economic) and that furthermore supports Wharton's efforts to forge and "enact" a particular version of herself. That Wharton's father should be tied directly to nearly 8 percent of her overall library collection marks him as a significant, material force in her life; that he should account *only* for 8 percent of her total library signifies the extent to which systems of inheritance fail to furnish explanatory models where this particular library collection is concerned.[23]

Indeed, the vast majority—more than 92 percent—of Wharton's library appears to have been acquired outside the spheres of inheritance and legally sanctioned transfers of wealth. This point actually lends credence to some of Wharton's claims about self-making, since it can be argued that she acquired most of her books without help from her family, through connections and associations that she forged for herself en route to becoming an author. Wharton's web of friends and affiliates fanned out and multiplied over time, revealing a network structured not primarily by inheritance and birthright but, more than anything else, by professional affinities. If we focus on other parts of the network visualization—on Wharton's affiliates based in France, for instance—we get a different image of the social ties represented by her library collection. In an example, Morton Fullerton, with whom she later had an affair, started out as a literary contact: she met him through Henry James, and he appears clustered on the graph near other members of Wharton's Franco-American cohort, which also included Paul Bourget and Gaillard Lapsley.[24] All four of these men contributed volumes to Wharton's library: James gave her several copies of his own work, some of which remain unopened to this day, while others feature tender inscriptions and appear to have been much read; Fullerton, as I explain in chapter 4, gave her books that are helpful in deciphering the long arc of their relationship; and Lapsley and Bourget bestowed works by both themselves and others. Lapsley, for instance, gave Wharton a copy of William Gerhardie's novel *Futility* (1922), and Wharton went on to write an introduction for the American edition that followed that same year. For this reason, her library retains two copies of *Futility*—one from Lapsley, and one from Gerhardie, whose inscription reads, "To Edith Wharton from W.A.G., *ceaselessly* grateful, 7.11.23."[25] Similarly, Wharton acquired the copy of Paul Bourget's novel *Les Deux Soeurs* (1905) that he had originally presented to Henry James with the inscription "à Henry James son ami Paul Bourget." Wharton was in the habit of appropriating her associates' books in this way, especially on the occasion of their respective deaths. She acquired her first-edition copy of *Ulysses*, one of the most valuable books in her collection (but a work that she nevertheless despised), in this precise way, seizing it from Walter Berry's relatives following his death in 1927.[26]

Wharton's library, when rendered in terms of human engagement, thereby encourages us to see reading and collecting as networked, social acts. Wharton read the works of her friends, associates, and contemporaries; she received suggestions about what to read in the form of gifts; she reciprocated and found new audiences for her work by giving gifts in kind; and she forged new relationships with people through reading. Consider that when Wharton first met Henry James at the tender age of twenty-five, it was at the house of the artist Edward Boit, a Bostonian living in Paris and an "old friend" of her husband, Teddy. This encounter resulted, arguably, from the sphere of contacts that had been put in place by the circumstances surrounding Edith's birth—that is, by her parents, their class status, and their affiliates. Wharton's family members were as much the architects of this moment as they were of her marriage to Teddy in the first place. But it was an unsuccessful encounter; James ignored her, and in *A Backward Glance* Wharton dubs the whole thing a "failure" in light of her inability to secure his attention.[27] It wasn't until years later, as Wharton tells it, that she and James got to know each other as literary professionals, at which point "suddenly it was as if we had always been friends, and were to go on being (as he wrote to me in February 1910) 'more and more never apart.'"[28] Two people who had nothing to say to each other fifteen years earlier went on to describe themselves as being inseparable, spurred by conversations that centered mostly on the reading of books. Reading, in fact, figured more prominently in their conversations than writing: "I always tried to keep my own work out of his way, and once accused him of ferreting it out and reading it just to annoy me," Wharton explains.[29] And, of course, were it not for her literary associations with Henry James, Wharton would have likely never met Morton Fullerton. In this way, it appears that many of Wharton's most important and intimate associations came as the direct result of her activities as a *reader,* rather than from her writing.

Wharton's social network also extends beyond the realms of lived intimacies and close relations, though, to include deceased figures. Her library features scores of association copies—that is, books previously owned by or associated with famous individuals and authors—in addition to less illustrious, secondhand editions. For example, a set of association copies originating from the Napoleonic writer known as "Madame de Staël" appears among the collection library; an inscription, written by de Staël's daughter, Albertine, reveals that it was presented to a "Monsieur de Salaberry" in 1814 on behalf of de Staël herself ("de la part De Mad. de Staël"). In all likelihood, Wharton received this set through her association with the Comtesse d'Hausonville, who was married to de Staël's grandson, and at whose suggestion Wharton established a workshop for displaced and impoverished women through the Red Cross during the First World War. Indeed, the set may have been a gift offered in appreciation of Wharton's wartime service; regardless of its origins, it illuminates more of the actors operating within Wharton's network and helps to shed light on some of its outer peripheries. So, too, does a twelve-volume set, dated 1826, of Edward Gibbon's *The History of the Decline and Fall of the Roman Empire,* which features the bookplate of John Wilson-Patten, Baron of Winmarleigh. The Winmarleigh armorial crest appears just beneath Wharton's own, indicating that she probably bought or acquired the books some time after Wilson-Patten's death in 1892. The entire set is gorgeously bound in calfskin, and we might well wonder about Wharton's reasons for acquiring it, given that she already owned a complete set of Gibbon's *Decline and Fall* (this one in seven volumes). The link to Wilson-Patten that survives through the twelve-volume edition, though, calls to mind a particular sector of Wharton's social network, one that is sometimes overlooked by scholars and historians: her associates in England.

Wharton's transatlantic migrations are often seen as centering on France and the United States, but many of her close associates were British, and for a time, even, she had seriously considered settling in England. The social ties connecting Wharton to members of the British gentry are furthermore substantiated by the inclusion of a typewritten letter that appears tipped in to one of the volumes in the 1816 set of Gibbon's masterwork. The letter is dated October 22, 1947, and is addressed to Lady Clark, wife of Kenneth Clark, from a British bookseller named Martin Breslauer, who writes to inform her of a possible rare book purchase. "You may remember an extremely rare work describing the funeral solemnities of Michel Angelo, which appeared in my catalogue 59," the letter reads. "You sent an order for the book, but unfortunately the copy had already gone. I enclose a cutting of the description as it appeared in the catalogue." Breslauer then goes on to describe the binding, which a handwritten caret specifies is "by the great French binder Lortic," indicating that the item in question was custom bound by the renowned craftsman of that same name working in postrevolutionary France. This volume, which is now more than two hundred years old, thereby illustrates—not through its content but through such material additions as bookplates and letters—a process of exchange that spans centuries and extends throughout the echelons of the British aristocracy. In this particular instance, we are not talking purely of the exchange of material goods: we are talking about the social mechanisms that are responsible for broadcasting a particular body of knowledge, for it is evident that people have read and interacted with these books. Wharton, displaying the kind of fustiness that characterizes much of her reading, has added a penciled correction to the first volume (changing a "was" to a "were"), and penciled markings appear similarly throughout volumes nine and eleven. What all of this—including the letter from Breslauer to Lady Clark—reveals is how a long line of people were handling, reading, and engaging with the text of these volumes over the course of two centuries.[30]

Richard Wendorf, offering a gloss on Walter Benjamin's ideas, comments that "every passion borders on the chaotic but the collector's passion borders on the 'chaos of memories.'"[31] In the case of Wharton's library, the "chaos of memories" does not pertain solely to Wharton. Rather, what we have here are networked spheres of memory and memorialization (an idea I will develop further in chapter 4) that permits us to see how books serve not just as vehicles for the transmission of printed information but as connecting lines on a graph that link living readers to their deceased counterparts and form connections between objects and extensive chains of subjective attachment. Objects make history happen in the minds of those who are living in the present, a point that furthermore surfaces in Wharton's story "The Other Two." Waythorn orders his wife to return a set of pearls that were given to her by her previous husband, Varick, but in a photograph that sits on his own dressing table she is pictured wearing the pearls. This prompts Waythorn to wonder, "Had Haskett [Alice's first husband] ever given her any trinkets" and, if so, "what had become of them . . . ?"[32] Wharton's strategic use of objects in this story reminds us of the ways in which things speak to legacies of networked association, legacies that furthermore prove difficult to pave over and erase, given modern humans' interests in hoarding, collecting, and accruing. The object that causes the most trouble for Waythorn in this story is neither the pearl necklace nor the photograph of it but "a made-up tie attached with an elastic."[33] Haskett wears this very sort of tie, which seems to advertise and expose the plain facts of Alice's schemes for social ascendancy. She started out with a husband who wore a fake tie, she graduated to pearls, and now she finds herself wedded to Waythorn, who is suddenly confronted with the knowledge that he might be, after all, just one more rung on her improvised ladder. This knowledge is made possible through a collection of objects, which proclaims in plain tones the truth of Alice's travels about the various, networked realms of modern social existence.

According to Levine, we tend to view networks as "violat[ing] the bounded enclosures that either imprison or protect us,"[34] including the kinds of fictive enclosures that receive legal designation, like marriage. And while Levine furthermore asserts, via a discussion of Emily Dickinson, that this is not always the case, such violation certainly entered into the picture where Edith and Teddy Wharton were concerned. Cornelia Brooke Gilder explains that during the period in which the Whartons built The Mount and settled in Lenox, Edith Wharton's network branched out in two different directions, encompassing, on the one hand, her "very loyal staff" and, on the other, "her intellectual friends." This situation constituted a problem for the very reason that Teddy's own family was centered in Lenox and that Teddy's mother took issue with Wharton's preference for surrounding herself with intellectual compatriots. "As an emerging celebrity author, she was sidelining Teddy for her adoring circle of male intellectual friends—Howard Sturgis, Walter Berry, Henry James—to say nothing of disappearing to Paris for an affair with Henry James' journalist friend Morton Fullerton," Gilder reports.[35] In other words, Teddy's mother saw Wharton's network of literary affiliates as having a deleterious effect on the couple's marriage, which was, by this point in time, fast approaching disintegration anyway.

Wharton's Library, by the Numbers

Wharton's social network had mushroomed in the wake of her 1905 publication of *The House of Mirth*, which launched her career as a literary author. Her library was also growing during this time, as indicated by a survey of the volumes in her library according to publication date. This graph makes visible the collection's four-hundred-year span and reveals a demonstrable

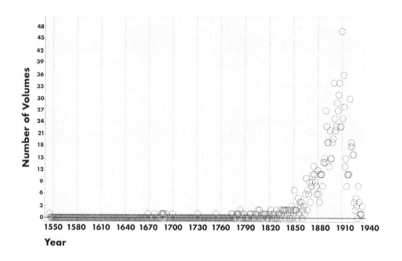

Wharton's library volumes by edition and date of publication.

spike in the number of books and editions acquired that date from the latter part of the era that Winship previously identified (1880–1916). In particular, the years 1910 and 1911 are well represented among editions in the collection. These were significant years in Wharton's life: they saw the purchase of her first Parisian home in the Rue de Varenne that precipitated her permanent relocation to France, the heartbreaking sale of The Mount estate in Massachusetts, and the beginnings of her divorce from Teddy. Wharton's library features several works that would have been new in 1910 and 1911, including some titles relating to the Irish Literary Revival, which was taking place just across the Channel. Wharton acquired first edition copies of Lord Dunsany's *A Dreamer's Tale* and Yeats's *Poems: Second Series* during this time, alongside other works like the French poet Henri de Regniér's *La Miroir de Heures* and a massive, eighteen-volume set of Flaubert's complete works, dated 1910.

But what this graph, alongside the body of metadata lifted from the Wharton library database,[36] likewise reveals is that Wharton did not concern herself chiefly with the purchasing of new titles. In fact, the majority of the volumes that she purchased or acquired during these years of heavy activity were new editions of old texts.[37] This observation helps to shed additional light on her habits as a reader, even as it obscures our view of her relationship to the field of contemporary literary production. For instance, George Sand's novel *Elle et Lui* was more than fifty years old by the time Wharton acquired a copy of it in 1911. The same goes for Ralph Waldo Emerson's *Journals,* which were originally published in the 1830s. Other new acquisitions dating from the years 1910–11 include a number of books on Beethoven (all of them later editions or reprints), Joshua Reynolds's *Discourses on Art* (1769–90), works by Machiavelli, philological texts by the German classicist Ludwig Friedlaender (1862–71), and the Occitan poet Frédéric Mistral's *L'Isles d'Or* (1875). On the one hand, volumes by the likes of Sand and Mistral suggest that Wharton's interests in the French literary canon were expanding and deepening in connection with her expatriate lifestyle during this period; at the same time, we can see Wharton as rejecting the rigidity of nationalism in favor of reading across a broadly European, cosmopolitan (though consummately white) canon. Wharton's being in Paris ought to have exposed her to the likes of Colette, whose *La Vagabonde* was published in 1910 and whose work ought therefore to have furnished a kind of contemporary context for Wharton's own. But while Wharton owned a copy of *La Vagabonde,* she did so only by virtue of her association with Walter Berry: his tastes were more liberal than hers, and it is his 1923 copy of Colette's novel that can be found today at The Mount.

When Wharton read her contemporaries, then, it was often the result of a desire to honor the social connections she had with them. Many of the volumes that she acquired in 1910 and 1911 came to her as gifts: her longtime associate John Hugh Smith, for one, presented her with a copy of *The Oxford Book of Ballads,* while a fledgling interest in the Spanish–American philosopher George Santayana grew in response to a gift from William Henry Schofield, a Harvard academic who was living in Paris and lecturing at the Sorbonne at the time. Henry James gifted her with copies of his newest works, including the novel *The Outcry* (1911), which had started as a play but was never produced, and Wharton's copy remains laterally unopened today on a shelf at The Mount. Likewise, the French literary scholar Ernest Seillière gave her copies of his own work, each with a lavishly complementary inscription like "à Madame Edith Wharton Hommage respecteux": one of these was a study of the writer Jules Barbey d'Aurevilly, famous for his short story collection *Les Diaboliques,* which was published in 1875 but which Wharton likewise acquired and read in 1910. Wharton, it must be remembered, was approaching fifty during this time, so figures like Seillière (who was born in 1866) fit in nicely among a milieu that had not just literature but also a certain generational outlook in common. This was a group that had been formed by the nineteenth century, even if it was living in the twentieth, a fact that may help to explain why Wharton's library's nineteenth-century holdings continued to grow even as new writers, like Colette and like James Joyce, were launching a direct challenge to nineteenth-century literary conventions under the rubric of a new movement called "modernism." Though her own success resulted exclusively from books she published after the year 1900, Wharton remained circumstantially allied to the nineteenth century by virtue of her friends and associates, some of whom (like James) were much older than she.

Wharton's library, though it grew considerably throughout the early part of the twentieth century, grew primarily backward, extending further into the nineteenth century and beyond. This occurred even as modernist figures like Ezra Pound demanded that writers look toward the future in order to "Make it new!"[38] Wharton, by comparison, maintained an interest in making it *old* and in using her characteristic brand of socially incisive realism as a means of reappraising the past. Consider, for instance, that it was also during this period that she began work on *Ethan Frome* (1912), a novella that employs a frame narrative in order to grant readers access to what is, essentially, a work of historical fiction. Ethan is fifty-two years old when we first encounter him at the start of *Ethan Frome*—close to Wharton's age—but he is twenty-eight for the majority of the narrative that follows. Wharton's desire to represent historical periods in her fiction thus appears linked to a concomitant interest in reading and studying historical texts. This point merits special emphasis because it is one that often remains neglected in many discussions of the history of readership: while best-seller lists, literary prizes, and promotional programs (like the Book-of-the-Month Club) succeed in granting us a picture of what the publishing industry looked like at a particular point in time, they do not always bequeath an authentic view of the connections between publishing and readership, or between authors and readers. Indeed, we must reckon with the fact that, for many readers at many points throughout history, best sellers and new releases would have held less allure than classic texts. Lynch, for example, points to the ways in which readers in the middle part of the eighteenth century, thanks in part to the emergence of a fledgling kind of literary criticism, gravitated toward old texts. "The reading of old books with the assistance they afforded was esteemed precisely as a means through which the present generation might assert and retain its affiliations with the generations preceding it," Lynch argues.[39] Readers who sought access to guarded realms of cultural capital—or, for that matter, to the economic categories associated with those realms—would, like Wharton, have likely gravitated toward classic texts, which had the virtue of having already been designated as important, thanks to a process that Bourdieu labels "consecration."[40] Likewise, literary criticism, which was gaining strength and legitimacy as an enterprise throughout the nineteenth century, was primarily concerned with texts written a hundred years (or more) previously, a situation that amounted to tacit encouragement for the reading of old texts over new ones. One need only consult the works of Matthew Arnold or, as previously mentioned, William Hazlitt—two early literary critics whose works can be found in Wharton's library—to see how this might have been the case for readers like her in the early twentieth century.[41]

Indeed, discussions of popularity and sales often furnish only half the story. Gordon Hutner, in his *What America Read,* assesses the neglected "middle ground" of middle-class realist fiction beginning in the 1920s and extending through to the middle point of the century. These "bourgeois novels," Hutner claims, constituted the primary literary vehicles "through which Americans were most likely to enter into and perhaps to participate in the public life of the century's middle decades."[42] Hutner sets his sights exclusively on those novels published during the decades that he surveys, a strategy that enables him, for example, to "survey the middleclass realism that was praised throughout the decade [of the 1920s] for its efforts to confront modernity,"[43] but which takes for granted the idea that a significant portion of the reading during this time period centered on new publications. One of the advantages, meanwhile, of studying a library collection as a whole is that it allows us to interface between large-scale data sets (dates, copies sold, awards won) and readers' individualized behaviors.[44] Wharton, as I have argued elsewhere in the preceding chapters, was certainly interested in "confronting" modernity, and the novels that she published into the 1920s furthermore show how this was the case. Yet it would appear that those confrontations did not comprise the bulk of her own reading or studies during this era—one that likewise saw her rise to success as a popular author. Rather, it seems that those confrontations formed dialectically, in response to her deepening studies of history.

Wharton's relative disinterest in popular fiction is especially significant given Hutner's insistence on viewing her novels as touchstone examples of popular "middleclass realism." Realist authors like Wharton, according to Hutner, helped to broker a transition from what he calls the era of "American Victorianism" to the dawn of an era better known for its associations with both modernity and modernism. Wharton and her ilk excelled in offering a particularly mollifying brand of bourgeois realism, the purpose of which, Hutner argues, was to "guide middle-class readers through contemporary bewilderments." To that end, Hutner asserts, "Whatever these novelists' identities, their patron saint was William Dean Howells, not Henry James; Edith Wharton, not Djuna Barnes."[45] In pairing Wharton with Howells, and in severing her from both modernist writers like Barnes and more "literary" authors like James, Hutner is suggesting that *as a novelist* (if not necessarily as a reader or consumer), Wharton ought to be seen as allied with the realist writers of her day. Her library, though, suggests otherwise. Wharton did own one novel by Howells, a first-edition copy of his *A Modern Instance,* published in two volumes and acquired when Wharton was all of nineteen years old, and she likely would have encountered his work in magazines like the *Atlantic* (where she would later be published). But if her own work was influenced by Howells, that influence does not appear to have resulted from the protracted study of his fiction. Meanwhile, in lieu of Howells, Wharton owned multiple works by authors like Flaubert (twenty-five volumes) and Zola (four volumes), both foundational examples of what Hutner labels "bourgeois realism"—albeit *French* bourgeois realism, not American—and thus both better candidates for the kind of "sainthood" that Hutner describes.

In tying his discussion of what America read to a discussion of what America published, Hutner turns contemporaneity into a recurrent punchline and thus simplifies the link between subject and object with respect to historical readership.[46] Wharton's library puts pressure on those claims of contemporaneity and shows, conversely, how reading during this era still primarily meant reading the Western canon, especially for upper-class readers like her who saw the accumulation of cultural capital as a kind of precondition—not for social success, per se, but for "quality" breeding and true refinement. The literary education that Wharton received as a child courtesy of her governess, Anna Bahlmann, similarly centered on the reading of classic, historical texts, as indicated by much of their correspondence: in an 1876 letter to Bahlmann, a thirteen-year-old Wharton cites Goethe, Tennyson, the Icelandic *Edda,* and the poetry of James Russell Lowell.[47] The last of these references is the most modern of them all, though Lowell's "Prometheus"—which Wharton mentions directly—was published in 1843 and so was already thirty years old by this point. This education, much like her father's modest library of "classic" texts for gentlemen, formed the basis of her habits as a reader, which tended toward conservative forms of appreciation and greeted anything that appeared suggestive of innovation or newness with a measure of old-fashioned suspicion.

There is a gendered dimension to Wharton's reading habits that becomes clearer when we stop to consider two factors: that she, unlike most of the men she knew, was never permitted to attend school; and that she was often one of the only, if not *the* only, female among her circle of literary compatriots. Whereas Howard Sturgis was educated at Cambridge, Henry James studied at Harvard, and Walter Berry was a graduate of Columbia, Wharton's lack of education held the potential to differentiate and to mark her from her associates, as did her gender. This combined set of circumstances meant that a discernible gap existed between her and the great minds that had furnished the substance of her improvised, less formal education. Though Wharton went on to develop an appreciation for female writers like George Eliot and George Sand (two writers whose pseudonyms reveal the extent of their own struggles with gendered exclusion), they were not chiefly or automatically folded into her literary upbringing, even though another woman supervised that upbringing. Rather, we might see Wharton's investment in reading and collecting the Western canon as evidence of a need to account for perceived shortcomings—ones that gendered inequality had helped to engineer in the first place. In reading old books and relying on historical settings in her stories, Wharton became engaged in a process of rewriting and thus reclaiming some of the history that she had been previously denied access to or inclusion in.

To that end, it's no surprise to see that history ranks alongside poetry and literary fiction as one of the best-represented subject categories in Wharton's library.[48] A graphic depiction of Wharton's library volumes by subject shows how her reading tastes skew primarily toward literature and history, with essays making up another large part of the collection.[49] Toward the middle, we see subjects like drama, biography, science, and religion clustered between the fifty and seventy-five volume marks. After that, a rather steep descent lands us among subjects like art history, horticulture, design, and psychology. It is crucial that we approach this graph with the understanding that certain categories are bound to appear less represented. This unevenness has to do with the way that Wharton divided up the collection and willed it to her heirs based *by* subject. Ramsden reports that this division appears to have been "slightly haphazard" and cites how "a substantial section of French history, some Italian history (especially of the Papacy and the Jesuits), Gibbon, several standard works of American history, and a smattering of English history came to Colin Clark,"[50] despite the fact that all of the history books were marked for transfer to Wharton's second heir, William Tyler. What Ramsden's findings—much like the graph—suggest is that the library's extant collection of history volumes, though substantial, is far from complete: Tyler's portion, which was supposed to have primarily included works of history in addition to art and archaeology,[51] was, to recall the discussion of inheritance from chapter 1, destroyed in the London Blitz of 1941.

It seems likely, therefore, that Wharton, at the time of her death, owned more works of history than of literature. This conclusion, while it helps to explain the depth of her investment in writing historical fiction, also lends greater nuance to our studies of her behaviors as a reader and her tastes relating to her identity as an autodidact. Wharton scholars have made careful efforts over the years to account for the ways in which Wharton's fiction appears to correspond to her extraliterary reading habits, with critics like Donald Pizer declaring that "even the casual reader of *The House of Mirth* is made aware throughout the work that Edith Wharton had been reading widely in social evolutionary theory of her day."[52] Yet as some of the visualizations featured in this chapter help to make clear, Wharton's reading of history and historical texts would appear, even, to far outshine her much-documented interest in evolutionary theory (included here under the

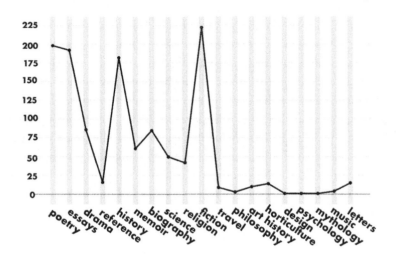

Wharton library volumes by subject.

general heading of "science"). We might wonder, therefore, what kind of influence, if any, *that* reading of history had on her intellectual and creative trajectories. For the purposes of this study, I am more interested in delving into the context that would have supported or made such reading possible in the first place. Can we view Wharton's rather thorough engagement with history and with historical texts as par for the course during this era, or must it be viewed as idiosyncratic? And what did the reading of history hold for people like her during the early twentieth century, faced as they were with the irreversible fact of living their lives under the conditions of an antihistorical modernity?

In his essay on the rise of national book trade in the United States, Michael Winship works from a chart showing new titles and editions released between 1880 and 1916 and divided by subject. The chart was crafted from two sets of data published in *Publisher's Weekly*, first in 1911 and then again in 1917. In other words, these data were originally prepared within the same time frame that saw Wharton's library book acquisitions spike (1910–11), and its reliance on subject divisions more or less corresponds to those used in the illustration here (biography, history, travel, fiction, and so on). The chart thus surveys publishing by subject—if not necessarily sales or consumption—from the perspective of the publishing industry, which Winship explains had not yet begun to diversify to the point where individual publishers were specializing in particular subjects. Rather, Winship observes, publishing firms "issued works of all subjects and genres, competing with each other in what often proved to be an oversupplied market."[53] Among these were works of history, which consistently accounted for only a humble share of the market of newly published books (about 4 percent) for almost four decades, from 1880 until 1914. Things changed slightly in 1916 as the United States prepared for entry into the First World War and the publication of history texts suddenly increased, taking up just more than 7 percent of the market. Wharton's history books, by comparison, account for nearly 8.5 percent of her library based on the figures shown in the graph, though one may reasonably assume that the real proportion might be slightly higher given that the graph was drafted from a representative sample and so is not comprehensive. It would be undoubtedly higher were we able to add William Tyler's inheritance to these calculations.

Wharton appears to have ranked as an above-average reader of history, then, if not extravagantly so. Her earliest interactions with the subject came in response to reading her father's library books, where "the principal historians were Plutarch, Macaulay, Prescott, Parkman, Froude, Carlyle, Lamartine, Thiers."[54] But it is important to keep in mind that given her exclusion from formal schooling and her status as a woman, that reading would have nonetheless been considered rather atypical. For instance, Edward H. Clarke's *Sex in Education,* published in 1873 on the heels of progressive cries for the expansion of coeducation,[55] argues against educating females alongside males. Coeducation, Clarke feared, would force women to compete intellectually with men, resulting in the depletion of their delicate female bodies and, in time, in illness and death as well. Instead of coeducation, Clarke halfheartedly explores the prospect of what he calls "special and appropriate education," a phrase that he uses to describe a form of education based both on gendered segregation and on the development of separate curricular agendas for boys and girls. Clarke calls for a kind of education that observes, and thus also reifies, "physiological" differences between men and women: "in the education of girls, as well as boys, the machinery and methods of instruction shall be carefully adjusted to their [physiological] organization," though he admits that such educational schemes are likely to be costly and burdensome for schools.[56]

Though coeducation was on the rise during this era, Wharton's own educational history rather suggests that Clarke's claims—however extreme they might seem to us today—continued to hold weight in late nineteenth-century America. Upper-class parents who could afford to keep their daughters away from the ghastly coeducational arena of public education were encouraged toward the kinds of segregation espoused by Clarke and obliged to see their girls privately educated at home, or else in boarding schools.[57] Such was the case for Wharton, who began her studies under the tutelage of Anna Bahlmann in the spring of 1874, only months after the publication of Clarke's *Sex in Education* and amid an array of public discussions that were still swirling in response to it.[58] It is additionally fascinating to note that Clarke closes his arguments about coeducation in his book with a quotation from Friedrich Schiller's play *Wallenstein* in a translation by Coleridge that reads:

> Leave now the puny wish, the girlish feeling
> Oh, thrust it far behind thee! Give thou proof
> Though'rt the daughter of the Mighty—*his*
> Who where he moves creates the wonderful . . .
> Meet and disarm necessity by choice.[59]

Clarke offers this quotation in connection with his advice to American women, that they "become convinced of the evils they have been educated into, and out of which they are determined to educate their daughters."[60] Clarke is calling for the resolution of false consciousness and "puny wishes" regarding women's education, and for a return to conservative approaches to the subject. His use of the Schiller quotation, though, gains an aura of tragedy when read in light of Wharton's own education: her copy of Schiller's *Gedichte,* which includes *Wallenstein,* dates from 1874, the year that she started her studies in private with Bahlmann. This coincidence, I think, invites us to see how a shadow of gendered exclusion hung over Wharton's studies from the start.

As Goldman-Price points out, upper-class women's education (such as the kind Wharton received) during the late nineteenth and early twentieth centuries centered not on *education* per se but on *cultivation.* "Schooling might not be the proper measure of learning" where such women were concerned, Goldman-Price observes.[61] This point receives elaboration via a conversation that Goldman-Price had with the granddaughter of Wharton's close friend Daisy Chanler, who explains the situation thus: "Looking back at my own education, I have realized that the point was to be cultivated, rather than educated," a process that manifested primarily in the study of subjects like "French and German, and Italian if possible," in controlled social interaction, and in the memorization of "much poetry by heart."[62] In other words, upper-class women during Wharton's time (and throughout subsequent generations) were primed for success in social intercourse and received training in subjects that might prove beneficial to their social, rather than their intellectual, development. By the looks of it, the education that Wharton received as a child through Bahlmann did not differ dramatically from this prescribed, gender-specific course of instruction. What did differ was the attitude that Wharton appears to have adopted in relation to that training.

Wharton embraced the study of languages not simply as potential fodder for social success but as a legitimate intellectual enterprise. This is a final point that surfaces in response to large-scale readings of her library as a corpus. A pie chart shows all of Wharton's library books divided by language, revealing that, while the majority of the library comprises English-language editions, nearly a third of the collection includes books written in French. German and Italian account for smaller but still significant and identically proportioned shares of the collection. While this, too, would appear to confirm some of what we already know about Wharton's educational background, it also helps to show how, in her particular case, linguistic education goes beyond mere social training and becomes a basis for interfacing with the kinds of hybrid networks produced by a modern, globalized world. Language functions as a powerful mechanism in such networks—it excludes and alienates on the one hand while it admits and makes social exchange happen on the other. It also serves as a gateway to the amassing of certain, nation-specific forms of cultural capital. Wharton heaps derision on those characters in her fiction who appear unaware of larger linguistic or cultural traditions outside their own. In *Hudson River Bracketed,* the dilletantish Vance Weston attends a gathering of New York literary aesthetes, whom Wharton depicts as being the antitheses of the new, modern cosmopolitanism. "Zola—who's he?" a partygoer asks in response to a reference to the French naturalist. "Oh, I dunno. The French Thackeray, I guess," another gauchely responds.[63] All four of Wharton's remaining copies of Zola's novels are French-language editions, in light of which this scene appears representative of her pride in both her linguistic and literary training, subjects that she saw as intimately connected.

Wharton's identity as a polyglot, and her sympathetic interest in the philological tradition, transcended the standards of polite education for upper-class women during this time. Whereas *that* style of education was designed with the primary purpose of making the woman herself more interesting, Wharton's marshaling of her linguistic training succeeded in making the study of language, history, and culture more interesting and thus also more important as an enterprise in *her* eyes. The mastery of a given language translated into a desire to tackle and master other areas of intellectual development as well, which is why, in that same scene from *Hudson River Bracketed,* Wharton draws a line between being unfamiliar with French writers like Zola and being unfamiliar with the history of science. The conversation about Zola pivots to a discussion of the pioneering scientific researcher Gregor Mendel. "Why, [life] is a series of jumps in the dark. That's Mendel's law, anyhow," one guest volunteers. "Gee! Who's Mendel? Another new novelist?" is the reply that greets this outburst. "Mendel? No. He's the guy that invented the principle of the economy of labour. That's what Mendelism is, isn't it?"[64] Wharton became acquainted with Mendel's theories of genetic mutation through her reading of William H. Drinkwater's *A Lecture on Mendelism,* printed (and acquired by Wharton) in 1910, during that previously mentioned period of intense procurement. That Wharton's unnamed characters in this scene appear to be confusing Mendel's theories with those of Frederick Winslow Taylor is supposed to function as proof of the depleted state of intellectual curiosity among young Americans. They are not well read or worldly but, even worse than that, they exhibit no desire to make themselves otherwise. In such instances we see the professed autodidact in Wharton appearing to mount her soapbox in preparation for a sermon.

The gendered specificity of Wharton's education resurfaces at last in her fiction as a gendered burden. Halo Tarrant, in *The Gods Arrive,* performs a number of managerial and administrative duties on behalf of

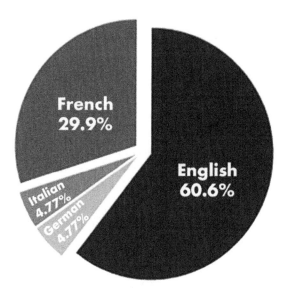

Wharton library volumes categorized by language.

Vance Weston, who, by the opening pages of this sequel, has become both a distinguished novelist and also her lover. As the couple proceeds to move about the European continent, Halo's duties include translating and speaking for Vance (who is seen grappling with the Spanish language and searching for his lost Spanish grammar book), arranging for hotels and transportation (the result of her better command of the language), secretarial work (she transcribes and edits Vance's manuscripts), housekeeping, shopping, and gardening. Halo reflects that "the distance was yet too great between her traditional culture and Vance's untutored curiosities" and assumes these duties in lieu of trying to educate Vance to assume them for himself.[65] Halo assents in this novel to the burdensome work of being the lover of an acclaimed (but uncultured) novelist, even though her training and education have primed her for something better.[66] Her frustrations appear to match up with Wharton's own frustrations about being wed to a man who was, by all accounts, also not her intellectual equal. Thus Wharton's library helps to reiterate a question raised by novels like *The Gods Arrive*: the point of elite women's education is to make them interesting, but interesting to whom, exactly?

This question returns us to a discussion of networks and to architectures of exchange. Social networks are governed by social codes, by what is essentially reducible to the term "manners," which Lionel Trilling describes as "a culture's hum and buzz of implication." Novels—especially novels written by socially preoccupied authors like Wharton—document the "evanescent context" that structures and surrounds historical processes of social exchange.[67] Because of that very "evanescence," these eras, along with the manners that once subtended and defined them, become more obscure over time, and this is where archives and libraries enter into the picture. Archives help to reanimate and to give voice to that larger "buzz"; letters, records, receipts, notes, and drafts help us to gauge the less explicit components of social discourse, components that are only ever the result of processes of social negotiation and so apt to change dramatically over time. But, as Trilling points out, "there is not a single system of manners but a conflicting variety of manners, and one of the jobs of a culture is the adjustment of this conflict."[68]

Wharton's library, as I see it, brings such conflicts to the fore, highlighting interstices and places where competing networks overlap, or else collide and bring each other into crisis. One of the regnant systems of manners that has weighed heavily on many of my observations throughout this chapter has to do with the behavioral codes that govern gender; another involves social codes arising from the history of education in America; still another relates to economic class; and still another descends from familial systems of attachment and from the circumstances of one's birth. Each of these spheres of human relations comes with a set of historical rules, but those rules rarely prove equivalent when they are brought into confrontation with each other. Thus Wharton's oeuvre, much like her era, appears governed by the need to adapt and adjust, socially speaking, to a variety of positions—some of them old, some of them new. Lily Bart in *The House of Mirth* fails when her adaptive capacities are put to the test. She refuses to make the kind of adjustments to her social interactions, her behavior, or her worldview that might, in time, result in her achieving some measure of stability. By contrast, though, Halo Tarrant, who appears at the close of Wharton's oeuvre in both *Hudson River Bracketed* and *The Gods Arrive*, is nimble, able, and responsive. Some scholars tend to neglect or else downplay the significance of these later works of Wharton's, dismissing them on account of their sentimental undertones and their Dickensian reliance on serendipitous reunions.[69] But I would argue that these works, like Wharton's library, show a Wharton who is learning to live with networks.

The world of *The Gods Arrive* feels small, and it is made to feel smaller by virtue of sprawling social networks that extend all the way from the rural Midwestern plains to the South of France. But social networks are not the only reason that the world has started to feel small for Wharton. Indeed, Wharton is aware of the ways in which these networks rest on the expansion of global systems of economic exchange, as when her Vance observes the faces of a passing crowd on the streets of Monte Carlo. "[They] were not all young or beautiful; the greater number were elderly, many ugly, some repulsive; but almost all wore the same hard glaze of prosperity."[70] The advance of global capital has had a leveling effect and inducted members of the upper class, like Wharton, into a worldwide coterie of privilege. Meanwhile, though, poorer individuals (represented elsewhere in her fiction by characters like Ethan Frome and Charity Royall from *Summer*) appear to languish as the victims of an outmoded, regional myopia. Their salvation lie not so much in physical escape or migration, though, since, as a disenchanted Vance puts it, "It's the same everywhere."[71] Rather, their salvation, Wharton believes, is to be found in the socially networked act of self-definition through education, or reading. Wharton folds complaints about the decline of reading into both of these two later novels, which center on an assessment of the field, or network, of literary production. Central to that field is the function of *reception* and the roles played by individual readers. Thus, even while these two final novels are about the development of a young writer's path to success, they are really about the future of reading and the social networks that are necessary to support and sustain such a future.

After running into Lorry Spear, the somewhat roguish brother of his lover Halo Spear, on the streets of Monte Carlo, Vance Weston meets up with another character from his past. Floss Delaney was his muse, and likewise his constant torment, during his younger days back in Illinois. By the time Vance meets her again on the French Riviera, he has succeeded in becoming a celebrated novelist. But the moment of their reunion is soured by Floss's "ingratiating" statements about his books. "[My father] has read your books," she explains. "That means you haven't?" Vance asks in return. "Well—I will now" suffices as her watery reply.[72] This exchange corroborates my earlier point about Wharton's own reading habits—namely, that social connection often provides a handy basis for the enlargement of one's intellectual spectrum and helps to hold readers accountable, in certain instances. But if social intercourse itself functions at the behest of manners and codes, and if manners dictate that reading and study ought not to be taken seriously or valued, what is the future of reading as a social act going to look like? This is the question that Wharton raises in these final two novels, and it is one that stems from an inspection of the links between milieu and cultural production. Wharton has learned to live with networks by the time of writing *The Gods Arrive*; this is why they surface like a set of infrastructural arrangements—part of the scenery, if you will—in these books. Lorry comments that Monte Carlo is "the place where nobody ever comes any more, yet where you meet everybody you know,"[73] suggesting that Wharton has veered away from seeing such meetings as serendipitous or ironic in her writing. They are now an expected part of the modern landscape. This compares to Foucault's observation that the twentieth century, unlike the one that came before it, distinguishes itself via a marked fascination with "juxtaposition." Writing a few decades after Wharton's death, in the 1960s, Foucault notes how the concept of the network haunts and defines the modern century, in particular with relation to history: "We are at a moment, I believe, when our experience of the world is less that of a long life developing through time than that of a network that connects points and intersects with its own skein." Foucault furthermore asserts the need for new interpretive models (and creative ones too, by extension) for the rendering of these complex "ensemble[s] of relations."[74]

Wharton attempts such an undertaking in novels like *The Gods Arrive,* wherein Vance is confronted by the need to choose between networks and by the consequences of their repeated collisions. Though he rises among the ranks of an elite European social circle—one that he has been granted access to *through* Halo, who, unlike him, received a head start in being born into prominent family—that success does not gain him an audience for his books. His new friends show little interest in reading what he writes, though they are brimming with opinions about how it should be written. He spurns Halo's company, when her education and training made her an ideal audience for his writing in the first place, and his writing suffers for the lack of a productive and inspiring social context. As he toils away on his latest novel, he remarks, "I don't believe it is a book—just a big dump of words. And not mine, anyhow,"[75] reinforcing the point that social interaction is inevitably bound to processes of artistic production, in Wharton's eyes. At the conclusion of *The Gods Arrive,* Vance and Halo return to the scene of Vance's artistic making, a crumbling old gothic house known as "The Willows," which I discussed in chapter 1. Thus Wharton ends the story of Vance and Halo by having them prepare to return to the library that served initially as a point of genesis—of their relationship (it is in the library that Vance first meets Halo), of Vance's career as a writer, and of their networked travels throughout the varying spheres of human relation. And continuing the theme of genesis that appears attached to the library as a concept, Halo admits to Vance at the last that she is pregnant with his child.

Libraries and networks are therefore alike in being cast as productive in Wharton's work. This chapter has sought to make clear the ways in which a library, as a networked entity, had an active hand in producing the person that was Edith Wharton: to that end, it seems significant to mention that Wharton dedicated *The Gods Arrive* to her friend Walter Berry, the person who, next to her father, was the largest source of books in her collection and who died years before the novel's publication. This chapter has also aimed to disrupt the supposedly "personal" readings that arise from the inspection of a personal library collection by showing how Wharton's library reflects larger trends in publishing, in readership and the history of engagement with printed text, and in networked acts associated with intellectual development and cultivation. Wharton's library is at once both representative and wholly atypical: it reflects and enacts some of the standards of its era with regard to gender-segregated education, publishing trends, and popular works even as it defies others. Such contradictions render it a rich site for investigations into both the making and collecting of books and the making of a modern person like Wharton.

4

·················

The Library as Tomb

Monuments and Memorials
in Wharton's Short Fiction

> Much concerns a man, forsooth, how a few sticks are slanted over
> him or under him, or what colors are daubed upon his box. . . . It is
> of a piece with constructing his own coffin,—the architecture of the
> grave, and "carpenter" is but another name for "coffin-maker."
>
> —Henry David Thoreau, *Walden*

WE HAVE SURVEYED THE WAYS IN WHICH LIBRARIES APPEAR synonymous with gestational origins. Wharton, as the preceding chapters have shown, viewed her father's library as a primary site of her education and, hence, her formation as a person and as a literary producer. "Whenever I try to recall my childhood," she explains in *A Backward Glance,* "it is in my father's library that it comes to life,"[1] echoing Alberto Manguel's observation that libraries, even those that are not our own, invite narcissistic reflection by offering "a tantalizing wisp of intuition of who we are as readers, a glimpse into the secret aspects of the self."[2] Similarly, the novelist Ray Bradbury connects the library to processes of maturation and growth when he describes it as an "embryonic place where a person [can] sit with the vibrations of lives off the walls, all around him."[3] But what Bradbury's description also makes clear is that libraries succeed in nurturing not just the beginnings of the life of the reader but also the afterlives of the authors contained within its walls. Insofar as the library can be seen as a cradle and a space of protective incubation, so does it beg to be seen as a tomb and a space of immortal enclosure.

Wharton, certainly, perceived the links between libraries and posterity. In *Summer*, for example, which I discussed at length in chapter 1, Charity Royall wonders if Honorius Hatchard, whose name graces the "queer little brick temple" of the memorial library that employs her, "fe[els] any deader in his grave than she d[oes] in his library."[4] To Charity, everything about the Hatchard Memorial Library reeks of the grave: the books "moulder" on the shelves in "cobwebby" ranks;[5] the library's name appears etched in "tarnished gold";[6] and the building itself resembles both a "mausoleum" and a "vault."[7] Though the library is dedicated to the memory of Honorius Hatchard, a long-deceased local author, Charity views it less as a usable space and more as "prison-house" and a vessel for her own, living internment.[8]

In a similar way, Wharton describes her childhood memories of her father's library as having been framed by a kind of communion with the dead. Unlike the fictional Charity, though, she revels in the prospect of that communion. "The dead were my most living companions," she reports in *A Backward Glance*. "I was a healthy little girl who loved riding, swimming and romping; yet no children of my own age, and none even among the nearest of my grown-ups, were as close to me as the great voices that spoke to me from books."[9] The dead are, for Wharton, a companionable presence; dead writers grant her a "secret ecstasy of communion" that frankly outshines her interactions with the living and transforms the library into a space of sacred intimacy and conversation. This is why Wharton, in her descriptions of libraries, often turns to the language of spirits and specters, as when she recalls that "words and cadences haunted [her father's library] like song-birds in a magic wood, and I wanted to be able to steal away and listen when they called."[10]

The sensation of being "haunted" and of being allowed to engage with that which, strictly speaking, no longer *is*, shapes much of the modern discourse surrounding libraries. Lynch, for example, argues that libraries are an essential component of the gothic storytelling,[11] and Lefebvre takes it one step further in viewing modern social spaces like libraries as tacitly organized around anxieties about mortality. "Social space 'incorporates' social actions," he tells us, and death itself comprises a social act.[12] What's more, Western culture appoints and builds social spaces that are meant to memorialize the dead in the form of monuments. "Only through the monument," Lefebvre argues, "can the space of death be negated, transfigured into a living space."[13] Often monuments are reduced to their functional role as spaces designed for the storing and commemorating of the dead. But sometimes monuments take the form of libraries: the Hatchard Library in *Summer* is one example of how a library comes to stand for a famous deceased figure; so are presidential libraries, which, in the United States, function less as libraries in the traditional sense and more as archives and museums; and so are the various memorial libraries that appear sprinkled across the Western world commemorating figures like Karl Marx, whose memorial library in London previously also housed its namesake's daughter's ashes for a few decades while plans for a Marx family gravesite were under dispute.[14]

To a great extent, then, the point of a library—much like the point of a monument—is to provide the living opportunities for interfacing, and intermingling, with the dead. Barbara Johnson sees that interfacing as "one of the reasons behind a monument" and argues that a monument exists "to express the inexpressible, to remember the unarticulable."[15] This is similar to the way that the art historian Alois Riegl, writing in 1903,[16] sees symbolic expression as a defining characteristic of monumental tributes to the dead. "In its oldest and most original sense," Riegl asserts, "a monument is a work of man erected for the specific purpose of keeping particular human deeds or destinies (or a complex accumulation thereof) *alive* and present in the consciousness of future generations."[17] What this means, in essence, is that a monument performs the function of enclosing or entombing so that the subject—whether it is a deceased person or a historical event—might remain "alive" in the minds of those who are still living. But it is Riegl's note about "complex accumulation," in particular, that strikes me: for one, it recalls Baudrillard's point about collecting, particularly the notion that the collection is itself devised to stand as a monument to the collector. "All objects that are possessed submit to the same *abstractive operation* and participate in a mutual relationship in so far as they refer back to the subject," Baudrillard observes. It is this constant manner of referring to (or pointing toward) the subject that allows a collection of objects to function, in

Baudrillard's view, as a "*system,* on the basis of which the subject seeks to piece together his world, his personal microcosm."[18] What's also significant about all of these linkages between subject and object, though, is Riegl's willing reversal of Baudrillard's point: where Baudrillard sees the life of the subject emblematized and represented by the collection, Riegl sees human subjectivity as a "complex collection" of "destinies and deeds." Such deeds leave few material traces, though, and thus it is the monument's job to translate the immaterial "collection" of actions that is the story of a human life into a solid, physical structure that persists in taking up space throughout the centuries.

A monument announces a deceased figure's claims to the continued occupation of "living" space.[19] In doing so, it furnishes evidence for a whole legacy of previous physical occupation. As Riegl sees it, monuments offer "evidence" of the fact that something or someone once "happened": "This evidence may be a monument of writing, which, through reading, stirs images contained in our consciousness, or a monument of art, whose content is perceived directly through our senses."[20] As such, monuments to the dead do more than just take up space—they invite the living to engage with the dead through sensory experience. This, Riegl argues, is similar to the way that books invite communion with the dead. Critic Gillian Silverman hits on this point in her work *Bodies and Books* when she characterizes books as "the repositories of ghosts" that possess the ability to "conjure up an author who is absent, inaccessible, and, very likely, dead."[21] Where monuments afford visitors the opportunity to enter into and occupy space that has been claimed in the name of the dead, books create such space metaphorically, through "images contained in our consciousness," to recall Riegl's words.

Yet in both of these accounts—Riegl's and Silverman's—the focus falls almost exclusively on the connection between author and reader. It is the reader who enters into and inhabits the space of the author, affecting a kind of transmigration that places the reader inside the space of the author's body and allows her to see the world through the author's eyes, much in the way that a tourist enters into and inhabits the space of the dead body via a physical monument. This invitation to occupation prompts Silverman to call the book "a technology of intimacy" that "binds time and distance" and connects the reader to the author.[22] This drawing of a straight line between author and reader, though, neglects the ways in which books function as objects in the physical world by privileging, and thus oversimplifying, the link between producer and consumer. After all, a book, especially if it is an old book, does not enter into the life of a single reader but rather, over time, passes through the lives of many readers. As such, it makes sense to reframe our discussion of the ways in which books monumentalize the dead around an understanding of communities of readership. Yes, the book provides a link between the dead author and the living reader, but so does it connect a host of previous readers, both living and dead, to the contemporary act of reading.

Edith Wharton's library collection speaks directly to such histories of communal interaction. We saw in chapter 3 how Wharton's library re-enacts the social networks that buttressed her career and successes as an author. It is my aim in this chapter to carry that discussion of community into a discussion of memorialization and entombment. In particular, the chapter explores the myriad ways that the library collection comes to stand as a monument to the deceased collector by reading Wharton's library and work through the lens of both curation and memorialization. Wharton's library, I argue, can and should be read as a kind of monument: but *a monument to whom?* To her father, from whom she inherited the basis of her library collection? To classic literature and to the many authors who wrote the books contained therein? To the people—many of them friends and relatives—who owned the books before her? Or to herself?

The answer falls somewhere close to *all of the above*: Wharton's library collection serves to immortalize not just communities of authors, owners, and readers but also the very acts and practices that were so sacred to Wharton's understanding of herself as a literary producer. The library erects a monument to the acts of reading and intellectual cultivation—acts that, Wharton feared, were fated for deletion at the hands of modern technology and modern life in the early part of the twentieth century. Wharton furthermore weaves these anxieties into her fiction, most especially in the short story "The Angel at the Grave" (1901) and in her novella *New Year's Day* (1924). In the first of these examples, Wharton contemplates the prospect of communion with the dead author; in the second, it is communion with the dead *reader* that structures and drives the narrative that she is telling. In this chapter, I analyze both of these stories in concert with a reading of libraries as vessels for the containment of the dead. I focus on the ways in which books and print materials enable the living subject to assume a curatorial role in crafting the archival components of their own posthumous legacy.

The desire to curate and to control is, I believe, directly related to the mythos of "self-making" that is the subject of this book's overall investigations into the meaning of the library collection. And there is no arena that has been subjected to discussions of curation and control quite like the library. The library emblematizes human fantasies of order, and fantasies are not, as Anne-Sophie Springer and Etienne Turpin argue, "the products of spontaneous invention." Rather, fantasies, like libraries, "require care, cultivation, and discipline."[23] This chapter therefore examines fantasies of communion alongside themes of cultivation and control, viewing the library as a space that enacts the life of the collector even as it monumentalizes, entombs, and condemns.

Keeping the Archive Alive: Entombment in "The Angel at the Grave"

Published as part of the collection *Crucial Instances* (1901), "The Angel at the Grave" tells the story of Paulina Anson, whom Wharton describes as having been "born . . . into a museum."[24] Paulina is the granddaughter of the late Orestes Anson, a philosopher and writer of some renown whose former residence in a small, unnamed New England town has for generations caused fans and scholars to flock to the site. "The most searching inroads of village intimacy hardly counted in a household that opened on the universe" is Wharton's way of describing how Paulina's isolated village became a locus of worldly knowledge and cosmopolitan attraction.[25] "The Angel at the Grave" anticipates many of the narrative ingredients that would, later on, form the basis of Wharton's *Summer*. In each we have a secluded New England village; we have a young woman who feels "stuck" within her rural environs; and we have a library. Unlike in *Summer,* though, the library in "The Angel at the Grave" is also a house.

Paulina Anson lives, along with two of her aunts, in the house that once belonged to her grandfather, though the bulk of that "living," it turns out, takes place on the upper floors of the building. This is because the ground floor holds Orestes Anson's library, a site that, prior to Paulina's occupation of the house, "had already acquired the publicity of a place of worship."[26] Indeed, the library forms the center of the house and Wharton describes the monkish arrangement that sees Paulina and her aunts living "on its outskirts, as it were, in cells that left the central fane undisturbed."[27] Here Wharton makes unapologetic use of the language of worship: the word "fane" refers to a temple or shrine, and it descends from the Latin root *fanum,* from which we also get the word "profane" (referring to acts that take place "before" or "outside" the temple and, thus, outside of accepted, sacred practice). Paulina and her aunts occupy "cells" located on the "outskirts" of the temple that is Orestes Anson's library and public memorial, and they are thereby obliged to serve as the custodians of both his monument and his legacy. Except, in the case of this particular monument, such custodianship comes with a set of expectations: though Wharton explains that Paulina's aunts are "unexcelled" in their roles as "recorders of their parent's domestic habits" and as "pious scavengers of his waste-paper basket,"[28] we learn that they are "not intellectual" and so are incapable of making sense of his philosophical writings. This situation leaves Paulina in charge of caring for their famous relative's intellectual bequests, since she is "the only person in the family who [can] read her grandfather's works."[29]

How exactly Paulina acquired these skills of interpreting and understanding philosophy remains the subject of speculation. Wharton explains that "fate seemed to have taken a direct share in fitting Paulina for her part" as both "the custodian of this historic dwelling" and "the interpreter of the oracle" of Orestes Anson's works.[30] It's an unlikely fate, for we also learn that Paulina is the daughter of the Anson family black sheep, a woman who was "so unworthy" of her family legacy that she "married a distant cousin, who had taken her to live in a new Western community where the *Works of Orestes Anson* had not yet become a part of the civic consciousness."[31] Paulina was born in that uncultivated "Western community," only to be shipped back east after the death of her infamously unworthy mother. What all this amounts to, of course, is a narrative of self-madeness and intellectual "orphanhood," to recall the words of Irene Goldman-Price, who, as previously mentioned, describes Wharton in precisely these terms in her introduction to the volume *My Dear Governess.* Much like Wharton, Paulina Anson appears molded by the twin hands of fate and self-invention. She might possess a noble last name, but her abilities are the result of cultivation, not inheritance, and we readers are encouraged to view her as the sole author of her own talents.

Wharton's descriptions of the "elm-shaded" New England village[32] that serves as the setting for this story make it sound rather a lot like Concord, Massachusetts, which was the seat of transcendentalist philosophical thought in mid-nineteenth-century America. This setting makes sense, too, given Wharton's preoccupation with themes of self-madeness: Concord gave rise to an entire philosophy of self-madeness, after all, that saw the publication of touchstone works on the subject like Ralph Waldo Emerson's essays (especially "Self-Reliance") and Henry David Thoreau's *Walden*. Too, Concord served as the hub for a network of intellectuals who, though they may be less well remembered than Emerson and Thoreau, crafted their own contributions to a philosophical plan that emphasized self-cultivation and individual betterment. Among the transcendentalist movement's founders was Orestes Brownson,[33] whose name and biography mark him as a likely inspiration for Wharton's Orestes Anson, but whose writings fell out of popularity following the decline of the movement (and his own conversion from Unitarian Universalism to Catholicism) in the 1850s. Whether or not Wharton is describing Concord, and whether or not Brownson is Anson, is beside the point: what matters is the way that Wharton emphasizes and encodes historical antecedents to modern narratives of American self-madeness in this story. The moment that was transcendentalist Concord becomes the moment of genesis for a modern ethos of self-cultivation, and the timeline that Wharton constructs in "The Angel at the Grave" (Paulina is past forty at the time of the story's telling) locates Paulina's grandfather right in the middle of that "moment"—that is, back in the 1830s. What's more, this timeline places Paulina within Wharton's own generation, as she would have likely been born in the 1860s.

We see Wharton wrestling with generational legacies of self-madeness in "The Angel at the Grave." Paulina, in being a direct descendent of Orestes Anson and an indirect descendent of the values and teachings of his transcendentalist ilk, inherits an appreciation for self-cultivation, discipline, and autodidacticism. This condition mirrors the way in which many of the transcendentalists laid proud claims to their American colonial ancestors: Joan W. Goodwin, for instance, in her biography of Sarah Alden Bradford Ripley (a peripheral but nonetheless significant character in the transcendentalist scene), notes that Ripley's "ancestry included the pilgrim names of Alden and Bradford," much like many of "those who created what came to be known as the American Renaissance."[34] Wharton's own lineage, of course, included a roster of "old" American names, but none of them were particularly famous. Lee explains that Wharton's most prominent colonial forebear, her great-grandfather Ebenezer Stevens, appears in John Trumbull's paintings of the Revolutionary War (specifically, in *The Surrender of Burgoyne* and *The Surrender of Cornwallis*).[35] But so far as Wharton's intellectual heritage might be concerned, it's clear that she saw herself as a fictive (rather than consanguineal) heir to the legacy of transcendentalist thought. Her library also supports such claims for invented kinship: in it, we see copies of Emerson's *Essays* and *Poems*, both of them much marked and littered with marginalia, alongside copies of Thoreau's works.

Wharton, I would argue, saw herself as an "interpreter" of American transcendentalist thought to the same extent that the fictional Paulina sees herself as the "interpreter" of her grandfather's philosophical teachings in "The Angel at the Grave." What's more, such acts of interpretation, Wharton furthermore asserts in this story, demand these degrees of generational distance and separation. Paulina actually benefits from the condition of having never known her grandfather: "There were no little personal traits—such as the great man's manner of helping himself to salt, or the guttural cluck that started the wheels of speech—to distract the eye of young veneration from the central fact of his divinity,"[36] Here Wharton is suggesting that intimacy is the enemy of intellectual sympathy and understanding. Paulina's aunts—their intellectual deficiencies notwithstanding—could *never* have assumed the role of interpreting or promoting Orestes Anson's philosophic legacy properly: their relationships with him would have prevented them from doing so. It is therefore the burden of that intimacy, rather than their own intellectual shortcomings, that consigned the Anson spinsters to lifetimes of "needlework and fiction," while Paulina "stepped into immediate prominence as the chief 'authority' on the great man."[37] Familiarity, Wharton is suggesting, can be an obstacle to purer forms of camaraderie and understanding.

Given the proven hazards of intimacy, then, it's no surprise that Wharton ends up promoting a vision of genius in this story that sees the artistic producer as "orphan," as necessarily placed at a distance from networks of affinity and social interaction. Such a commitment to antisocial means of self-improvement furthermore squares with Emerson's understandings of "character," which he sees as a prerequisite to the formation of genius. "Character is nature in its highest form," Emerson argues, and for this reason it is best served by the experience of isolation: "[Character] is best where no hands but nature have been laid on it."[38] To Emerson's mind, character is forged by a willful embrace of "noncomformity," and this is why he praises "the total solitude of the critic," whose originality of mind is shaped by "the Patmos of thought from which he writes, in unconsciousness of any eyes that shall ever read [his] writing."[39] Emerson invokes a reference to the Greek isle of Patmos, a small island in the Aegean Sea where St. John the Theologian is said to have sat in isolation and written the Book of Revelations. I highlight this line among the many lines in Emerson's treatise on "Character" that speak to the connection between social isolation and a well-nourished mind because it is one that Wharton has likewise underlined in her copy of his *Essays*.

Wharton's copies of both Emerson's *Essays* and *Poems* date from the 1880s, and we know from her letters and journals that Emerson's work formed a cornerstone of her educational upbringing.[40] Lewis explains that Wharton "admired [Emerson's] essays in particular" and that they served as a "major influence" on her development as a writer—even more than Stendhal, whom Wharton often named as her favorite author.[41] And in "The Angel at the Grave," we see that Paulina's grandfather's fame is due in part to *his* association with Emerson. Paulina laments the fact that, over time, as her grandfather's ideas have fallen out of fashion, he has ceased to be seen as an author in his own right and only as "the friend of Emerson."[42] Distance, Wharton therefore shows us in "The Angel at the Grave," is the essence of esteem. But what's also significant is the way that the archive, as a space and as a construct, engineers forms of distance while also affording certain levels of intimacy. Inside Orestes Anson's library, Paulina receives "nourishment" through her interactions with the physical objects that were once her grandfather's possessions. Surrounded by "spare ornaments" like "steel engravings by Raphael Morghen," "the black walnut desk with its bronze ink-stand modeled on the Pantheon," "paneled walls," "polished mahogany," and "portraits of triple-stocked ancestors," Paulina's imagination "brim[s] with the richest hues."[43] These objects are in fact as much a part of Orestes Anson's archive as the documents and books that draw historians, critics, and "ladies with inexplicable yearnings . . . for an interpretation of phrases which had 'influenced' them" to the spot.[44] And Paulina, in serving as the appointed custodian of these items, cannot help but feel duly protective of them.

That protectiveness, though, proves to be an impediment to socialization and to Paulina's chances at a "normal," socialized existence. When a young man appears on the scene and begins courting her, Paulina is horrified by his impertinence when they are alone together within the space of the library. "From the outset," Wharton narrates, "it had been impossible to fix Hewlett Winsloe's attention on Dr. Anson. The young man behaved with the innocent profanity of infants sporting on a tomb."[45] Here, once again, Wharton employs the language of worship and sacramental practice. Though there is nothing truly "profane" about Winsloe's actions, Paulina registers disgust at his refusal to be "possessed" by the space of the library in the way that she is.[46] Winsloe cannot sympathize with Paulina's feelings of "piety toward implicit demands, toward the ghosts of dead duties walking unappeased among usurping passions."[47] For this reason, when Paulina learns that marrying Winsloe requires moving away to New York and, thus, *vacating* the space of the Anson library, she rejects his offer.

Wharton thus invests her descriptions of the Anson library with the language of monumentalization. Phrases like "ghosts of dead duties" and words like "possessed" serve to intensify feelings of control and entombment. Ultimately, she condemns Paulina to a life spent inside the tomb—to the condition of being buried alive, in effect—when she has Paulina reject Winsloe's proposal of marriage. Even as the villagers speculate that Paulina's refusal of Winsloe was rooted in fears about her aunts' disapproval of him, Wharton tells us that, in fact, "such disapproval as reached her was an emanation from the walls of the house, from the bare desk, the faded portraits, the dozen or so yellowing tomes that no hand but hers ever lifted from the shelf."[48] Her aunts, in other words, hold no sway over Paulina, but ghostly "emanations" coming from the library, and from its deceased subject, do. These "emanations," more than anything else, appear to prompt Paulina's decision to stay.[49] She is aware of having assumed the role of medium in conveying her grandfather's legacy to the world: Orestes Anson, dead in his grave, speaks through her and only through her.[50] For this reason we see that the moment of Paulina's conscious assumption of this role coincides with the moment of her evolution into a writer. Paulina, seized by a "mystic conviction" and believing that she is more or less inhabited by the spirit of her dead grandfather, placidly transitions from the role of reader into the role of writer in an effort to "fortify her position." She begins work on an exhaustive biography of her grandfather, which she symbolically refers to not by its full name, *The Life of Orestes Anson,* but simply by the name *Life.*[51]

To her work on *Life* Paulina offers the wholesale sacrifice of her youth and her social existence. Wharton thus ceases to describe the Anson house as a monastic enclave and, instead, labels it a "plot" in a move that invokes the grave of the story's title and suggests that its occupants are, in fact, already deceased.[52] Paulina, at any rate, might as well be dead: Wharton informs us that she is forty years old by the time she finishes work on *Life* and has succumbed to conditions of increasing seclusion. "She had traveled little in her life, and it had become more and more difficult to her to leave the House even for a day," Wharton writes,[53] taking care to capitalize the word "House" in a way that marks the Anson family domicile as a living entity that appears imbued with human-like agency. Paulina ultimately ventures outside the House's enclosure, though only for the sake of ferrying *Life* to the office of a literary publisher in Boston (the same publisher that, generations before, oversaw the printing of Anson's complete *Works*). En route, she takes the opportunity to reflect on her years of confinement and isolation, suddenly seeing the manuscript *Life* for what it is—her life's work, on the one hand, but likewise her condemnation and death, on the other. "It was not so much her grandfather's life as her own that she had written," she reflects,[54] and she finds little consolation in the prospect of seeing that life appear in print at long last. Here Wharton reinforces the connection between the printed book and the dead body of its author in permitting Paulina these moments of contemplation on the subject of her own mortality. Paulina seems to perceive that the act of writing, much like the act of reading, grants life even while the inert physical object that is the product or basis of such actions might be associated with finality and, thus, death.

But it is that inertness that spells out the fact of death for Paulina, less than the medium of print itself. Paulina's manuscript ends up getting rejected: the publisher informs her that, while the public still regards her grandfather with a modicum of polite curiosity, their tastes for his work have subsided. As Paulina makes the journey home, she comes to the realization that the "silence which had gathered round her task" and her work in writing *Life* had been "the hush of death."[55] Wharton is quick to point out that we are not talking about the death of Orestes Anson: "Not *his* death! The very walls [of the library] cried out against the implication," she writes.[56] Rather, it is the "hush" signaling the death of the "world's loyalty" to Paulina's grandfather that has settled about the House and about Paulina's life, too.[57] But Paulina has already made the discovery that life can only be lived through action and activity, and so she begins her work again, starting over at the beginning and "re-reading the *Works*" in an effort to breathe new life into her own existence, if not necessarily into her grandfather's reputation.[58] Wharton offers, in this scene, an image of compulsive repetition: Paulina is preparing herself for another trip around the track that ended, previously, in disappointment and failure. But why?

The answer to such a question lies in the phrase that Wharton first used to introduce Paulina as a character: "born . . . into a museum." Paulina is herself *part* of the monument, part of Orestes Anson's archive.[59] If we return to that initial description, we see that Wharton additionally styles Paulina as "cradled in a glass case with a label."[60] Paulina is as much a part of the public exhibit that has been designed to commemorate and preserve her grandfather's authorial legacy as the furniture, the books on the shelves, and the neglected sheaves of documents. Thus it is clear that the act of maintaining and preserving the Anson library is, for Paulina, a crucial act of "self-preservation."[61] She cannot renounce her position as the collection's proprietor and go on living, for the two activities are in fact intertwined. What's more, in reassuming her quest to document and record the life of her grandfather, Paulina stumbles on a discovery. The members of her grandfather's circle ("The little knot of Olympians" with whom he associated) are, in fact, almost indistinguishable from each other when viewed from the perspective of the written page. "Amid that clamor of far-off enthusiasms she detected no controversial note. . . . They were continually proclaiming their admiration for each other."[62] In other words, the public's interest in the works of Orestes Anson waned not because they judged his ideas to be irrelevant or untrue but, rather, because they judged them to be uncontroversial and, as such, unimportant. What's more, Anson's associates and contemporaries, Paulina reasons, had not managed to stay famous thanks to their written work but thanks to their reputations as men. Actions, it seems, really do speak louder than words and Paulina, in the final sections of "The Angel at the Grave," is forced to reckon with the realization that she has neglected to act and, thus, neglected to *live* her own life.

Paulina thereby arrives at the conclusion that she has, in a certain way, always been dead. This deduction coincides with her sudden ability to see the Anson library for what it is: a tomb. "She looked up one evening from her reading and it stood before her like a ghost. . . . She sat in the library, among the carefully tended books and portraits; and it seemed to her that she had been walled alive into a tomb hung with the effigies of dead ideas."[63] Wharton offers us these images of immurement—that is, of living entombment—in order to critique the simplistic equation between the dead author and the living reader. It is not enough to read, Wharton is saying, nor is it enough to reproduce or represent what one has read. One must create *anew*. The problem, for Paulina, is that she has no idea how to go about creating anew; she has received no education or training in such tasks and she lacks for an experienced guide. Even as she dismally reflects on the experience of having "kept vigil by a corpse" all her life, she struggles to imagine any alternatives to the life she has lived.[64] And though she has arrived at the conclusion that ideas, like humans, stay relevant and alive only through controversy, debate, and conflict, she has not developed an eye for conflict, which is to say an eye for *critique*. She does not know how to go about being the person of "character" that is the subject of Emerson's fascination, the figure who possesses the "foresight of an order of things so excellent as to throw all [current] prosperities into the deepest shade" and who, in doing so, appears solid and "imparts a sense of mass."[65] Wharton also marks this last line of Emerson's in her copy of the *Essays,* a fact that furthermore hints that the fictional Orestes Anson, if he is guilty of anything, is guilty of having suffered from an insufficiency of character—a condition that he furthermore bequeathed to his granddaughter.

At this moment, as Paulina succumbs to grief for all the wasted years of her life, "The Angel at the Grave" takes a sudden, final turn. A stranger calls "to see the house," though it has been years since anyone has bothered to do so.[66] Paulina begins the old process of readying the temple for public inspection; she instructs the servants to "draw up the library blinds" and she frets over the room's cold and "inhospitable hearth."[67] Paulina's actions in this scene are overwhelmingly custodial and domestic in nature: she is more concerned about the state of the hearth and the temperature of the room than she is about the status of her grandfather's legacy, which looks suddenly as though it might be on the brink of revival. These domestic priorities are, however, indicative of the way that Paulina now concerns herself only with transmission and maintenance—with secondary, rather than primary, activities that, for all that they have contributed to the promotion of her grandfather's philosophy, might well have been limited to dusting the furniture and arranging the books. The strange visitor, though, whose name is Corby, announces that the room's frigidity, along with "the seclusion, the remoteness, the philosophic atmosphere," lends an air of authenticity to the tomb of a neglected intellectual like Anson. "There's so little of that kind of flavor left! I should have simply hated to find that he lived over a grocery, you know," he tells Paulina.[68] These statements serve to establish Corby as an ambassador from the realms of modernity; he discerns a clear difference between the modern world in which he lives (where people—even famous people—live above groceries) and the antiquated, mausoleum-like surroundings that have nurtured Paulina's existence. And whereas Paulina has languished in that realm of "dead ideas," modernity has fitted Corby for the task of identifying opportunities for innovation and, thus, for reclaiming the legacy of Orestes Anson.

Corby informs Paulina that he has not come to see Anson's philosophical manuscripts but, rather, to view an early pamphlet—a mere scrap of ephemera, it would appear—that he wrote in the 1820s providing "an account of the *amphioxus*." Paulina stumbles through an articulation of her knowledge of the item, asking aloud "It's an animal, isn't it—a fish?"[69] It is, indeed, a fish and, according to the stranger, a key to a recently emergent strain of evolutionary theory, "Sainte Hilaire's theory of the universal type," that, several decades before, went uncelebrated thanks to "cowardly publishers."[70] Paulina locates the pamphlet and offers it obligingly to Corby, all the while marveling at the fact that she, who knew the entirety of Orestes Anson's archive better than anyone else, and who alone appeared to have been marked for the task of interpreting and promoting his intellectual legacy, might have overlooked this item. Wharton suggests, though, that

Paulina's failure to recognize the pamphlet's importance is primarily due to a lack of training and experience on her part: though Paulina recalls having once "struggled through the unintelligible pamphlet," she remembers also that the "subject and phraseology were alien to her and unconnected with her conception of the great man's genius," a fact that caused her to "avert[] her thoughts from the episode as from a revelation of failure."[71] These statements compound our understandings of Paulina as a "failed" person, for not only has she "failed" at the task of keeping her grandfather's reputation alive, it seems she has likewise "failed" to identify opportunities for carrying out that work. This is because Paulina lacked training and experience with the language of evolutionary theory—a nascent field in the middle part of the nineteenth century[72]—and so wasn't able to recognize Anson's *amphioxus* pamphlet for what it was, a contribution to emergent forms of scientific discourse.

Paulina even tells Corby that the pamphlet was intended for destruction and that she found it "among some papers that my aunts were burning up after my grandmother's death. They said . . . he'd always meant to destroy the whole edition . . . But it was something *he* had written; to burn it up was like shutting the door against his voice."[73] As such, Paulina, as both quintessential custodian and keeper of the flame, held on to the pamphlet, in spite of her grandfather's and family members' wishes. She did so not because she understood its arguments or perceived its value but rather because she viewed it, like everything else in the Anson archive, as a materially important part of *him* and his legacy. In this way we see that Paulina's understandings of her responsibilities have stagnated at the level of custodianship and domestic control, a fact that places her on par with her "waste-paper basket" scavenging aunts and strips her of her claims to more "intellectual" talents. What's more, Wharton is suggesting that this stagnation happened because Paulina became content to limit her intellectual interactions to those that involved communion with the dead; the Boston publisher previously indicated as much when he rejected her manuscript. And like Orestes Anson himself, whose ideas fell out of favor in being viewed only through the lens of adjacency to a historical movement, Paulina's own capacity for intellectual understanding has decayed over time as the result of her effective entombment within the walls of the Anson library. That entombment, Wharton shows, has kept Paulina sepa-

rated from the rest of society and thus eroded the capacity for intellectual ⟵
achievement that was, originally, her "fate."

Several critics have observed that Wharton ends "The Angel at the
Grave" rather ambiguously. Paulina narrates the story of her wasted years
to Corby, who responds in tones of soothing reassurance. "Don't you see
that it's your love that has kept him alive?" he asks, explaining that but
for Paulina's years of vigilant sacrifice "he *would* have been dead!"[74] He
then seeks her permission to begin work on a scholarly article on Anson's
amphioxus pamphlet, with her help and support, and tells Paulina that he
will come again to the house the next day. "I'll have everything ready," she
responds. "And the fire shall be lit for you."[75] Lee, like many other critics,[76]
chooses to interpret this ending through the lens of romantic optimism.
"Miss Anson is rescued from desolation by a bright young man who comes
in quest of her grandfather's one scientific discovery. . . . Wharton, unusu-
ally, allows for a consolatory comic ending here."[77] In pronouncing this
ending as "consolatory" and "comic," though, Lee's reading misses a lot.
For instance, take Paulina's last spoken response to Corby: "the fire shall
be lit *for* you." From this we see that Paulina has not only resigned herself to the role of domestic custodian for the Anson library but that she is
furthermore conscious of the fact that any fires that are to be lit—be they
actual or metaphoric—are not for her chief benefit or comfort. She has
proven incapable of acting on her grandfather's behalf, and through her
conversation with Corby has come to acknowledge and name all the ways
in which she has *failed* in her efforts to do that. What's more, it's clear that
Paulina's youth and energy has been, for the most part, expended; though
Wharton does not tell us how old her protagonist is now, we see that Paulina readies herself for her meeting with Corby by, first, "la[ying] aside her
walking stick" and donning her "Mechlin cap."[78] Time has all but run out
for Paulina, whereas, in comparison, Wharton relies on a host of youthful
adjectives to describe Corby, labeling him a "fresh-eyed sanguine youth"
who appears "clearly independent of any artificial caloric" and whose presence is described as "robust."[79] Corby's speech is likewise strewn with slang
terms that confuse Paulina's "unaccustomed ear," and he has a "rapid eye"
that moves hungrily, almost greedily, about the library while Paulina,
Wharton tells us, responds "slowly" and appears to struggle both physically
and cognitively.[80] Indeed, Paulina is too old to embark on the kind of task

that Corby is proposing. She also lacks experience and familiarity with the modern market of ideas, assets that would likely prove essential to her ability to assume an authoritative role in that process.

Wharton takes pains in "The Angel at the Grave" to explain that Paulina's fate was sealed from the very start. Consider, for example, the fact that readers first meet Paulina in the same place where they last see her—in the Anson library. Wharton craftily encodes the details of Paulina's fate on the very first page of the story when she tells us that Paulina Anson has, over time, become the "solitary inmate of the Anson House";[81] her aunts' deaths, it appears, occur somewhere in the middle of the story but they warrant no formal statements from the narrator. In the last line of "The Angel at the Grave," Paulina is still there, standing in the middle of the "empty room," watching Corby's "buoyant figure hastening down the elm-shaded street" and away from her.[82] This circular narrative structure hardly denotes progress and optimism; rather, it thematically reinforces feelings of compulsive repetition. Paulina, we have already seen, is drawn toward the very prospect of repetition, chiefly because she can't help it—her life has been structured and grounded by routine and it is all she has ever known. This is why she performs the same custodial tasks, day in and day out, within the space of her grandfather's library; this is why she rejected Winsloe, who threatened to interrupt her routine by removing her from the space of its enactment; this is why she delivers the manuscript of *Life* to the grandson of the publisher who first represented her grandfather generations before; this is why, after having *Life* rejected, she resolves to begin the work once again and to start in on a new version of the same manuscript project.

What's more, Paulina, in suffering from a desire to repeat, typifies the nineteenth-century literary heroine who finds herself trapped within patterns of domestic cyclicality. Critic Jennifer Fleissner explains that female characters of this kind define "the domestic realist tradition associated with New England," a tradition that, by the 1890s, is supposed to have waned with the onset of naturalist literature. But according to Fleissner, not only do such characters and conventions persist into the 1890s and beyond, they serve as ballast to male literary archetypes who, during that same period, appear "running off from the worlds of New England fiction to rediscover the conflict and uncanniness of raw nature." Meanwhile, the compulsive, domesticated female figure exhibits these same qualities "within the domestic mode itself, as the classic story of feminine growing up becomes a perverse tale of compulsive behaviors."[83] Indeed, this is true for Paulina, who was weaned on processes of interminable cyclicality and, as such, seems doomed to repeat them from the outset. If Paulina is at all satisfied by Corby's propositions to let her help him in his research, the satisfaction can only come from the dawning awareness that she is starting the cycle over again, that she is returning to what feels "normal" for her. In this way, Paulina exhibits what Berlant would label a pattern of cruel optimism, since what she desires (repetition and cyclicality) is actually an obstacle to her "flourishing," in Berlant's words. "All attachment is optimistic," Berlant reminds us,[84] and in "The Angel at the Grave," we see Paulina preparing to recommit herself to a set of attachments (to her secondary role as custodian; to a subjugated position, that of an intermediary to genius; to the House itself, which was the original obstacle to her flourishing in the first place) that she already knows leads not to satisfaction but, rather, to a satisfyingly familiar course destined to end in disappointment.[85] If there is a moral to be found here, it is that a happy ending does not wait in store for those who resist change, insist on the comfort of routine, and wall themselves off to the opportunities for growth that come via social engagement.

Many critics disagree with Lee's reading of the story's ending and argue, instead, in favor of a more pessimistic interpretation. Both Josephine Donovan and Emily J. Orlando emphasize the ways in which Wharton's ending reinforces a set of patriarchal messages. Donovan points out that at the conclusion of "The Angel of the Grave," Paulina's "own work remains unpublished and therefore on the margins, silent" and that Paulina herself has achieved little aside from serving "as a vehicle for the transmission of a patriarchal tradition."[86] Orlando, meanwhile, adds to Donovan's critique in observing that the story centers on a depiction of "a woman quietly laboring behind the scenes while two men—Orestes and George—are credited with the fruit of her work."[87] Orlando furthermore echoes Donovan when she argues that Paulina's prime function has been to "keep[] a watchful vigil at the grave of a patriarch" and, by extension, patriarchy as well.[88] Both critics see Paulina through the lens of complicity; she is complicit in maintaining patriarchal authority (which she herself never attempts to challenge), and for this reason she is likewise complicit in her own incarceration and immobility. What all that complicity points to, though, is a thematic emphasis on qualities of self-madeness.

Paulina's fate might be a dismal one, as both Donovan and Orlando attest, but it is a fate that she herself has had an active role in engineering. The suggestion, then, is that Paulina's fate might have been otherwise; she might have chosen *not* to assume the role of custodian and to devote her youth to watching over the Anson archives, just as she previously chose *not* to marry Winsloe. But, I would argue, Paulina's reasons for doing so stem in large part from her understandings of herself as a self-made creature. For people like Paulina, people who have forged their understandings of personal identity from the cauldron of autodidacticism, isolation, and, yes, reading (rather than through imbricated systems of formal education taking place within public, social settings), the so-called ghosts of dead duties might, in fact, appear preferable to flesh-and-blood relationships with living humans. This, I think, is what lurks at the center of Paulina's decisions to stay and remain within the tomb of the Anson archive; she distrusts living, social attachment and with good reason—her mother was the family outcast who was disallowed familial support and who died young and poor, leaving Paulina to her own defenses. In comparison to such an arrangement, the specter of Orestes Anson looks like a relatively safe place to invest one's hopes for communion and intellectual engagement.

Wharton's point in this story is that material objects and possessions—archives in particular—have the capacity to improve upon our memories of their owner–subjects. Archival collections offer seemingly complete or coherent reminders of the incomplete or incoherent personages that they purport to represent. The Orestes Anson of Paulina's imagination, we must assume, is leagues better than the Orestes Anson of the "guttural clicks," the one who, let's not forget, excommunicated his daughter from the family and cut her off without "the traditional penny," as Wharton puts it.[89] Orestes Anson's primary legacy is, clearly, one of female subjugation; his daughters, like his wife, were required to attend to him and to flatter his status as an author, and the one who dared to challenge this convention was punished accordingly. And this is why a stranger must be appointed to serve as the caretaker of his literary legacy. In "The Angel at the Grave," the first of those caretakers is Paulina, but, as Orlando observes, she "relinquishes that control to Corby when she hands over the pamphlet."[90]

This means that, to a certain extent, Paulina is passing the torch, but she is also succumbing to the temptation to repeat the cycle of submission and servility that has defined her life (and also kept her from living it). After all, preserving the archive is, as I have already argued, central to Paulina's sense of self-preservation in this story, and this means that Paulina isn't going anywhere, apart from moving aside in order to make some room for Corby.

Indeed, Paulina looks to be settling more deeply into her predestined role as part of the exhibit, as taking her place among the many objects that comprise Orestes Anson's proprietorial legacy. The issue of Paulina's useful-ness as an object, I believe, causes the trouble for many readers and makes Wharton's ending appear ambiguous. In allowing herself to become a part of the archive that she formerly oversaw and curated, Paulina, it can be argued, may yet experience the satisfaction of being useful. The problem, though, is that her usefulness comes at the price of her agency and produc-tive capacity, a fact that furthermore indicates her transition from subject to object at the end of this story. Paulina becomes useful *to* Corby in the exact same way that the proffered pamphlet does, and thus the handing over of the pamphlet signals a handing over of herself as well. Paulina, in becoming a part of the archival hoard, comprises but one ounce of its multitude of raw materials—materials that will prove useful to Corby's research and creative energies. That condition of usefulness thereby makes her his property in the eyes of capitalism, at least. Consider, for instance, Marx's comment that, under capitalism, "private property has made us so stupid and inert that an object is ours only when we have it, when it exists as capital for us, or when . . . we use it."[91] Paulina has proven unfit for the task of converting the raw materials of the archive into the form of new and marketable commodities, but Corby now appears poised to do pre-cisely this, based on his understanding of existing market niches (science, we see, is ascendant at the turn of the century while spiritual philosophy is accordingly descendent). Paulina thereby cedes the active role of reader and medium to Corby, who, as a modernized subject, understands what she cannot, namely, that the forward progression of knowledge depends on showing the world what is *new,* not simply preserving what is old.

But if Paulina's interactions with Corby don't solidify my reading of her transition from subject to object, a closer analysis of the story's title, I believe, ought to. In calling the story "The Angel at the Grave," Wharton appears to position Paulina as accessory to her grandfather's genius, watching over the shrine of his accomplishments with fastidiousness and loyalty. But what the story's title doubly describes is an ornament—a stone angel—attached to the monument's edifice. If Paulina is truly the "angel" of the story's title, Wharton suggests, then this makes her functionally tantamount to statuary, designed to beautify and designate the space of the monument but, at the same time, necessarily immobile and inert. This is the image that Wharton leaves us with at the conclusion of "The Angel at the Grave": Corby leaves Paulina alone in the empty room, looking "as though youth had touched her on the lips."[92] But here, as elsewhere in this story, Wharton opts for the passive construction ("had touched"), which signals that Paulina is a thing that does not act but, rather, reacts or else is acted upon. The blush of youth that touches her lips is not that of hope or of optimism but rather of an old, weathered monument that has just been visited for the first time in years and, perhaps, received a bit of sprucing up on account.

Collections and Communion in *New Year's Day*

According to Riegl, one of the purposes of a monument is "to keep a moment from becoming history."[93] Monuments to the dead, whatever form they happen to take, operate with fantasies of atemporality and permanence in mind. But as we have seen with "The Angel at the Grave," such hopes for permanence require active participation on the part of the living. It is not enough for a monument to exist in, or as, space; rather, it must exist as *usable* space in order to speak and "live" in the present moment. Barbara Johnson approaches the discussion of monuments via the rhetoric of access, explaining that insofar as "a monument marks the boundary between life and death, it does so by making the dead belong to the public."[94] The space of the monument must, therefore, be made accessible to the public that would seek to own and use it.[95]

Often, though, age and preservation appear to stand in the way of usability (as with the Hatchard Memorial Library in Wharton's *Summer*). Riegl asserts that, where monuments are concerned, preservation and use tend to appear antithetical to each other since "what is required to keep a monument 'alive,' in use, is not necessarily concessions to either use value or its aesthetic counterpart, newness value, but rather a sacrifice of virtually everything that constitutes age value."[96] Efforts to transform monumental space into something that can be used right now often result in the paving over and alteration of history and of the space that was. In this way, preservation and use persist in appearing conceptually divided, prompting disagreement over the question of what is to be done about an unused monument? Monuments, much like libraries, are suggestive of conditions of dormancy; both, it seems, require use and activation in order to be deemed valuable. Foucault, for instance, sees libraries in this way when he argues that their ascendancy in nineteenth-century culture resulted in "a new imaginative space" wherein "fantasies" may be "carefully deployed." He notes that a library's "treasures lie dormant in documents" and that "only the assiduous clamor created by repetition" can free a library from the conditions of dormancy and "transmit to [audiences] what only happened once."[97] That emphasis on processes of transmission and repeatability binds Foucault's library to Riegl's monument as, in both cases, usability and relevance form the necessary ingredients for making what once happened happen *again*. The survival of libraries, like the survival of monuments, therefore depends on the successful cultivation of contemporary audiences and users.

"The Angel at the Grave" is, in this very way, haunted by anxieties of impermanence and irrelevance. In that story, Wharton fuses two images— that of the unused library and that of the unremembered grave—to craft a composite portrait of authorial anxieties about immortality. But there are some, and William Wordsworth is among them, who would argue that great authors do not even need monuments. The test of an author's claims to immortality, Wordsworth contends, ought to lie in his work alone and not in any edifice or space dedicated to his honor. A great writer "raise[s] for himself a monument so conspicuous, and of such imperishable materials, as to render a local fabric of stone superfluous and, therefore, completely insignificant," Wordsworth claims, pointing out that, for this reason, copyright protections on authors' works are far more important than gravestones.[98] As Wordsworth sees it, average men and women are more deserving of monuments than great artists, since, in most cases, no written record is likely to survive them. This concern—the safeguarding and curation of a common legacy, not a grand one—animates much of Wharton's later writing and connects "The Angel at the Grave," one of her earliest works of fiction, to *New Year's Day,* one of her last.

New Year's Day was published in 1924 as part of the volume *Old New York,* and it showcases the development of Wharton's anxieties regarding the link between audience and an author's claims to perpetuity by focusing on a reader, not an author. The novella concludes the *Old New York* collection, the four segments of which chart the changing demographics of nineteenth-century New York society by focusing on four different decades (the 1840s, 1850s, 1860s, and 1870s). The collection reads, significantly, as just that—as a "collection," or archive, of dated impressions and historical sketches. Each of the four segments poses as a document of a particular era, and the four volumes, which were originally packaged and sold as one in matching "flower-patterned dust jacket[s]" and a "period gift box," appear designed for functionality "as both fine literature and elegant objects," according to June Howard.[99] The suggestion, in fact, is that the actual collection *is* a collectible: the dust jackets, packaging, and original illustrations by Edward Caswell combine to mount a claim for a position of honor on any owner's bookshelf. Likewise, these aesthetic details appear to hail the owner or reader in question and to mark them as being, like Wharton, a remnant of nineteenth-century America.

Themes of collecting surface among the individual vignettes in *Old New York.* In *False Dawn,* the lead novella, which takes place in the 1840s, twenty-something Lewis Raycie embarks on a "Grand Tour" of Europe with the express purpose of acquiring a collection of paintings on behalf of his well-endowed New York family. His father is looking to secure his own social legacy by founding a Raycie gallery that will feature "a few masterpieces" doubling as family "heirlooms." The elder Raycie charges Lewis with procuring "a few original specimens of the Italian genius. Raphael, I fear, we can hardly aspire to; but a Domenichino, an Albano, a Carlo Dolci, a Guercino, a Carlo Maratta" are to be featured alongside "one or two of Salvator Rosa's noble landscapes."[100] In this scene, Wharton makes her distaste for the collector who seizes without taste and hoards without enjoyment abundantly clear: the elder Mr. Raycie is the story's undisputed villain. He rules his family like a tyrant, betraying, even, the spirit of American democracy in his quest to found "a Family" (with a capital F) on antidemocratic standards like "primogeniture," inheritance, and ritual.

Wharton's own copy of *New Year's Day,* showing dust jacket and illustrations by Caswell. EdithWhartonsLibrary.org. Courtesy of The Mount.

Wharton derisively reveals that Mr. Raycie, "though not a wholly unread man," is too ignorant and too uncultured to appreciate that which he is able to purchase and collect.

In the end, though, ignorance wins the day in *False Dawn.* On his travels, the younger Lewis encounters a modern aesthete named John Ruskin—yes, *that* John Ruskin[101]—and returns home with a valuable collection not of masters but of early Italian religious primitives. Lewis's philistine father, like the rest of the Raycies' New York milieu, shuns him and his purchases; they wind up rotting in a relative's attic for decades before being discovered and eventually sold for a fortune. Wharton's point in this story is that art, to the same degree as monuments and libraries, must play an active role in educating and thus procuring its own audiences. An audience's refusal to learn, though, can often spell the death of art and of the history it represents.

Wharton thereby grafts themes of grief onto her discussions of collecting and artistic appreciation in the *Old New York* novellas. Howard observes that "a whole world of hope and grief is implied" by *False Dawn*'s narrative and that strains of "disappointment, loss, the waste of human potential" structure the story that it is trying to tell.[102] One source of all that grief, in Wharton's view, stems from the discrepancy between value and sincere appreciation, or real *use.* The Raycie descendent who discovers the priceless lot of Italian primitives does not care to keep a single one of them, except "in the shape of pearls and Roll-Royces" and a "new house in Fifth Avenue."[103] The sufferings that young Lewis Raycie experienced decades earlier when he was disinherited by his parents and spurned by society thereby appear to have been ultimately in vain: his own family, and the larger society that still encircles it, has not learned. They do not appreciate the paintings that were the cause of his torment and so happily trade them for Rolls-Royces. Wharton reaches a similar conclusion in the novella titled *The Spark,* wherein the protagonist, Hayley Delane, recalls a previous Civil War experience that once put him in contact with "Old Walt," meaning the poet Walt Whitman. Delane, though, is incapable of appreciating Whitman's poetry (and objects, specifically, to its homosexual themes) when he discovers it years later. He tells the narrator "I rather wish . . . you hadn't told me that he wrote all that rubbish";[104] he would, it seems, prefer ignorance over the challenges of understanding.

In *New Year's Day,* Wharton develops and adds to these anxieties regarding use and appreciation, and here, too, grief is paramount. Unlike in the other novellas, though, that grief is not resultant—that is to say, it is not the tragic product of mismatched values, nor is it an accidental byproduct of one character's obstinacy or refusal to understand. Rather, grief in *New Year's Day* is a motivating factor: Lizzie Hazeldean inherits her husband's library upon the occasion of his untimely death, and she wants more than anything to read his books and to gain access to him through them. But Lizzie, it would appear, is not a reader by nature. Indeed, "It was an old joke between [Lizzie and Charles] that she had never been able to believe anyone could really 'care for reading.'" Lizzie's disinclinations are not progressive, either, but static seeming and historically entrenched. Lizzie's husband's passion for reading, Wharton tells us, "remained for her as much of a mystery as on the day when she had first surprised him, mute and absorbed, over what the people she had always lived with would have called 'a deep book.'" Indeed, Wharton labels Charles Hazeldean "a born reader," and in so doing she tacitly applies the opposite designation to his wife: Lizzie is a born *non*reader.[105]

This focus on innate, quasi-biological propensities for reading and intellectual study is characteristic of Wharton who, all throughout her oeuvre, tends to separate and define characters in this way. Recall that, in "The

Angel at the Grave," Paulina Anson possesses an instinctive talent for reading and interpreting her grandfather's philosophy, while her aunts, by comparison, are deemed "not intellectual"; likewise, in "The Pelican," another
early short story, Wharton introduces us to Mrs. Amyot, a professional
lecturer who is not "intellectual" by nature but who achieves popularity
in harnessing "two fatal gifts: a capacious but inaccurate memory, and an
extraordinary fluency of speech."[106] In both of these cases, Wharton takes
pains to identify not just those characters who exhibit innate intellectual
talents but also those who do not. In both stories Wharton builds narrative
conflict by exploiting the tensions between the "born intellectual" camp
and its less worthy (and less authentic) adversary. This, of course, is consistent with the kinds of conflict that Wharton herself experienced—or,
at any rate, believed she had experienced—as a "born intellectual" hailing
from a resolutely "non-intellectual" household. In *A Backward Glance,* she
describes the horror that her parents, most especially her mother, suffered
when forced into confrontation with real-life "intellectuals" and literary
producers. "My parents and their group, though they held literature in great
esteem, stood in nervous dread of those who produced it," she explains, in
part because they regarded "authorship . . . as something between a black
art and a form of manual labor."[107] Wharton writes these expressions of
horror and repugnance into much of her earlier fiction, not only because
they provide such fertile ground for narrative conflict but also because they
lend support for the story she would tell about herself, a story that hinges
on themes of self-invention and independent heroism. Too, in foregrounding themes of biological destiny in her writing, Wharton reinforces the
deeply ideological notion that some, like her, are simply "born" with it.[108]
Others, meanwhile, are clearly not, and Wharton reserves a special kind of
venom for would-be intellectuals like Mrs. Amyot in "The Pelican"—that
is, for charlatans whose successes tend to come cheaply.

There is a difference between "nonintellectuals" like Mrs. Amyot and
"nonreaders" like Lizzie Hazeldean, and it has to do with sincerity and
effort. Where Mrs. Amyot, much like the infamous members of the all-
female Lunch Club in Wharton's short story "Xingu" (1916), *pretends* at
intellectualism and markets herself as a "thinking woman," Lizzie appears
in *New Year's Day* as guileless and stripped of all pretension. Wharton tells
us that prior to marrying Charles Hazeldean, Lizzie "had never before lived

in a house with books in it" and that her upbringing had stressed neither intellectual cultivation nor "useful accomplishments."[109] She is, in short, a sympathetic type of "nonreader," who, given a different set of circumstances, might have succeeded in being anything but. For Lizzie is not unintelligent; indeed, the narrator of *New Year's Day* remarks, "If she could not read books she could read hearts."[110] Rather, with Lizzie, Wharton gives us a hint of the same "disappointment, loss, waste of human potential" that Howard previously ascribed to other characters who appear in the collection. But what are the circumstances of Lizzie's "wasted potential," and who is to blame for them? The answer to this question can be found in the collection's title: *Old New York*. Lizzie is a victim—albeit also a culprit—of the society in which she lives, a society that had begun, by the later part of the nineteenth century, to run up against an inimitable array of modern challenges. One gets the impression in *New Year's Day* of a culture that is materially writhing in its death throes, even as its standards, opinions, and tastes appeared poised for smooth transference to the next generation.

Lizzie defies and offends her New York society by appearing at once both too old-fashioned and too at home in modernity, as when Wharton opens the novella with the line "She was *bad* . . . always. They used to meet at the Fifth Avenue Hotel,"[111] branding Lizzie as noncompliant from the outset in the eyes of her milieu. Here, though, Wharton furtively gestures toward a double standard that lies concealed within her opening line: Lizzie is singled out as being "bad" through the use of the pronoun "she," yet Henry Prest, her lover, who comprises 50 percent of the pronoun "they," remains free from censure. As such, Wharton introduces a level of gendered critique that bears upon her novella's analysis of themes of tradition and social impropriety. It's different for women, Wharton is saying, in a move that suggests that Lizzie's shortcomings as a "born reader" may have a lot to do with her likewise having been born a female.

Like Paulina in "The Angel at the Grave," Lizzie's gifts lie not in her intellectual abilities but, in fact, in her capacity for care. This much is suggested by the narrator's remark about her talent for "read[ing] hearts," though Wharton's project in *New Year's Day* revolves around an exploration of the ways in which a person's talents may likewise engineer their ruin. Lizzie cares too much—for her husband, especially—and this is part of what makes her appear so unfashionably old-fashioned. It is because she cares that she prostitutes herself to Henry Prest in an effort to gain money to pay for her ailing husband's medical treatments. Prest, though, mistakenly assumes *he* is the subject of that care until Lizzie informs him, following her husband's death, of the truth. "You thought I was a love-lorn mistress," she tells him, "and I was only an expensive prostitute."[112] In forsaking the bonds of marriage, Lizzie has done a very modern thing. Clare Virginia Eby sheds light on Wharton's fascination with the "modernization" of marriage in her analysis of Wharton's novel *The Glimpses of the Moon*,[113] which was published just two years before the *Old New York* novellas. But in forsaking her marriage bonds for the benefit of her husband, and out of love for him, Lizzie reveals herself to be, at the last, a rather traditional and sentimental kind of woman. Her choice to henceforth remain celibate and to lock herself away in her dead husband's library furthermore speaks to outmoded forms of devotion that rather place her on a level alongside Paulina Anson.

Also like Paulina, Lizzie assumes a domestic role with regard to the library, as when, on her way home from her tryst with Henry Prest at the Fifth Avenue Hotel, she stops to purchase a handful of roses. The flowers, which are "two perfect specimens of a new silvery-pink rose"[114] are, like Lizzie, products of a burgeoning modernity; plant hybridization grew as a field in the later decades of the nineteenth century, and the first successful hybridized rose (called "La France" and bred specifically for its silvery pink color) had appeared in 1867—that is, just prior to the temporal setting of *New Year's Day*. Wharton would have been aware of discussions of hybridization, since she owned a first-edition copy of Hugo DeVries's *Plant Breeding: Comments and Experiments on Nelson and Burbank* (1907), to which she has added marginal notes and markings.[115] Significant among those markings is a set of vertical lines and a penciled "x" that appear on page 187, next to a discussion of the invention of "new characters." DeVries's text reads: "It is a much discussed question whether new characters may be produced by crossing. Of course, there is no doubt that new varieties and new races may originate in this way, but this is not the same point. It is well known that the larger number of hybrids simply owe their character to a new combination of qualities."[116] It seems that Wharton, who was an avid gardener, may have been contemplating the metaphorical links between modernity's creation of new plant species and its creation of new human "characters."

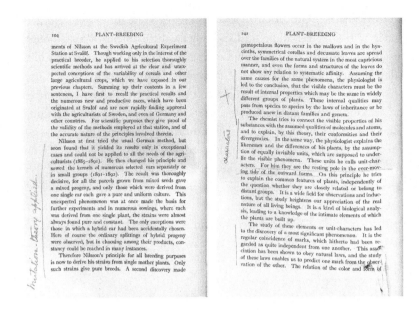

Pages from Wharton's copy of DeVries's *Plant-Breeding,* including penciled markings and marginalia that she added. EdithWhartonsLibrary.org. Courtesy of The Mount.

Lizzie is hard at work in *New Year's Day* exhibiting a "baffling combination of qualities," to recall DeVries, much in the same way that her roses do. Consider that she purchases them for her husband in a gesture of gallantry that runs against traditional, scripted notions of gendered behavior. When she arrives home with the flowers, she "tenderly unswathe[s] them" within the shrine-like confines of her husband's library and then places "them in a slim glass on her husband's writing-table" so that they may greet him upon his arrival.[117] This humble but profound gesture of care contrasts sharply with Lizzie's discovery of a "long florist's box" that awaits her inside her own bedroom. The box contains "a bunch of roses," along with an envelope that she "[flings] into the fire without so much as a glance at its contents" before "push[ing] the flowers aside."[118] The flowers, which are from Henry Prest, offend her because they are meant to mark the occasion of her most recent infidelity with him. Even more than that, though, they impinge on the consecrated atmosphere of the Hazeldean household, which has been the site of Lizzie's relationship with Charles from the very beginning. Later, after Charles has died, Henry Prest visits Lizzie at the home that she shared with her husband and proposes marriage to her. At first, Lizzie responds by "gazing about her as if she had the sudden sense of unseen presences between them."[119] She is aware, in this scene, of the "presence" of her husband, whose soul appears attached to the space of his home. She then tells Henry Prest, "This room is sacred to me."[120] Her reaction compares in many ways to Paulina's in "The Angel at the Grave," who similarly recoils at her suitor's insensitive behavior when they are together in the library. In both cases, it is clear, these spaces constitute sanctuaries dedicated to the preservation of memory, making the formation of new and usurpative social bonds appear anathema to their very functions.

Following Charles's death, Lizzie's chief role with respect to his library becomes that of curator. After she rejects Henry Prest's proposal, and subjects him to a brazen explanation of her original motives for following through with the affair, she resigns herself to a life that shall henceforth be lived inside the tomblike enclosure of her husband's library. Wharton's protagonist first entertains a glimpse of what that life will look like while she is seated alone in the library, in the wake of her conversation with Prest.

> "If I only cared more for reading," she moaned, remembering how vainly she had tried to acquire her husband's tastes. . . . "Well—there are always cards; and, when I get older, knitting and patience, I suppose. And if everybody cuts me I shan't need any evening dresses. That will be an economy, at any rate," she concluded with a little shiver.[121]

Lizzie fails to see the usefulness of her husband's library; she cannot bring herself to imagine that she will, in due time, develop into an ardent reader. But what's revealing about this inner monologue is that at no point during it does she consider selling the books or giving them away. Though Lizzie suffered, in the years before she met Henry, from recurring bouts of financial insolvency, she does not so much as entertain the option of selling them, nor does she relegate them to a relative's attic (as is the case with Lewis Raycie's Italian primitives in *False Dawn*). This suggests that quality of "dormancy" that I mentioned earlier in connection with Foucault; Charles's books, for Lizzie, contain potential, even if they are not immediately useful to her. Indeed, Wharton is suggesting in this scene that preservation and maintenance have the potential to pay off in the long run for the very reason that a willing audience is not always immediate but might, in fact, be forthcoming down the line. Wharton thus invests Lizzie's narrative with a spirit of hope that helps to make *New Year's Day* a fitting conclusion to the *Old New York* novellas. Society is plagued by an ignorant impatience, Wharton is saying; it does not yet realize the worth of its own hoard of history, or of its collected possessions. But it may yet, given time.

Accordingly, Wharton's narrative brightens somewhat toward the end of the novella. The narrator, who reports from an unnamed present and so looks back on the 1870s, and who is decades younger than the now-aging Lizzie Hazeldean, meets her through a friend. The two young men then begin to frequent Lizzie's residence, forming part of a small circle of "her intimates," which, significantly, includes only men. Eventually the narrator discovers Lizzie's husband's library. "I remember, on the evening of that first 'jolly supper,' coming to an astonished pause before the crowded shelves that took up one wall of the drawing-room. What! The goddess read, then? She could accompany one on those flights too? Lead one, no doubt? My heart beat high." Because she *collects* and possesses books, the narrator supposes, she must be a keen reader, too. But in this he is wrong. "It took me no long time to make the discovery," he states. "She turned but languidly even the pages of the last Ouida novel; and I remember seeing Mallock's *New Republic* uncut on her table for weeks."[122] Here, though, as is so often the case with Wharton, allusion is everything.

→ William Hullock Mallock's *The New Republic* was first published in 1877. It is a novel devoted to the satirical portrayal of a group of art critics, scholars, and aesthetes who were connected to Oxford University in the early 1870s. Among the figures it satirizes are John Ruskin (previously featured in the novella *False Dawn*) as well as Matthew Arnold, Thomas Carlyle, William Kingdon Clifford, Thomas Huxley, and John Tyndall. Wharton owned all of these authors; their works, including Mallock's novels, are still part of her library collection today. As such, to the same degree that *Old New York* functions as a collection of dated impressions of nineteenth-century New York life, so does it encode a bibliographical world that informed and shaped those impressions for readers like her. Those bibliographic references impose standards of contemporaneity on the fictionalized events of *New Year's Day* and the other novellas: if Mallock's *The New Republic* was published in 1877, and Charles Hazeldean has been dead since the early 1870s, then that can only mean that Lizzie Hazeldean, in spite of not being a "born reader," has continued to collect and buy books. What this means additionally is that her curatorial interest in maintaining the library collection is not structured by sentimental imperatives alone. She has continued to buy books because she views the collecting of them as important—that is, she sees the act of collecting as a form of investment that will, eventually, appreciate in one way or another. Lizzie is in this way the very antithesis of the Raycie family in *False Dawn*; where the Raycies refuse to wait, being too shortsighted and impatient to foresee the value of what they have collected, Lizzie continues to procure and to curate her husband's library collection with nascence and potential in mind.

Does Lizzie benefit as the result of maintaining the collection, though? Wharton, I think, encourages us to view her actions in an advantageous light. For starters, the collection forms the basis of her relationship with the young narrator, who enters her life and becomes the first (save for Henry Prest) to learn "the truth" of her story. The narrator praises Lizzie's skills as a curator, noting that her collection includes "the accumulated treasures of English poetry, and a rich and varied selection of history, criticism, letters, in English, French and Italian . . . books evidently assembled by a sensitive and widely-ranging reader."[123] The narrator's praise, in fact, makes it almost impossible to view Lizzie as an unintelligent person or a "nonreader," and this furthermore suggests that she has nonetheless developed into a more intelligent and cultivated person in the wake of her husband's death.

In time, however, the narrator's praises for Lizzie begin to invoke the language of monumental preservation. He observes that she has "kept [her life] empty" on purpose for the sake of filling it with the memory of her husband, and that the library has helped her to do that. She strikes the narrator as looking "like a guardian of an abandoned temple" who has devoted her life to "sweeping and tending what had once been the god's abode." But, the narrator reflects, these activities have substituted for the cultivation of a richer, inner life, and "Her tastes, her interests, her conceivable occupations" all exist "on the level of a middling domesticity," which is to say they are not, in the end, fulfilling. The parallels to Paulina Anson in "The Angel at the Grave" are, in this context, immediate and clear: Lizzie, like Paulina, has allowed herself to become possessed by the "ghosts of dead duties" and has not sought ways to establish a meaningful existence for herself within the modern world. Lizzie lives in what the narrator deems "cold celibacy" and prefers to "shut herself up in a lonely monumental attitude."[124]

Wharton, though, had great respect for solitude, as I previously explained in connection with her admiration for Ralph Waldo Emerson. It wasn't just from Emerson, however, that Wharton learned to see the charms of privacy; Matthew Arnold, who is one of the figures satirized in Mallock's *The New Republic,* wrote extensively on the subject. A copy of Arnold's *Notebooks* can be found in Wharton's library at The Mount, dating from 1902 and containing multiple marked passages. One of them, which contains lines written in French not by Arnold but by the nineteenth-century French theologian Jean-Baptiste Henri-Dominique Lacordaire, reads thus: "I regard with joy the loneliness around me: it is my element, my life. One does nothing except in solitude: it is my great axiom. A man is made within a person and not without."[125] Next to this section, Wharton has added a set of vertical pencil markings, indicating her enthusiasm for Lacordaire's point that solitude, in fact, is a more promising means of achieving contentment than the society of others. It is a point that rings true, given Lizzie's efforts to achieve what the narrator labels "inner satisfaction" through social engagement. Those efforts are ultimately unsuccessful, and as "she [grows] older," she begins to "fill[] her depleted circle with a less fastidious hand. One met in her drawing-room dull men, common men, men who too obviously came there because they were not invited elsewhere."[126]

Salvation for Lizzie arrives at long last not in the guise of social attachments but in that of the printed word. Though Howard contends that the significance of *New Year's Day* lies in part in "Wharton's high valuation of a character who does not read," to me, this pronouncement oversimplifies things: Lizzie *does* read—or, at least, she tries.[127] It's simply that reading does not come easily to her, and this is to some extent an unfortunate result of her upbringing. Though not a "born reader," she keeps step with the literary publishing world and continues to purchase new books, actions that establish her as a reader manqué. Too, at the close of the novella, which coincides with the close of Lizzie's life, Wharton explains that "there had even been found for her, among the books she had so often tried to read, those books which had long looked at her with such hostile faces, two or three (they were always on her bed) containing messages from the world where Charles was waiting."[128] That is to say, Lizzie discovers in books and in reading messages conveyed from beyond the grave. To the same extent that her husband's library has functioned as his tomb, so has it been hers, sealing her off from the perils and pain of social interaction with the living world. And her reward, at last, is these "messages," these words of insight and comfort that come to her not from the living—not even from the narrator, who has been granted access to her story and who purports to understand her—but from the dead. The prospect of communion with the dead, which Lizzie has previously only glimpsed in the pages of the books she has read and tended, becomes real to her at the last.

The Well-Wrought Epitaph: The Library as Literary Monument

Upon first encountering it, visitors to Wharton's library at The Mount often want to know what it is worth. They inquire as to the collection's total value and ask questions about the most "expensive" books on the shelves. Such questions, I think, are to a certain extent intuitive; the library *feels* different from the other spaces at The Mount, and visitors can usually sense that difference. It is, for instance, the only part of The Mount that features iron railings and automatic alarms—the sort of trappings commonly found in museums and used to restrict space and to cordon off objects of "worth." In the mansion's other rooms, visitors may touch and move about and even sit on the furniture if they like, and the library's railings serve to impart feelings of restraint. The room's contents, these physical features furthermore suggest, are worth a lot and so must be protected.

Some visitors arrive at The Mount already acquainted with a version of the library's story and with some of the facts associated with its worth. Thanks to a series of high-profile news articles that appeared in the early 2000s in venues like the *New York Times* and the *New Yorker,* the library's "worth" has been the subject of popular speculation and, in many cases, popular derision, as when Rebecca Mead, writing for the *New Yorker* in 2008, comments that the library collection's purchase price (roughly 2.6 million U.S. dollars) amounted to "twice that of [its] appraised market value"—an observation that news outlets have been quick to recite ever since. A "Save the Mount!" campaign, which solicited donations via online outlets like Slate.com, contributed to the media maelstrom surrounding The Mount back in 2008 and introduced readers to the ongoing saga of the estate's financial woes.[129] More recently, in the fall of 2015, the *Guardian* reported that The Mount had at long last succeeded in paying off its formerly mountainous debts; the article, however, reinforces the view that the purchase of the library was largely to blame for those debts, even though its purchase accounted for less than a third of the nonprofit's total deficits at the time of its acquisition.

For four consecutive summers while I was digitizing items from Wharton's collection in connection with the EdithWhartonsLibrary.org project site, I spent long days working inside the library. The iron railings separated me from the groups of inquisitive visitors that, once every hour, came trooping through in the company of tour guides. Sometimes an allusive remark would serve to express a visitor's disdain about the library "not being worth" the money that had been reportedly spent on it; others, meanwhile, would bombard their guide (or me) with questions that circled back to discussions of *cost* and *worth*: How much does a first-edition *Ulysses* cost, anyway? Did Wharton have all of her books custom bound or just the expensive ones? I came to see these forms of scrutiny as inspired by the space of the library itself, with its railings and its climate control and its overt physical enforcements. At the same time, I also came to see them as tied to a very specific kind of contemporary illiteracy: most of us in the twenty-first century no longer live with and among books, so we struggle when faced with estimations of their worth. As a researcher who specializes in book history, I often receive inquiries from strangers who want to know how much a particular book—one that has been, so the story usually goes, discovered in a relative's attic—might be worth. In a similar way, visitors to The Mount sense that Wharton's library has value, but they are hard pressed when asked to conceive of its value in terms that defy the logic of monetary worth or simple cost.

The ambiguities associated with value and worth bring us back to the discussion of monuments and tombs. Wordsworth declares that a monument's purpose is to furnish a record of "departed worth" and that it is the job of a tomb's epigraph, in particular, to articulate and publicize the details of that worth. An epitaph performs a social as well as a private function: it "naturally turns . . . upon personal or social sorrow and admiration," with the result being that an insufficient epitaph, like a poor monument, suggests "either that the dead did not possess the merits ascribed to him, or that they who have raised a monument to his memory . . . were incapable of perceiving those merits."[130] That is to say, monuments and epitaphs advertise worth to the same extent that they advertise deficiencies, may those deficiencies be direct (on the part of the deceased) or by association (on the part of his or her associates). A person whose death is marked by an unworthy monument or a trite epigraph is really no person at all, according to such logic.

Wharton's library at The Mount speaks as a monument and so seeks to advertise the worth of its subject. The problem is that it speaks in a language that has become anachronistic and so largely indecipherable to modern audiences. Unlike the actual Mount—meaning unlike the physical estate, which includes the house but also the grounds, the gardens, the outbuildings, and the sprawling views of its Berkshires environs—the library speaks via messages that require parsing and interpretation. In this way they are very like those that Lizzie Hazeldean receives from beyond the grave at the conclusion of *New Year's Day*. While the language of big houses and lavish estates is one that we still know and recognize today, in the twenty-first century we have, by comparison, lost the knack of deciphering the particular dialect of cultural capital that is specific to the practice of book collecting. This loss, by the way, is precisely what Wharton feared when she set about amassing her private library in the late nineteenth and early twentieth centuries. It's important to remember that she was not the only one suffering from such fears, and that Wharton's concerns for the fraying links between self-cultivation, reading, and book collecting comprise a single, localized instance that connects to a set of larger trends. For instance, Susan Sontag similarly describes Walter Benjamin's fears regarding the disappearance of what she labels the "freelance intellectual." Benjamin, when he wrote the essays in the 1930s that now form the work known as *Illuminations*, "thought that the freelance intellectual was a dying species; indeed, he felt that he was living in a time in which everything valuable was the last of its kind," according to Sontag.[131] This, as I have shown, is furthermore the case with the characters that populate Wharton's *Old New York* novellas—characters that Wharton devised during the same era that Benjamin was contemplating his own feelings of personal and categorical endangerment. Lizzie Hazeldean is conscious of feeling insufficiently modern and out of step with time, and so retreats to her memories of the 1870s with the help of her husband's library. The *Old New York* novellas, even, when taken together present a "collection" of impressions and memories that resists narrative coherence in favor of presenting a scrapbooklike array of vignettes. The overall suggestion is that this collection is meant to preserve and embalm images of "the way things used to be" in old New York, regardless of whether the "things" in question are, or ever were, preferable in the first place. The desire to preserve at any cost, when it appears divorced from evaluative concerns in this way, amounts to a kind of compulsion. The *Old New York* novellas, much like the books in her library, became for Wharton a means of hoarding personal impressions of the past when faced with overwhelming change and anxieties about endangerment.

Those anxieties, I think, help to explain why we see Wharton, in her fifties and sixties, exerting new levels of control over her library books. I mentioned in chapter 1 that Wharton never had a custom bookplate designed to mark her library books at The Mount. This is, of course, in spite of the fact that she proved to be an exacting and zealous overseer where the creation of the library space was concerned. Previously, Wharton had used bookplates to mark her books at Land's End, the first residence she shared with Teddy, which was located adjacent to her mother's property in Providence, Rhode Island. But it was not until her purchase of the house that she dubbed "Pavillon Colombe," which she bought following the First World War, when houses on the Parisian outskirts were "going cheap," according to Lee,[132] that she saw fit to revive the practice. No doubt the war had served to heighten feelings of general endangerment for those living on the continent; too, Wharton's divorce, which became final in 1912 (and which cost her The Mount), may have taught her the virtues of adopting a firm, proprietorial outlook toward one's possessions. Whatever her motivations, she had the American printer Daniel Berkeley Updike[133] design custom bookplates for both of her French residences later on, in 1924, and today, her library collection shows that she put them to vigorous use during the last decade and a half of her life. And bookplates have quite a lot in common with epitaphs.

In practice, both epitaphs and bookplates serve the function of drawing attention to the facts of a person's existence. Wordsworth actually laments this quality in epitaphs; though they are supposed to speak pronouncements of "departed worth," Wordsworth observes that, as a genre, they are for the most part doomed to insufficiency. This occurs, on the one hand, as the result of cliché, since "to be born and to die are the two points in which all men feel themselves to be in absolute coincidence."[134] On the other, though, that insufficiency also results from the pressure to create something permanent, according to Wordsworth. "The thoughts and feelings expressed [in an epitaph] should be permanent also," he argues—that is, just as permanent as the physical monument that is erected for the same purpose.[135] Yet most epitaphs fall spectacularly short of this goal, and Wordsworth notes that the most common type limits itself to a record of the "facts," or dates, of a person's life.[136] The same, I think, is true of bookplates, which, at minimum, attest to mere "facts" of ownership (this person lived; this person died; this person owned this particular book). Laqueur furthermore notes that "it has always been the case that names have stood in for, or pointed to, the bodies of the dead," and in his *The Work of the Dead,* he places special emphasis on the historical practice of tying names, which endure, to bodily remains, which do not. Names and dead bodies are "spectral mates," because a number of institutions throughout history, along with the people who act on behalf of them (insurance agents, lawyers, representatives of the state), deem it so.[137]

But where "records of worth" might be concerned, the connection between epitaphs and bookplates deepens. Both, to start, purport to express some kind of private sentiment: in the case of epitaphs, that sentiment is one of subjective grief (I am mourning the loss of this person); in the case of bookplates, that sentiment is one of personal attachment and physical interaction (I touched, held, and owned this book). Both try to broadcast private sentiment to a larger, public audience. As Wordsworth puts it, "An epitaph is not a proud writing shut up for the studious: it is exposed to all," and through it "the stranger is introduced through its mediation to the company of a friend."[138] A bookplate, I would argue, does something similar in that it converts the private act of reading into a public appeal for camaraderie. One does not, after all, add the "fact" of their name to a book in order to simply mark it as theirs; indeed, one does so while acting on the awareness that, someday, the book in question must inevitably *cease* to be theirs. As such, I think it makes sense to view bookplates not simply through the lens of ownership but as doubly representative of insecurities about the ephemerality of ownership. Bookplates, like epitaphs, are nothing if not appeals for posthumous remembrance. What's more, just as an epitaph may signify the "worth" of a deceased person, so may a bookplate functionally increase the worth of the book to which it is attached. A deceased famous person's bookplate makes even the most worthless book worth something, in the end.

Given their relationship with practices of posthumous remembrance, then, the analogy comes full circle: bookplates are to epitaphs as libraries are to tombs. This is as much the case for characters like Paulina and Lizzie, who reside in library-like tombs located within Wharton's fiction, as it was for Wharton personally: upon her death in 1936, Wharton was buried in a cemetery outside Paris, in a "plain, rather ugly grave."[139] Yet it is clear from Lee's account of her visit to Wharton's grave that, today, that space of physical internment lacks a contemporary audience base. Lee explains that she found it "covered with weeds, old bottles, and a very ancient pot of dead flowers" indicating that "clearly no one had been there for a long time. It struck me as an unvisited and lonely tomb."[140] The audience that is now best able to receive and to decipher Wharton's legacy is, I would argue, an audience of contemporary readers, scholars, and students—an audience who may, if they choose, visit the tomb that is her library at The Mount and bear witness to the epigraphic "fact" of her existence on the inside covers of the books that she owned. Wharton's grave in France lacks an audience because, in being simply a grave, it is located inside a modern cemetery and cemeteries "speak of finitude," as Laqueur puts it.[141] By contrast, Wharton's library at The Mount speaks not of finitude but of activity—of enduring forms of engagement and discourse.

Wharton's books, whatever they are worth in dollars, are worth more because she touched, read, and interacted with them. The bookplates furnish evidence of that interaction in places where pencil markings and annotations may not, and it is because of Wharton's decision to add bookplates to her books—to "secure" an insecure legacy of herself as the owner of them—that they are still around today. George Ramsden, the British bookseller who was responsible for compiling the library collection, started out in the early 1980s, a half-century after Wharton's death, with a trunkful of books containing bookplates with her name on them. When he sold his whole collection of Wharton books to The Mount in the early 2000s, its worth (that is to say, Ramsden's asking price) rested on questions of legitimacy that could, for the most part, only be laid to rest with the help of bookplates. Indeed, the act of designing and applying a bookplate is not unlike that of selecting a quotation for one's grave, or that of picking out a tombstone. It amounts to a form of posthumous curation, wherein the subject assumes an active role in selecting and managing the components of how they will be remembered.

A handful of books on the shelves at The Mount do not feature Wharton's bookplate. They are worth mentioning for what they reveal about the actions of other people who have had roles to play in curating the collection and in crafting images of Wharton's continuing legacy. Some bookplates have simply gone missing over the years, the result, perhaps, of a book's having been passed from person to person, of its having been read and used, or else of precisely the opposite, of its having been neglected and ill used. In a few books one can see where a bookplate must have previously been: a lightened rectangular mark graces the pastedown, and its shape roughly matches that of one of Wharton's bookplates. With other books, though, the origins are much less clear, and thus perhaps even more fascinating. Ramsden's *Edith Wharton's Library* lists a nearly complete set of the works of George Eliot, which he alleges belonged to Wharton. While Ramsden notes in his catalog that the set "lacks *Middlemarch* (3 vols.),"[142] the collection that he sold to The Mount—and which was installed within the library back in 2008—contains the missing three volumes of *Middlemarch,* which match the edition details listed by Ramsden for the rest of the set. There is no indication that these three volumes ever belonged to Wharton, though; rather, Ramsden procured them and added them to the collection because he wanted to see the complete set of Eliot's works on the shelves at The Mount. Mind you, there is no subterfuge at work here, and Ramsden admitted to having done this, but his actions cast doubt on the overall "value" and price of the collection, given his disregard for authenticity in this particular instance. Indeed, Nynke Dorhout, The Mount's librarian, speculates that there are more items in the collection of "questionable provenance," as she puts it; she doubts, for example, that *any* of the volumes in the Eliot set belonged to Wharton, since no bookplates (or evidence of

Wharton's copy of George Eliot's *The Mill on the Floss,* showing where a bookplate was removed from the pastedown. Photograph by the author.

previous bookplates) survive to mark them as her property, and since edition details are not mentioned specifically in any of her letters or writings. The same goes for a complete set of the works of Daniel Defoe, which Dorhout believes were likely never owned by Wharton either. Ramsden also admitted to adding a copy of *Madame Bovary* to an eighteen-volume set of Flaubert's works that would have been incomplete were it not for the addition of that "false," but matching, singular volume.

I find these counterfeit additions interesting because they inspire a multitude of questions. For instance, if Ramsden was willing to substitute inauthentic volumes and place them among Wharton's own books, then authenticity must not have been a motivating factor for his acquiring them in first place. In which case, the question becomes, what *was* the motivation, then? In an interview I conducted with him, he told me that he had never read anything by Edith Wharton before he started collecting the components of her personal library. Why did he do it, then? And why did he devote almost three decades of his life to overseeing that task? And how did his motivations bear upon his methods of acquisition?

Here the story I have been telling throughout this book—a story that hinges on considerations of collecting, hoarding, value, and worth—swerves and becomes not just a historical tale but a contemporary one. The story of Edith Wharton's library as it relates to Edith Wharton specifically has concluded but, as the ensuing Conclusion ought to make clear, it is far from over.

Conclusion

· · · · · · · · · · · · · · · ·

The Afterlives of Edith Wharton's Library

In the spring of 1984, nearly half a century after Wharton's death, a portion of her library came up for sale via auction. The seller was Maggs Bros. Ltd., a London-based dealer of rare and antiquarian print materials that had acquired about two thousand of Wharton's original library books after purchasing them from the Clark family. Sir Kenneth Clark, entrusted to keep the collection on behalf of his son Colin, who was Wharton's designated heir, had passed away only a year before, in the spring of 1983. But it was not Colin who orchestrated the sale of the books to Maggs following his father's death; rather, Colin's older brother, Alan, a parliamentarian with an irascible temperament and a notorious reputation, oversaw the sale, culling the Wharton books from his family's library at Saltwood Castle, where they had sat gently deteriorating for decades.

Alan Clark had little regard for the Wharton collection and little regard for their original owner, despite her close relationship with his father. That, and he needed the money: as reported in the *New York Times,* "[Clark] spoke proudly of having inherited a fifty-room, seventeenth-century castle and an estate worth tens of millions of pounds," but he publicly lamented the taxes levied on such an inheritance. Speaking to a reporter, he once described the "agonizing" experience of selling his family's valued possessions in order to pay the taxes on Saltwood, remarking, "You'll never know what it's like having to do without the Turner."[1] The Wharton books, though they were intended for his younger brother, Colin, wound up being included in the estate that Alan had inherited after his father's death, and he pounced almost instantly on the prospect of selling them, even while he expressed regrets at having to sell other items from his father's collection.

Alan was an amateur historian and author of books about the First World War, among other subjects, but he was known for adopting an indifferent stance toward intellectual pursuits. He once called his own Oxford education "a waste of time and petrol,"[2] and such feelings appear to have characterized his attitudes toward Wharton's library books, too. The Clarks' portion of the collection consisted of a motley assortment of works of history, fiction, philosophy, gardening, and other subjects, almost all of which featured either Wharton's bookplate or signature. But by the time Maggs Bros. acquired them in 1984, the vast majority were judged to be in poor condition as a result of having been "kept in the Castle Library, where conditions were far from ideal." The Maggs auction catalog describes the collection as "suffer[ing] from damp and occasional worming." Indeed, many of the Wharton books that are now housed at The Mount bear witness to their long years at Saltwood: mildew and rot mar the pages, worm tunnels extend from cover to cover, and bindings are in shreds. But setting aside these numerous physical deficiencies, Maggs knew that they had acquired something special and rare through their negotiations with Alan—a significant portion of a famous author's library, complete with "presentation copies" and books containing "annotations in the hand of Edith Wharton, with occasional transcription of significant passages on the endpapers."[3]

Those who deal in rare books are often tempted to break up owners' collections for the very reason that individual items tend to fetch higher unit prices when they are displayed by themselves, as unique instances presented without distracting accompaniment. Maggs, though, elected to resell the Wharton library collection in toto, complete with a "quantity of odd volumes" that are mentioned (though not actually listed) in the auction catalog, comprised of books that may have belonged to Wharton but lacked identifying marks.[4] One can imagine the types of investors that Maggs might have had in mind for the sale: scholars, well-endowed hobbyists, Wharton fans from around the globe, and experienced collectors would have all been eager to step up and secure the collection. But in the end Maggs sold the library collection to a bookseller who, at the time, was totally unfamiliar with Wharton's work. George Ramsden would later describe himself as having been "possibly slightly mad" at the time of the purchase, in spite of, or perhaps due to, that stated unfamiliarity.[5] "Of course," he went on to clarify in an interview I conducted with him, "I started to read, after I acquired it. The more I read of her books, too, the more central libraries seemed to be—to her, to her writing. Which only got me more interested."[6] Ramsden succeeded in securing the Wharton library remnants from Maggs for the price of £45,000 (about $80,000 at the time); the money came from his father, who, while he handed over the funds, acerbically dismissed his son's interests in book collecting by saying, "Do you know how many horses I could have for that price?"[7]

George Ramsden was born in 1953 into a respected family. His father, the Rt. Hon. James Edward Ramsden, was the last person in the country to hold the office of minister for war (1963–64) before he retired from politics at the age of fifty. In the spring of 1984, when George Ramsden bought that first, very sizable chunk of Wharton's library from Maggs, he was thirty years old and still in the beginning stages of his career as a bookseller. After studying at Cambridge, he had taken a job at Heywood Hill, a renowned London bookshop that boasts its own connections to the British aristocracy,[8] where he worked for three subsequent years, from 1977 until 1980. It was during that time he first heard the name Edith Wharton uttered with any kind of critical esteem. "Wharton's reputation was in the doldrums then, but they [the staff] rated her. They were always recommending her books to customers."[9] Eventually he found himself tasked with collecting quality volumes to sell in the Heywood Hill shop; he once returned from a trip with six early English editions of Wharton novels, which pleased his mentor at the shop, John Saumarez Smith. Ramsden's skill for collecting eventually led him to open his own bookstore in 1981.

That store, Stone Trough Books, was originally situated in Camberwell Grove, a serene street in southeast London that appealed to Ramsden's preference for peace and quiet over steady customers. "There were very few bookshops in South London," he explains in an interview, noting that this fact made it "an ideal location for quiet bookselling and collecting." Here, as in many instances, what is significant is Ramsden's insistence on a kind of fusion between the practices of selling and collecting; indeed, in an essay he wrote reflecting on his career as a collector, he admits that he was never "at ease with the carriage trade or good with it," even while he excelled as a collector.[10] While working at Heywood Hill, he had stumbled on the discovery of his vocation as a collector without, as he put it in another interview, "imbibing any of the positive sales pitch practised there."[11] Such repeated admissions of disinterest in the book trade suggest that Ramsden had, over time, become accustomed to viewing himself as a connoisseur-turned-accidental-pro. Given such self-awareness, it would appear that whatever motivations might have compelled his original purchase of the Wharton library collection, they did not chiefly include sales.

When he bought it from Maggs, Ramsden was looking to *own* Edith Wharton's library, not to sell it—at least initially. Upon installing the books (in the upper floor of his Camberwell shop, out of sight from the public), he realized that the collection was far from complete and set immediately to work on rectifying that condition. "I was driven by an instinct to get it right," he told me, alluding to a perceived, inherent connection between cohesion and integrity. Indeed, Ramsden was the sort of man who exuded a passion for integrity, as I learned during my meetings with him. But setting things right meant that he could not, in the meantime, even entertain the idea of selling off any of the individual Wharton volumes. In response to my asking whether or not, in moments of desperation, he had ever been tempted to do so, his response was adamant: "Certainly not. I wanted them all together, to represent her as well as they could. I would show them to people sometimes—not too often, actually—but I wasn't going to sell any of them. They needed to be together."[12] One of the lucky few to glimpse the Wharton collection during its tenure at the Camberwell Grove shop was the writer Ariane Bankes, who later published an account of her interactions with Ramsden in the British quarterly magazine *Slightly Foxed*. "If it was very quiet and there was no need to keep an eye on things downstairs, George would say, 'Why don't you come upstairs and see Edith?' Then you would be led up to a lovely room lined from floor to ceiling with Edith Wharton's library."[13] What's telling here is how Ramsden is purported to have used the library as a synecdoche for the person, for "Edith" herself. The invitation to "come and see Edith" suggests that Ramsden reveled in the prospect of seeing Wharton's library as the living embodiment of its deceased owner, in much the same way that many of Wharton's fictional characters—including Charity Royall, Paulina Anson, and Lizzie Hazeldean—view the libraries with which they are each, likewise, intimately connected.

When I met Ramsden in York during the spring of 2017, he made a similar offer to me, even though Wharton's library had, by that point, been residing at The Mount for more than a decade. He asked if I wanted to see where Wharton had "lived" after he had moved her library to the rural environs of Yorkshire, which he had done in 1990 while citing a reluctance to raise his children in London.[14] Though Stone Trough Books had followed him to York and been reborn in the form of a new shop under the same name, there was no room for the Wharton library there, and so, in the years preceding its sale to The Mount estate in Massachusetts, it had shared a roof with him at his nearby home, located just outside York. There, Wharton's two-thousand-plus books were given their own room and kept apart from the thousands of others that Ramsden owns. This sequestration was as much practical as it was sentimental: Ramsden had begun the rather painstaking work of cataloging the library's contents, and he needed to keep the collection organized. The catalog, which appeared in 1999 courtesy of his own imprint (also called Stone Trough Books), took almost a decade to complete, in part because Ramsden, fueled by that same passion for completion, kept finding more books to add to it and to the library itself. For it wasn't long after he acquired the collection that Ramsden discovered the location of many, if not most, of the remaining books from Edith Wharton's library: Saltwood Castle.

Certainly haste, combined with a minor kind of unscrupulousness, could be blamed for the Clarks' failure to include many of Wharton's original books in the collection that they sold to Maggs Bros. But other explanations are possible, too. For example, Alan Clark had been known to remove the bookplates from some of Wharton's books in an apparent attempt to disguise the facts of their origins. As Ramsden explains in an essay he wrote:

> Clark had a decided fondness for William Orpen's *An Onlooker in France 1917–1919*, from which he had once removed Edith Wharton's bookplate. Loose in the book was a postcard with colour illustration on silk of a town in flames, captioned "Bapaume, 1917." The sender wrote that a rat had got into his tent and eaten his birthday cake. Clark loved everything about this copy, even the stains on the faded green cloth.[15]

This was not an isolated instance: Wharton's entire collection of George Eliot's *Works,* which was omitted from the Maggs auction sale catalog and subsequently rescued by Ramsden from Saltwood Castle during one of his many return trips there in the 1990s, displays evidence of having had its bookplates intentionally removed. On the front pastedowns of these volumes one may find shiny squares formed by the residue of bookplate adhesive, as mentioned previously in chapter 4. These correspond in size and shape to Wharton's own bookplates for both her Land's End and Pavillon Colombe–Hyères residences.[16] Such disfiguration proved to be yet one more obstacle for Ramsden, who, in addition to having to make special trips to Saltwood Castle (located in Kent, a six-hour drive from York) had to contend with Alan Clark's infamously "splenetic" personality.[17]

Clark was loath to part with the books that ought, rightfully, to have been included in the original Maggs auction sale anyway, and he demanded that Ramsden pay him for the extra items or else secure replacements for them. Ramsden, relying on his skills as a professional collector, succeeded in tracking down some elaborately bound volumes to trade with Clark during his repeated trips to Saltwood.

> I was required to "replace the divot," i.e., fill in the gaps [on the library shelves] with something suitable, normally with an emphasis on appearance rather than content. In Clark's study, for instance, he favored the soft mellow tones of old calf, where as in the Great Library he'd diversify a uniform run of books with a splash of gilt. As we suited my imported volumes to the shelves, I remarked that it was like flower-arranging.[18]

Here Ramsden calls attention to the way in which, for Clark, the owning of books was something akin to owning works of art. In either case, it's clear that the main concern was aesthetics. Clark's chief objective was to have books that looked "right" in the Saltwood Castle library, with "rightness" referring to the quality of the bindings and, in some cases, the period of publication. This helps to explain why so many of Wharton's books fell into disrepair during their time at Saltwood, for in all likelihood no one was reading them.

In addition to removing the bookplates, we also know that Alan Clark dispatched several volumes from the Wharton library collection as gifts—or, in certain instances, as peace offerings. In Wharton's copy of the French philosopher Jean-Marie Guyau's book *Esquisse d'une Morale sans Obligation ni Sanction*,[19] I found a letter from Alan Clark, composed on his stationery and bearing a rather enigmatic message. "Dear Norman," it reads, "So sorry about last night—definitely enough by Tebbitt to spoil your birthday. Hope you like this birthday card—the bookplate is quite her. (Her entire library is at Saltwood.)" It is signed "A.," indicating that Clark gave this volume—which contains annotations and underlinings by Wharton—to a friend or colleague following some kind of altercation. One might well question Clark's scruples in doing so, too, not only because an annotated copy of a French philosophy text owned by Wharton may be seen as having significant scholarly value but also because professional appraisals often rate Wharton association copies as being worth thousands of dollars. In contrast to Ramsden's inclination to "get it right" and to secure the collection in whole, Clark appears to have been content with the idea of splitting up its contents, even as he boasted about owning the collection in its "entirety."

Ramsden visited Saltwood for the last time in 1999, just as he was finishing work on the *Edith Wharton's Library* catalog. He describes his nervousness in an essay he wrote remembering Alan Clark, explaining that, on his previous trip to the estate, "Alan had said, 'I find it admirable that you should devote your whole life to reconstructing Edith Wharton's library; it is also a *thundering* nuisance.'" But as a "sizable heap" of Wharton books was apparently at stake during that visit, Ramsden felt compelled to make light of Clark's earlier comment.[20] What I find particularly interesting about this story is the way that Ramsden additionally makes light of Clark's accusation that the reassembling of the Wharton library collection formed the core of his existence, i.e., Ramsden's "whole life." Ramsden, certainly, approached the task of completing the library with the kind of obstinacy that appears born from fanaticism. But the question we ought to be asking is, Why? How did Ramsden, who had never read an Edith Wharton novel back in 1984, come to organize his life around the task of reconstructing her library by the year 1999? And if the overall point wasn't simply to sell and make money off the library, what *was* the point? Though Ramsden would, in due time, reap a sizeable reward from his efforts to reconstruct the library, his intentions appear to have been less straightforward at the start. For even if he had not been familiar with Wharton, he *had* been acquainted with her authorial legacy, thanks in part to his association with a certain young woman, a Wharton aficionado who would later develop into a hobbyist scholar.[21] Ramsden's purchase of the Wharton library collection coincided with a period of his life that was characterized in part by his interactions with this young woman.

It is therefore tempting to read Ramsden's acquisition of the Wharton library collection through the lens of romance. Indeed, the library appears to invite such a reading, given the many ways in which its books speak to histories of sentimental attachment, desire, and heartbreak. Take, for instance, the books that Wharton received as gifts from her lover, Morton Fullerton. A 1911 gilt leather edition of Salomon Reinach's *Eulalie* includes a brazenly tender inscription from Fullerton, composed in Greek, which reads, "I proclaim that someday in story sweet-speaking Heliodora will surpass by her graces the Graces themselves."[22] The inscription comes from an epigram from *The Greek Anthology,* written by the poet Meleager, and is meant, it would appear, to suggest that Wharton, through her talents as a writer, may aspire to "surpass the Graces themselves." It reveals a somewhat surprising capacity for care and flattery on Fullerton's part, whereas much of his interactions with Wharton, even during the high points of their affair, were marked by a kind of "hurtful" callousness and "unreliability," in the words of Lee.[23] There is also Fullerton's gift of a lavish illustrated edition of Bédier's *Le Roman de Tristan et Iseut,* which features an inscription composed of lines from Wharton's own poetry. Wharton had presented him with a handwritten copy of a poem ("Ogrin the Hermit") that had been inspired by her reading of Bédier's version of the Tristan and Isolde legend. Fullerton's 1909 Christmas gift of an illustrated edition of that same text (she already owned a copy and had marked it thoroughly) was meant to echo and match Wharton's gift of the poem she had given him, the copy of which she had inscribed to him with the words "Per Te, Sempre Per Te."[24] Fullerton, in gifting an additional copy of Bédier's text along with this self-referential inscription, was attempting a similar kind of flattery in appealing to Wharton's vanity. And since Fullerton's own copy of the "Ogrin the Hermit" poem has been lost, his inscription to Wharton in this book comprises the only remaining copy of an original work by her, a fact that reinforces its significance and rather makes it a highlight of the collection.

There are other ways in which Wharton's library collection speaks to simmering legacies of love. Wharton had an abiding appreciation for the poet George Meredith, and in her copy of his 1862 work *Modern Love* (a collection of devastating ruminations on the subject of a failed marriage), there is an inscription that reads, cryptically, "To Sheelagh from George." This appears alongside the bookplate from a previous owner, Sheelagh Hancox. When I examined this book, I found tucked inside it a piece of paper with a quotation from Henry James's novel *The Portrait of a Lady*, apparently designed to accompany the book's presentation "To Sheelagh."

The quotation, which is typewritten and yet a decidedly modern addition to the volume (based on the condition of the paper, which is chemical wood pulp or "acidic" and so unlikely to last multiple decades without incurring visible signs of deterioration), replicates a few choice lines from James: "I lost no time; I fell in love with you then. . . . I don't know whether you suspected I was doing so, but I paid—mentally speaking, I mean—the great possible attention to you. Nothing you said, nothing you did, was lost upon me." The tone of these words is fervent and sincere, as is the context behind them; the quotation comes from chapter 12 of James's novel, when Lord Warburton proposes to Isabel. At that point in the narrative, Isabel is wracked by her own feelings of ambiguity toward Warburton. She "likes" him—that is the word that James uses repeatedly—but she does not feel passionately about his proposal and is, in fact, unsure of her feelings about marriage in general. She admits to being "not perfectly sincere" in her responses to Warburton, "for she had no doubt whatever that he himself was." At the same time, she observes that "the tone in which he replied would quite have served the purpose" to convince her that Warburton is a not a "loose thinker" but a man of intention.[25] But Isabel ends up refusing Warburton, to her own very great detriment. Instead she marries the duplicitous Gilbert Osmond, who siphons away her inheritance and leaves her miserable. Thus the aforementioned quotation, for all its sincerity, may be doubly read as expressing an ominous kind of warning: take me, for you may never receive a better offer.

I asked Ramsden about the Meredith volume and about the James

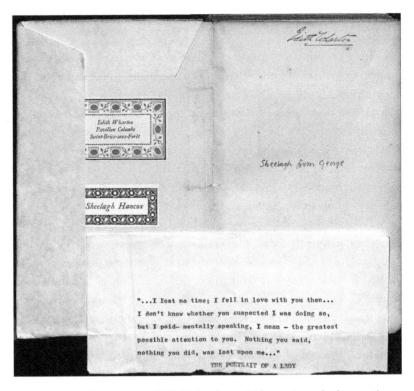

Wharton's copy of George Meredith's *Modern Love,* which contains multiple owners' bookplates, Wharton's signature, George Sims's inscription to Sheelagh Hancox, and a typewritten quotation from Henry James's *The Portrait of a Lady.* Photograph by the author.

text when I met with him. He claimed to have no memory of the particulars with regards to either, so I showed him a scanned image I had captured of the quotation, tipped into the pages of the Meredith book. Once again, his response was evasive, and he lost no time in steering the conversation back to Wharton, saying, "It fits in with her life, though, doesn't it?"[26] The "though" caught my attention in this instance because it suggested that there might be more to the story, and this turned out to be precisely the case. Sheelagh Hancox was the wife of another renowned English bookseller, Alan Hancox, whose Cheltenham-based store was for years seen as being a locus of literary life in the Cotswolds region. Sheelagh, though, had a close relationship with another bookseller, a friend of her husband named George Sims, and it was from him that she received the inscribed copy of the Meredith book. Sheelagh and Alan Hancox's marriage ended in divorce, a fact that makes this look like a particularly auspicious gift, in retrospect.[27] But I did not learn any of this from Ramsden, who, during our conversation, appeared eager to sidestep such personal matters and keep things focused on Wharton. We split a piece of chocolate cake while he shared with me his suspicions about Wharton's love life (he speculated, for instance, that Wharton had a romantic affair with her lifelong friend Walter Berry), seemingly offering these speculations in exchange for his reticence about the Meredith book inscription and the James quotation.

It was probably due to oversight that the James quotation remained in the book, anyway. Susan Wissler, who today is executive director of The Mount and who served as the organization's vice president and oversaw the sale of the library back in 2005, told me that Ramsden ended up retaining a significant collection of ephemeral materials (some of them Wharton's, some of them originating elsewhere) gleaned from individual library volumes. These materials included postcards, letters, bookmarks, torn shreds of paper, and other items that, as Wissler explains, she opted to let Ramsden keep in order to assuage his emotional distress over having to part with the library. I had hoped to examine some of these materials when I met Ramsden in York and thought that the typewritten James quotation might provide me a means of broaching the subject. But it became clear to me that Ramsden was not the "George" of the inscription; after all, his scruples as a collector would have prohibited him from gifting a Wharton book to anyone, no matter the person or the circumstances. And for all his speculations about Wharton's love life, Ramsden was disinclined to divulge personal information about himself or others in his network.

In the end, Ramsden did not end up showing me his stash of Wharton ephemeral materials, but he showed me other items that helped me to glimpse his personality and motivations as a collector. He let me browse the shelves of his shop, showing me postcards and bits of relevant correspondence, including a photograph that Cornelia Brooke Gilder had taken of a billboard advertising the arrival of Edith Wharton's library at The Mount. The billboard had featured a close-up image showing Wharton's copies of her own novels, arranged on the shelves of the library that she had herself designed, while, on the back of the photograph, Gilder had scrawled a warm message of thanks and congratulations to Ramsden. Similarly, at his house in Yorkshire (Ramsden resided, fittingly enough, in an old stone rectory with books piled in every corner and rooms haunted by the smell of wood smoke), he showed me the aforementioned room where Wharton had "lived" for almost ten years. The gaps left by the sale of the Wharton collection had long since been filled in, and Ramsden pointed out association copies once owned by Virginia Woolf and Henry James, along with rare editions of Whitman texts. His long-time friend, the editor and publisher Rupert Hart-Davis, had been the previous owner of some of these materials. And though it took some convincing on my part, Ramsden eventually let me see and handle one of his most prized possessions: a set of cricket pads that had belonged to the poet Siegfried Sassoon, complete with sweat stains. Meanwhile, Ramsden's reverence for these various items, and his nervousness about letting a stranger touch them, was more than evident. I estimated that he had about five thousand to seven thousand books in his possession, and that was before he led me out to the barn where, I discovered, another ten thousand or so were additionally kept. When I asked him what led him to amass a collection of more than fifteen thousand books, Ramsden told me simply that he considers books to be "great companions."[28] This response, which forms the refrain of the collector's credo,[29] struck me as being thoroughly Whartonesque, even if his habits as a collector might exceed Wharton's own.

If I learned anything from these interactions with Ramsden, it was that emotional attachments and sentimental imperatives had always been part of the equation for him where collecting is concerned. Indeed, Wharton's library shows us that this was the case for her, too, as it likely is for many bibliophiles. But an awareness of the emotional structures that subtend Ramsden's work in gathering, organizing, and cataloging the Wharton library collection shed some light, I think, on the conflicts that later arose throughout the process of selling it. It is to that narrative—to the story of how the library made its way back to the United States and to The Mount, at long last—that I shall now turn. It is, at points, an unpleasant one, but it forms a bridge between Ramsden's story and the discussions of value and worth that have thematically shaped the preceding sections of this book. Just as Wharton, in the early twentieth century, suffered anxiety over what she viewed as a process of gradual devaluation where books and reading were concerned, so Ramsden feared for the prospect of seeing a price tag attached to his years of labor and dedication. Such anxieties, as I have furthermore already argued, characterize and define the act of collecting: though the collection would purport to speak for the person who collected it, subjective attachments are doomed to translation via the crude and insufficient language of material value. A collection *means* most to the collector when it is still subject to becoming, still unfinished and in progress. But like all commodities, a collection incurs a pronouncement of value only through the process of exchange; it simply cannot be permitted to sit still forever.

What a Library's Worth

The year 1993 marked the beginning of Stephanie Copeland's reign as executive director of The Mount estate, which is overseen by the nonprofit Edith Wharton Restoration, Inc. As an organization, EWR had been steadfastly working to restore aspects of the estate since purchasing it—or 49 of the estate's original 113 acres, most of what remained intact—from a developer more than a decade previous, back in 1980. Those restoration efforts had cost the fledgling EWR deeply, with the result being that several projects had to be left in temporary abeyance. In the early 1990s, in addition to the renovations, Copeland found herself faced with a rather daunting new challenge: how to secure and pay for Edith Wharton's library books.

Even before Copeland appeared on the scene, Ramsden had been in contact with The Mount. A few years before he had written to see if The Mount might be, first, interested and, second, financially able to purchase the library collection, which was growing steadily as the result of his repeated trips to Saltwood Castle. Ramsden felt from the start that The Mount would be the ideal home for the collection; he wanted to see the books installed within the space that Wharton had designed specifically for their accommodation. But he was keeping his options open, which included exploring the possibility of selling it to an American university library. In 1993, as the two parties began to work toward the prospect of a sale, talks resumed in earnest between Ramsden and The Mount, under Copeland's firm stewardship. Copeland traveled to York to meet Ramsden and to view the collection on display at his house in Yorkshire. Having the opportunity to physically engage with the library itself, as opposed to a cataloged list of its components, proved a turning point for her. Whereas the board had been prepared to replicate Wharton's library with dummy editions in the event that Ramsden's price continued to place it beyond the organization's means, Copeland, upon seeing the library for the first time, became convinced that it was to be the most important purchase that The Mount could ever make. Like Ramsden, Copeland was swayed by the belief that the real books belonged inside the space of The Mount's library. The problem was the asking price, which Ramsden had originally set at $3 million, and which the EWR's board viewed as being wantonly excessive.

In order to test these suspicions, the EWR's board commissioned Peter Selley, of Sotheby's, to examine and appraise the collection. Selley carried out his appraisals from a distance and with the help of documents provided by Ramsden, which included drafts of the still incomplete *Edith Wharton's Library* catalog. After concluding his research, Selley assigned a value of £450,000–600,000 (roughly $880,000–1 million) to the collection based on material considerations alone and further argued in favor of capping the asking price at 1 million pounds (nearly 2 million dollars), given the state of the collection and its being so remarkably intact. Ramsden responded to Selley's appraisal by lowering his offer price slightly to $2.5 million, but Selley thought that The Mount ought to reject that figure given its marked distance from both the appraisal price and the proposed cap. Ramsden came away from this spate of dealings feeling angry and cheated; he insinuated that Sotheby's might not be properly qualified to evaluate the library collection. Copeland, in turn, encouraged him to reach out to a trusted adviser and have the collection reappraised, which he did. He invited Ed Maggs, of Maggs Bros. (the firm that had originally sold him the collection twenty years before) to visit his home in Yorkshire and issue an updated appraisal. Maggs did, but the result turned out to be devastating for Ramsden: 294,000 pounds, much lower than Selley's previous figure. In an effort to assuage Ramsden's feelings of offense, Copeland offered to let him choose yet another appraiser. Ramsden had come away from the Maggs appraisal claiming that the London bookseller had no experience selling library collections as a whole and so, like Sotheby's, was unqualified. He therefore selected Joan Winterkorn of Bernard Quaritch, Ltd., another London-based dealer of antiquarian books, to conduct the third appraisal. It wound up echoing Selley's initial evaluation, even after Copeland urged Winterkorn to raise the price. Winterkorn's final price, 605,000 pounds, left Ramsden hovering shy of even the $2 million mark once again.

Ramsden's pride, though, coupled with the depth of his emotional investment and his years of labor, prevented him from revisiting the $2.5 million asking price. He refused to go beyond his previously stated threshold. Tempers flared, and for a time the lines of communication between Massachusetts and York grew icily quiet. Both Ramsden and The Mount sensed that they had arrived at an impasse, resulting in repeated efforts on Ramsden's part, during the four years that followed, to sell the Wharton library collection to an American university. He approached a variety of institutions that had already laid claim to having some of Wharton's papers (most notably, Yale) but they all declined or else expressed interest in acquiring only parts of the library. Ramsden, meanwhile, continued to cling to his adamant refusal to see the library broken up.

By this point, Ramsden's catalog had appeared at long last in print as *Edith Wharton's Library,* with a glowing introduction by the British scholar and Wharton biographer Hermione Lee.[30] Given the historical context surrounding its publication, Ramsden's catalog begs to be understood not just as a list of the library's contents but likewise as a marketing device. It was designed, after all, to help *sell* the Wharton library collection—to mount a claim for its value and to aid in fetching the highest possible price. Not inconsequential to that argument are the material details of the catalog itself: it was printed in a limited run of 350 copies, bound handsomely in red cloth and featuring Wharton's embossed signature on the cover, with high-quality paper and tasteful typography. Furthermore, the whole volume was printed and bound via traditional letterpress by the noted English printer Smith Settle, a fact that explains its limited print run and marks it as being a volume that, like its subject, appears suggestive of exceptional worth. Much in the way that morocco leather and calfskin might have been, during a previous era, added to a book in order to make a statement about the value of its contents, Ramsden opted for fine material details that would aid his cause and speak to the value of his wares.

As a marketing tool, certainly, the *Edith Wharton's Library* catalog dazzles and impresses. As a scholarly tool, though, it proves somewhat insufficient.[31] To start, Ramsden constructed the volume without paying heed to accepted cataloging styles, adopting a somewhat idiosyncratic and, at times, inconsistent method for organizing titles and information. What's more, the catalog was incomplete the second it went to press. Ramsden continued to find more Wharton books even after his last visit to Saltwood in 1999, a fact that necessitated two separately published lists titled "Additions" (which feature their own idiosyncrasies). And both the catalogs and the "Additions" are full of factual errors. For example, Ramsden identifies Wharton's modern copy of Andrew Kippis's *A Narrative of the Voyages Around the World; Performed by Captain James Cook* as dating from 1799, the year that Cook died, when the title page shows that it was printed in 1904. Ramsden cites other dates incorrectly as well, and in certain cases he overlooks both material insertions (items that have been added to the books) and annotations appearing in margins or on endpapers. But all this makes a certain kind of sense when we recall that Ramsden was not a scholar but a collector, as does his decision to put more effort into the description of bindings and physical components and less into documenting marginalia. Quality bindings, after all, have historically come into play where evaluations of a book's worth are concerned, and Wharton's collection includes custom-bound editions from celebrated binders, like Chambolle–Duru, Lortic, and others, dating from the golden age of bookmaking.[32]

Ramsden's catalog appeared during the period of stalemate between himself and The Mount. During that time, Ramsden engaged Nicholas Barker, a former deputy keeper of the British Library and editor of *The Book Collector* magazine, to represent his interests and labor on behalf of the collection's $2.5 million asking price. Though he was not a licensed appraiser, Barker carried out an independent evaluation of the Wharton library materials, concluding that numbers might, after all, prove futile where attempts to estimate its real worth might be concerned. These documents, alongside Ramsden's finished catalog, formed the basis of a forceful marketing campaign that sought to reach beyond discussions of per-unit price by instead highlighting claims about the collection's inherent uniqueness. In his evaluation, Barker drew attention to the collection's size, observing that this was arguably its most important attribute, especially when viewed in comparison with other historical authors' libraries. Though Ramsden's stockpile of 2,700 books probably accounted for less than half of Wharton's overall library as it existed at the time of her death, Barker's point was that most writers' libraries receive much worse treatment because the vast majority of institutions simply can't afford to keep collections together. Ramsden reiterated this same point throughout our conversation, explaining:

> Part of the reason I was so obstinate . . . about the price, you know . . . is that there was nothing similar, nothing like that had ever been offered before. No one had ever bought an *entire* author's library, at least not of that size, ever before. I didn't have anything to use as a reference. Since then, even, I haven't seen an auction lot or a sale of that size, though some do acquire individual copies from writers' libraries, of course.[33]

Ramsden and Barker were unsuccessful in their attempts to sell the Wharton collection to another institution and so resumed their dealings with The Mount in 2003, at Stephanie Copeland's request. For a while, The Mount had been considering purchasing the collection jointly in cooperation with nearby Smith College, but this generated fierce division between Ramsden and Barker. The latter was committed to the prospect of making the library available to researchers, but Ramsden could not live with the idea of seeing it split up, even between neighboring institutions.

Talks resumed between The Mount and Ramsden, but a million dollars still meant the difference between Ramsden's demands and the appraisers' estimates. Ramsden held tight to the $2.5 million asking price, even while the majority of appraisals scarcely touched $1.5 million. Copeland, faced with the history of her own thorny interactions with Ramsden, reached out to her associate Christopher Tugendhat, a life peer with a seat in the House of Lords who also served on the European Advisory Board of Lehman Brothers, the now-defunct global investment firm. Citing a telling list of concerns, Copeland engaged Tugendhat to serve as the EWR's "man in London" and to help reason with the ever-sensitive Ramsden. It's evident that by this point the long years of negotiating and haggling had left Ramsden feeling wounded and resentful; he had begun to see himself as a victim who stood in danger of having his labor and emotional investments devalued, and he did not react kindly to Tugendhat's sudden arrival on the scene. Emails exchanged between Barker, Copeland, and Tugendhat dating from this period indicate the degrees of paranoia and bitterness that were now clouding the negotiation process. Ramsden, everyone saw, was close to digging in and taking the library collection to his grave. But Tugendhat knew Ramsden by association: he had served alongside his father in the House. In the end, thanks to Tugendhat and thanks to the providential appearance of a last-minute funding source, Copeland made a deal to purchase the library for £1 million even, or about $2.6 million total, given taxes and fees: Ramsden's price.[34]

The deal was done, and the library arrived stateside in 2006 amid fanfare and champagne toasts. Ramsden accompanied the books to their new home in Massachusetts, having first negotiated the right to see them arranged on The Mount's library shelves according to his liking. Mount staff members recall how he appeared overcome with zeal and that he devoted hours and hours to the task of arranging the library books, in keeping with Lynch's observation that fantasies of curation and arrangement, at heart, compel many collectors. "Any collector of rare books has a knack for arranging things so that the particularism of his relation with a specific copy of a text upstages his commonality with that text's fellow readers,"[35] Lynch explains, and in Ramsden's case this proved to be true, with sentiment taking precedence over schematics. But the library space, it turned out, could accommodate only about half of Wharton's collection, which had grown considerably in the wake of Wharton's permanent departure from The Mount in 1911. Ramsden, driven by that same desire to "get it right," wanted to make sure that the best books appeared on the library shelves to represent and speak for Wharton's tastes as a reader, collector, and thinker. The rest would have to be stored in The Mount's attic, which, while it might lack features like temperature control and ventilation, still meant that the collection would be secure and protected. The Mount's acquisition of the library thus brought an end to a long period of uncertainty and concern, with the *New York Times* reporting that it served to "round[] a circle begun a century ago, when Edith Wharton . . . packed up and left the United States to live in France." Tugendhat, speaking to the *Times,* echoed Alan Clark's earlier comments about the library's influence on Ramsden, and vice versa, calling it "a 'life-work' worthy of recognition."[36] What such pronouncements overlook is the fact that Ramsden was only fifty-two at the time of the sale and that his life was far from over, even if his work on the library had come to an effective end.

Even now, a decade later, stories proliferate with regards to Ramsden's emotional state at the time of the sale. Some Mount staff members insist that they saw him weep as the books were unpacked, while others marvel at the immense amount of time that he took in arranging them on the shelves (he is reported to have demanded solitude in connection with the task). Fears for the library's existence as a completed whole, I likewise discovered, continued to unsettle Ramsden: during my interview with him, he asked me repeatedly to describe physical aspects of the current library space, which he had not seen since 2006. He had heard, for instance, that The Mount had removed library books from two sets of shelves, citing security reasons (the shelves in question are positioned near the guard rail that is designed to contain visitors), and this prospect appeared to bother him deeply. This reaction was due in part to his preferences for the arranging of the library; he had chosen to feature volumes of poetry bearing Wharton's father's signature on these particular shelves. He asked me if I might lobby to have the books securely reinstalled on the shelves behind Plexiglas dividers or wire. As with Alan Clark, the prospect of having gaps on the shelves proved to be a source of great annoyance. I promised I would raise the issue during my next trip to The Mount, and Ramsden responded with a threat that, though half in jest, concealed some new information: if they didn't fill in the shelves, he would keep the remaining boxes of Wharton books for himself instead of sending them to Massachusetts.

This is how I found out about the *rest* of the Wharton library, the part that today resides in a basement in York. For it turns out that Ramsden, in spite of having completed work on the catalog, and in spite of having officially parted with the collection, had not been able to *stop* collecting. He had continued to search for and to secure volumes from Edith Wharton's library in the years following the sale, storing them away in the basement of Stone Trough Books and awaiting the day that he might, eventually, deliver them to the United States so that they could become part of the larger collection. I did not get the sense that he meant to sell these materials; in fact, he wanted me to take them with me to The Mount when I left England, in order to spare him the cost of having them shipped there. But there were simply too many—three boxes full, with titles relating to classical history, French literature, philosophy, and religion, and all bearing Wharton's bookplates. I left them there, in that basement room that is actually a bathroom, among a telling array of detritus: a bathtub filled with printer's proofs of the *Edith Wharton's Library* catalog, receipts, funeral programs, unwashed wine glasses, and, of course, more books—stacks and stacks of them. I had dreamed of returning to collect the remaining Wharton library volumes on behalf of The Mount but was ultimately prevented from doing so: Ramsden took his own life in the spring of 2019, at the age of sixty-five.

Aftermath

For Wharton's library books, the long journey home had been a celebratory one, with resoundingly a happy ending. But the story was not yet over for Stephanie Copeland and for the EWR. The funds that had appeared almost miraculously from an anonymous source during the final stages of those negotiations had been loaned, not donated, and The Mount now had two years to pay back the $2.5 million that had gone toward the purchase of the library books. The EWR's board, which had endorsed that purchase, began to scatter in the face of such a formidable challenge. By the summer of 2006, a year after the completion of the sale, all but one board member had resigned, and Copeland was left alone to take the fall for The Mount's struggling finances. The EWR wound up defaulting on its original loan, and that led quickly, and controversially, to Copeland's ouster: in the spring of 2008 she resigned as executive director at the behest of the newly installed board (which now included Christopher Tugendhat). Ramsden, though he had struggled throughout the bulk of his interactions with her, expressed regret for Copeland's dismissal when I spoke to him, saying, "When Stephanie Copeland got into trouble . . . I never got in touch . . . I'm sorry that I never got in touch."[37] Ramsden had gotten what he wanted in the end, but he seemed burdened by the knowledge that his own objectives had been achieved at the expense of others.

Copeland's prognostications about the library being the most important purchase The Mount could ever make turned out to be largely correct. In the late 2000s, while The Mount was teetering on the edge of foreclosure, the library was appraised once more, albeit this time under the auspices of capital that might be legitimately seized to pay off the organization's debts. That appraisal lists individual items whose worth stands in excess of $10,000, including works like Wharton's first edition of *Ulysses,* her inscribed first edition of James's *The Golden Bowl,* and an oversized preprint version of Adams's *The Education of Henry Adams,* which is one of only forty copies. In the end, The Mount succeeded in recovering its financial footing, rendering this last set of appraisals to be superfluous. But all these appraisals, when taken together, help to outline the worth of an investment that has been bequeathed to scholars and Wharton fans as a result of both Ramsden's and Copeland's actions. Even more than that, they highlight the unlikeliness of this story's conclusion and help to show just how implausible, and how providential, it is that Wharton's library should exist how and where it does today. The forces of history and happenstance, at various points throughout this story, appeared poised to eradicate the existence of this collection, just as the logic of *value* and *worth* worked to corrode the negotiations that were part of the process of bringing it home. What we scholars ought to therefore take notice of, then, are the myriad pressures that weigh upon processes of historical preservation where print materials, and especially large print collections, are concerned. Even more than that, we ought to take note of both the people involved and of their relative distance from formal scholarly institutions in order to better gauge and understand the mechanisms that, quite often, are adjacent to scholarly processes but nevertheless remain functionally neglected. George Ramsden, Stephanie Copeland, Christopher Tugendhat—these people are not scholars, but they played major roles in securing an important scholarly legacy. Were it not for them, there might not be *any* remaining copies of Wharton's poem "Ogrin the Hermit."

What a library means is thus inheritance writ large—across histories of social and cultural evaluations of worth, and in a language that is at once expansive and common but at the same time personal and intimate. What a library says it says not only through a stockpile of objects but also through shared histories of use, engagement, and even neglect, as well as through personal testimonies and forms of emotional attachment. Wharton's library, as the story I have been relating here helps to show, has meant a variety of things to the wide variety of people who have had a hand in its preservation. Where Ramsden saw it as a means of establishing his self-worth and an identity as a collector, Copeland and the rest of her ilk at

The Mount saw it as a way to solidify their claims to being the preeminent institutional stewards of Wharton's memory. And while, at every stage, the library collection has also meant *money,* what's clear given the history of these contested negotiations is that the translation of meaning into money is a messy and undeniably dangerous business. Such messiness results, I would furthermore argue, from a surfeit of meaning, as opposed to the reverse. James H. Billington, who previously served as librarian of congress, contends that "libraries are places for the pursuit of truth,"[38] and by that same logic it would appear that personal libraries often serve as the staging grounds for the investigation and shaping of personal truth. This was certainly the case for Wharton, who sought to forge declarations of personal truth from the processes of amassing and engaging with her library books, but it has likewise been the case for those who followed after her—even for Alan Clark who, in spite of his apparent indifference to the collection, succumbed to sentimental attachments and resorted to dishonest methods in his attempts to retain parts of it.

So far as the quest for truth may be concerned, then, libraries actually have much in common with universities. The modern research university, which rose and proliferated during the comparatively recent era of the nineteenth century, was similarly founded on the ideal of a shared and inherently communal search for truth. This is in part why today's research universities have been historically organized around and defined by their libraries, which serve as handy loci that enable all the varied activities and methods associated with the pursuit of knowledge. A modern research university's prowess has thus been secured based on the strength of its libraries' holdings, and it has been my task throughout this book to furthermore expose the ways in which this might have once also been true for individuals. While it's true that Wharton never made a name for herself as a book collector or as the direct result of her library, it's also true that we might not know her name today if it weren't for her library and for the education she received from it. Wharton's library granted her means of both direct and indirect access to the world of literary publishing, introducing her to authors, publishers, and other bookish associates both living and dead. That fact alone, I think, establishes the significance of libraries to any conversations that we might seek about the historical realities of authorship.

In light of that significance, then, what this concluding section has sought to also highlight are the countless forces that combine to render the idea of the library fragile and susceptible to extermination. Insofar as a library means cultural and individual inheritance writ large, so is it necessarily prone to the burdens that descend via systems of inheritance, which are anything but stable. T. S. Eliot, writing in the same decade that Wharton died (and authored her own final ruminations on the subject), ponders the question of communally inherited truth when he famously asks, "Where is the wisdom we have lost in knowledge? / Where is the knowledge we have lost in information?"[39] The concern is that, with the proliferation of the pursuit of knowledge, including the institutions that foster such pursuit, there has come a loss of general understanding. The "wisdom" that was to have been the communal legacy of previous ages and the people who lived in them has fallen by the wayside, while "new" knowledge can't help but grow and multiply. The result is more books but fewer readers, more items in the library catalog but less likelihood that anyone will touch or use them—a situation that predicts the fate of libraries in the twentieth and the twenty-first centuries.

As I discussed in greater detail back in chapter 4, successful inheritance depends on successful transmission and so requires a willing and able audience. Well-educated and understanding audiences, even more than good books, constituted a resource that Wharton and Eliot sensed might be in decline, given all the enthusiasm over the expansion of the reserves of human knowledge known as "information." Wharton, in the scrapbook-like collections of clippings that she arranged during the last decade or so of her life, appears to have been enthralled by the prospect of the reader who only reads to *gather* rather than to truly understand. Wharton collected advertisements for *The Elbert Hubbard Scrap Book,* a volume of "ideas, thoughts, passages, excerpts, [and] epigrams selected from the master thinkers of all ages" that was guaranteed to make the user (for the word "reader" seems suspect in this instance) "more interesting." Wharton, or else perhaps one of her servants, cut multiple versions of these advertisements out of the likes of *Time* magazine in the late 1920s; these new, *Reader's Digest*–style inventions must have galled and stunned her.[40] The *Hubbard Scrap Book,* like other publications of its kind, billed itself as a "whole library condensed into one fascinating scrap book . . . contain[ing] the best thoughts of the best minds of the last twenty-five hundred years."[41] As such, it promised to increase the buyer's ability to appear "interesting" by expanding their knowledge of classic texts. Wharton, when she encountered these ads at the age of sixty-four, must have enjoyed many a laugh at their expense.

At the heart of Wharton's anxieties about the future of books, book ownership, book collecting, and book reading—the very anxieties, in other words, that I have been documenting and describing throughout the length of this study—were, in effect, a cluster of worries about the *kinds of minds* that get cultivated as the result of different kinds of intellectual engagement. Wharton foresaw that the kinds of audiences who bought the *Hubbard Scrap Book* would not be the kind to find enrichment or value in the practices that she herself had held dear, which included the contextualized and responsible reading of history through engagement with historical texts. What this realization must have therefore also necessitated was a concern about losing an audience for her own works. If future generations of readers turned their backs on the values that had shaped Wharton's own, what would her novels and stories have to say to such people? Perhaps nothing at all. Wharton, like Eliot, revered the written word for its ability to bestow immortality, an idea that Eliot mulls in his poem "Burnt Norton": "Words, after speech, reach / into silence."[42] But Wharton also perceived that her claims for immortality rested on the estimations of vulgar, information-obsessed audiences of modern readers.

It is in this way that we see Wharton's activities as a reader intimately tied to her understandings of herself as a writer, and to our own, contemporary abilities to interpret and parse the meanings that lie not just within the body of her fiction but within the bulk of her library collection, too. Indeed, Wharton's library embodies some of the most compelling contradictions regarding the fate of art under the auspices of modernity, inviting contemplations on the topics of inheritance, transmission, worth, value, and canonicity, to name only a few. At the same time, it permits one to access a kind of anachronistic display that feels distinctly nonmodern, to a space that operates like an oasis of antiquity located at the very core of modernity's swirling machinations. It is a space that recalls and thus unites all the disparate cultural traditions of Europe, even though it exists in America; it is a modern space, structured by worldly and cosmopolitan desires, even while it aggregates and showcases history within its midst; it speaks, through these very contradictions, to what Lefebvre calls a "leap forward in the productive forces" that signals "a new mode of production,"[43] yet it embalms and entombs in an effort to preserve that which is old. And all of this is entirely in keeping with Wharton's fiction, which maintains a firm grasp on the dialectic relationality between old and new. One need only recall that Wharton became the first woman to win the newly inaugurated Pulitzer Prize in 1921 for a historical novel called *The Age of Innocence,* set in the 1870s, to grasp the pervasiveness of such a dialectic in her work. And one need only step inside the reconstructed space of her library at The Mount—a space that, thanks to the people whose names have appeared throughout this Conclusion, has become accessible once again—to witness the incessant interplay of past and present, of innovation and preservation, still at work there.

Notes

· · · · · · · · · · · · · · · · ·

Introduction

1. Rose Macaulay, "Losing One's Books," *Spectator,* 28 May 1989, 19, http://archive.spectator.co.uk/article/27th-may-1989/19/losing-ones-books.

2. Quoted in Irene Goldman-Price, ed., *My Dear Governess: The Letters of Edith Wharton to Anna Bahlmann* (New Haven, Conn.: Yale University Press, 2012), 51.

3. Goldman-Price, 51.

4. Wharton scholars disagree on the exact number of these Atlantic crossings: Meredith L. Goldsmith and Emily J. Orlando, for instance, report that she did so sixty-six times, while Sarah Bird Wright puts the number higher, at seventy. See Meredith L. Goldsmith and Emily J. Orlando, *Edith Wharton and Cosmpolitanism* (Gainesville: University of Florida Press, 2016), 4; and Sarah Bird Wright, quoted in Nancy Bentley, "Wharton, Travel, and Modernity," in Carol Singley, ed., *A Historical Guide to Edith Wharton* (New York: Oxford University Press, 2003), 51.

5. George Ramsden, *Edith Wharton's Library* (Settrington, UK: Stone Trough Books, 1999), xxi.

6. Edith Wharton, "Liste des Livres a Jean-Marie"; "Volumes à Relier," Box 50, Folder 1504, YCAL 42, Series 4, Edith Wharton Papers, Beinecke Rare Books and Manuscript Library, Yale University, New Haven, Conn. I'm additionally grateful to Shafquat Towheed, who, in a 2013 conference paper, details discrepancies between the Ramsden catalog and the packing lists mentioned here, identifying more than 170 titles from Wharton's library that have since been lost. See Shafquat Towheed, "Edith Wharton's Libraries" (conference paper, Writers and Their Libraries Conference, London, March 15–16, 2013).

7. Walter Benjamin, "Unpacking My Library," *Illuminations* (New York: Schocken, 1968), 59–67. Though it first appeared in 1931 in *Die Literarische Welt,*

Benjamin wrote this and many of the essays that appear in the volume *Illuminations* earlier, throughout the 1920s, a fact that helps to reinforce my arguments about contemporaneity where Benjamin and Wharton are concerned. See Howard Eiland and Michael W. Jennings, *Walter Benjamin: A Critical Life* (Cambridge, Mass.: Belknap Press, 2014): 362–63.

    8. Benjamin does not use the term directly in "Unpacking My Library," but in a 1925 letter to Gerhard Scholem he relates (in translation), "My bibliomania is strangely—but explicably—receding. I have not bought anything for months." See Theodor Adorno and Gerschom Scholem, eds., *The Correspondence of Walter Benjamin* (Chicago: University of Chicago Press, 1994), 262.

    9. Joseph D. Lewandoski, "Unpacking: Walter Benjamin and his Library," *Libraries and Culture,* 34.2 (Spring 1999): 151.

    10. Benjamin, "Unpacking My Library," 59.

    11. Benjamin, 60.

    12. Quoted in Ramsden, *Edith Wharton's Library,* xv.

    13. Benjamin, "Unpacking My Library," 60.

    14. Deidre Lynch, *Loving Literature: A Cultural History* (Chicago: University of Chicago Press, 2015), 14.

    15. Benjamin, "Unpacking My Library," 60.

    16. Benjamin, 63.

    17. Nietzsche, Friedrich. *On The Geneaology of Morals* and *Ecce Homo,* trans. Walter Kaufmann (New York: Vintage, 1989), 288.

    18. For example, Wharton famously outlined her plans for the novel *The Fruit of the Tree* (1907) on the fly of a volume of Nietzsche's complete works. Volume 9 of Nietzsche's *Werke,* held today at The Mount, features penciled notes that read "50 grains of veronal is the minimum fatal dose," which reflect the conversations that Wharton had with a local, Lenox-based doctor about how to convincingly stage an act of assisted suicide in that novel. Veronal was a brand-name barbiturate, and while some scholars have associated this penciled note with Lily's death in *The House of Mirth,* chronology would indicate otherwise: Wharton published *The House of Mirth* in October 1905 and the Nietzsche volumes are dated 1906.

    19. Lynch, *Loving Literature,* 10. Andrew Piper mulls a similar point, observing that, despite decades of study on the subject, "we have no idea what happens when people read." This quality of "opaqueness," Piper goes on to argue, actually comprises one of "reading's great gifts." See Andrew Piper, *Book Was There* (Chicago: University of Chicago Press, 2012), vii, x.

    20. Karl Marx, *Capital,* trans. Ben Fowkes (New York: Penguin, 1976), 932.

    21. Walter Benjamin, *The Arcades Project* (Cambridge, Mass.: Harvard University Press, 2002), 221.

22. Carolyn Levine, *Forms* (Princeton, N.J.: Princeton University Press, 2015), 18.

23. Benjamin, *The Arcades Project*, 210. Susan Sontag reverses the equation but arrives at the same argument with reference to Benjamin. She observes, for example, that "learning was [for Benjamin] a form of collecting, as in the quotations and excerpts from daily reading which Benjamin accumulated in notebooks that he carried everywhere and from which he would read aloud to friends." See Susan Sontag, "The Last Intellectual," review of "The Last Intellectual: Review of *Illuminations,* by Walter Benjamin," *New York Review of Books,* October 12, 1978, http://www.nybooks.com/articles/1978/10/12/the-last-intellectual.

24. Henri Lefebvre, *The Production of Space* (New York: Blackwell, 1991), 86–87.

25. Levine, *Forms,* 19.

26. Levine, 16.

27. Levine, 18.

28. Levine, 19.

29. Nathan K. Hensley, *Forms of Empire* (New York: Oxford University Press, 2016), 11.

30. Wayne H. Wiegand, *Part of Our Lives: A People's History of the American Public Library* (New York: Oxford University Press, 2015), 95.

31. Quoted in Wiegand, 95.

32. Colton Storm and Howard Peckham characterize the early twentieth century in this way. The authors explain that "the first American collector to gather a library that could stand comparison with the libraries of the greatest English collectors was Robert Hoe II," and that the sale of his library in 1911–12 "established a new and higher price for rare books" that marked the "dominance of American collectors" during this era. See Colton Storm and Howard Peckham, *Invitation to Book Collecting: Its Pleasures and Practices* (New York: R. R. Bowker, 1947), 33. Wharton herself owned a copy of Hoe's library catalog, published in 1898, which is held today at The Mount and contains her markings and annotations, suggesting that she had taken notice of the trend described by Storm and Peckham.

33. Lynch, *Loving Literature,* 13.

34. Jean Baudrillard, "The System of Collecting," in John Elsner and Roger Cardinal, eds., *Cultures of Collecting* (Cambridge, Mass.: Harvard University Press, 1994), 24.

35. With regard to new materialism, I am drawn to the methodological approach described by Bruno Latour as "a sociology of associations," which appears most on display in chapter 3, when I turn to the discussion of the library as network. However, insofar as Latour's ideas appear tacitly reliant on classically

materialist concepts (like superstructure and ideology), I tend to foreground those preexisting investigations and the critics who helped to launch earlier movements dedicated to the discussion of them. Such strategic foregrounding furthermore complements my interest in temporally specific forms of materialist critique and in establishing Wharton's contemporaneity to materialist critics like Walter Benjamin. See Bruno Latour, *Reassembling the Social* (New York: Oxford University Press, 2005), 7.

36. Carolyn Lesjak, "Reading Dialectically," in Andrew Pendakis et al., eds, *Contemporary Marxist Theory* (New York: Bloomsbury Academic, 2014), 414.

37. Lesjak, 420.

38. Lesjak, 414.

39. Lesjak, 414.

40. Michael Jennings, "Introduction," in Walter Benjamin, *The Writer of Modern Life: Essays on Charles Baudelaire* (Cambridge, Mass.: Belknap Press, 2006), 2.

41. Walter Benjamin, "The Paris of the Second Empire in Baudelaire," *The Writer of Modern Life*, 96.

42. Benjamin, 103.

43. The EdithWhartonsLibrary.org database furnishes an interactive online catalog for Wharton's library. I built it using the Omeka publishing platform with support from a number of research assistants (including students at the University of North Dakota) and volunteers at The Mount estate, and it can be accessed via the URL http://edithwhartonslibrary.org.

44. Geoffrey Galt Harpham, "Roots, Races, and the Return to Philology." *Representations* 106, no. 1 (Spring 2009): 44.

45. Daniel Pick, *War Machine: The Rationalization of Slaughter in the Modern Age* (New Haven, Conn.: Yale University Press, 1993), 75.

46. Wharton's wartime essays, collected in the volume *Fighting France,* for instance, showcase the elegiac depths of her understandings of the culture of her adopted homeland. Of the French people, Wharton writes, "No people so sensitive to beauty, so penetrated with a passionate interest in life, so endowed with the power to express and immortalise that interest, can ever really enjoy destruction for its own sake. The French people hate 'militarism.' It is stupid, inartistic, unimaginative and enslaving." Similarly, Alan Price, in his analysis of these wartime writings, explains that "it was the destruction of life and culture that she found blasphemous," a view that squares with Wharton's status as a "snob" with regard to "breeding and learning. She preferred an oligarchy of taste and erudition, a meritocracy of learning" (xv–xvi). This idea is furthermore reinforced in Shari Benstock's biography of Wharton, wherein she explains that, according to Wharton, "new wealth posed a dangerous threat to American society . . . because it came

'without inherited obligations, or any traditional sense of solidarity between the classes." See Wharton, *Fighting France* (London: Hesperus Press, 2010), 110; Price, *The End of the Age of Innocence: Edith Wharton and the First World War* (New York: St. Martin's Press, 1996), xv–xvi; and Shari Benstock, *No Gifts from Chance: A Biography of Edith Wharton* (Austin: University of Texas Press, 2004), 151.

47. Land's End was the name of the first residence that Wharton shared with her husband, Teddy Wharton. It was located in Newport, Rhode Island, and the couple took up residence there beginning in 1892. For a more detailed discussion and description of Wharton's bookplates, see chapter 1.

48. Price, *The End of the Age of Innocence*, xvi.

49. The term "unopened" refers to the state in which a book's pages have not been "opened," or cut away from, the adjoining pages that originally formed part of the larger, folded printing sheet. The word "uncut" is sometimes erroneously applied in such situations, but it in fact refers to whether or not the borders of the book's pages have been uniformly cut so as to create an even edge.

50. Edith Wharton, *The House of Mirth*, ed. Elizabeth Ammons (New York: W. W. Norton, 1980), 17.

51. Hensley, *Forms of Empire*, 20.

52. Carolyn Steedman, *Dust: The Archive and Cultural History* (Rutgers, N.J.: Rutgers University Press, 2002), 73.

53. The term "bookworm" is a generalization that refers to a number of wood-boring insects, chiefly beetles. For example, both the death watch beetle and the common furniture beetle are known to create wormlike tunnels in books, and in my work at The Mount I've seen countless instances of damage wrought by the likes of them.

1. The Library as Space

1. Benjamin, "Unpacking My Library," 66.

2. Hermione Lee describes the circumstances of this arrangement in detail, noting that "the bitter fall-out" resulting from discrepancies in *both* parents' wills would continue to "run on" and haunt Wharton into old age. See Hermione Lee, *Edith Wharton* (New York: Vintage, 2008), 61, 137.

3. Edith Wharton, *A Backward Glance* (New York: Touchstone, 1998), 66.

4. Benjamin, "Unpacking My Library," 67.

5. Benjamin, 66.

6. Baudrillard, "The System of Collecting," 8.

7. Edith Wharton and Ogden Codman Jr., *The Decoration of Houses* (New York: W. W. Norton, 1997), 151.

8. Lefebvre, *The Production of Space*, 86.

9. Lefebvre, 87, emphasis original.

10. Michel Foucault, "Of Other Spaces: Utopias and Heterotopias," trans. Jay Miskowiec, *Diacritics* 16, no. 1 (Spring 1986): 23.

11. Wharton's feelings for her father's library place her in conversation with the likes of Jorge Luis Borges, who asserts that "my father's library was the capital event in my life. The truth is that I have never left it." In this way, Wharton earns her place among a list of rank-and-file bibliophiles who similarly viewed their library collections as enduring family monuments. Yet it is interesting to note that Wharton's attachments to her father's library did not prevent her from donating some of his books to the Lenox Public Library. For Borges's comments, see Giraldi, "Why We Need Physical Books," *New Republic* 19 April 2015.

12. Lefebvre, *Production of Space*, 77.

13. Lefebvre, 83.

14. Foucault, "Of Other Spaces," 23–25.

15. Judith Fryer, *Felicitous Space* (Chapel Hill: University of North Carolina Press, 1986), 70–71.

16. While Fryer is careful to point out that Wharton's design schemes for The Mount likewise convey an understanding of "long-standing social traditions," her reading of the house itself places a concerted emphasis on exclusion and retreat, seeing the rooms as "a series of protective enclosures." Lee echoes Fryer's comments to this end when she describes the library, in particular, as designed "to ensure quiet" and as exuding feelings of "warmth and enclosure." To be sure, the library is structured as an *enclosed* space, but I would argue that it is nevertheless an approachable and congenial space—an accessible form of enclosure—and that Wharton furthermore designed it to appear thus. See Fryer, *Felicitous Space*, 70–74; Lee, *Edith Wharton*, 146–47.

17. Wharton and Codman, *The Decoration of Houses*, 152.

18. Bachelard argues that physical spaces "suggest the values of intimacy" and so require "a state of suspended reading" that is inherent in the task of "'writ[ing] a room,' 'read[ing] a room,' or 'read[ing] a house.'" Insofar as "the reader who is 'reading a room' leaves off reading and starts to think of some place in his own past," Bachelard maintains, these intimacies become diffuse and compelling, since they encourage the reader to examine their own intimate relationships with, and in light of, space. Lefebvre complicates this point, to some degree, by arguing that the "reading" of space both does and does not make sense. With regard to the latter point, Lefebvre says, "spaces are . . . 'over-inscribed': everything therein resembles a rough draft, jumbled and self-contradictory." I would argue, however, that these multiple, competing layers and levels of inscription make certain spaces

more, as opposed to less, readable. Foucault, meanwhile, advocates for "systematic description" where heterotopias or superimposed spaces are concerned. See Gaston Bachelard, *The Poetics of Space* (Boston: Beacon Press, 1994), 14; Lefebvre, *The Production of Space,* 142; Foucault, "Of Other Spaces," 25.

19. Kate Marshall, *Corridor: Media Architectures in American Fiction* (Minneapolis: University of Minnesota Press, 2013), 15.

20. Wharton, *A Backward Glance,* 35–36.

21. Goldman-Price, *My Dear Governess,* 2.

22. Edith Wharton, *Life and I,* in *Edith Wharton: Novellas and Other Writings,* ed. Cynthia Griffin Wolff (New York: Library of America, 1990), 1074.

23. Goldman-Price, *My Dear Governess,* 6.

24. Goldman-Price.

25. Piper, *Book Was There,* vii.

26. Edith Wharton, *The Fruit of the Tree* (New York: Scribner's, 1907), 22.

27. Wharton, 125.

28. Edith Wharton, *Ethan Frome* (New York: Penguin, 2009), 71.

29. Edith Wharton, *New Year's Day,* in *Old New York* (New York: Scribner's, 1952), 246.

30. Wharton, 298.

31. Edith Wharton, *Hudson River Bracketed* (New York: Signet, 1962), 49.

32. Critic Louis Auchincloss makes a handy and somewhat hasty connection between Vance and Wharton, viewing Vance as "an extension of Mrs. Wharton's vision of herself, freed from the impediment of her sex." But Auchincloss overlooks the most compelling (indeed, perhaps the *only* compelling) connection between Wharton and her male protagonist—that is, their mutual adherence to a mythos of "self-madeness." See Auchincloss's "Afterword" in Wharton, *Hudson River Bracketed,* 410.

33. Wharton, *The Fruit of the Tree,* 319.

34. In her study of various objects owned by the Brontë sisters, critic Deborah Lutz comes to a very similar conclusion regarding the ways in which these writers encode certain judgments about characters, given their relationships with books. In Brontë novels, Lutz claims, "if books appear[] well-used and spread around the house, this implie[s] a genteel erudition. . . . Likewise, we are not meant to lend much credence to characters who have books merely for show, with expensive spines, shiny because never opened. These volumes are just furniture, expressions of wealth." See Deborah Lutz, *The Brontë Cabinet: Three Lives in Nine Objects* (New York: W. W. Norton, 2015), 15–16.

35. Wharton, *Hudson River Bracketed,* 99.

36. Wharton and Codman, *The Decoration of Houses,* 3.

37. Edgar Allan Poe, "The Philosophy of Furniture," *The Works of Edgar Allan Poe in Five Volumes,* vol. 5 (New York: P. F. Collier and Son, 1903), 9; emphasis original.

38. Wharton and Codman, *The Decoration of Houses,* 29.

39. John Barrington Bayley, "*The Decoration of Houses* as a Practical Handbook," in Wharton and Codman, *The Decoration of Houses,* 254.

40. In the 1911 short story "Autre Temps . . . ," for example, Wharton's protagonist, Mrs. Lidcote, delivers the icy comment that "traditions that have lost their meanings are the hardest of all to destroy," indicating that Wharton also viewed education and understanding as a means of combating the compulsive obeisance *to* tradition. See Edith Wharton, "Autre Temps . . . ," in *Edith Wharton: Collected Stories, 1911–1937* (New York: Library of America, 2001), 85.

41. Wharton and Codman, *The Decoration of Houses,* 17.

42. Wharton and Codman, 18.

43. David Harvey, in his landmark volume *The Condition of Postmodernity,* arrives at a very similar conclusion, arguing that "The effect of continuous innovation is to devalue, if not destroy, past investments and labor skills." See David Harvey, *The Condition of Postmodernity* (Cambridge, Mass.: Blackwell, 1989), 105–6.

44. Bayley, "*The Decoration of Houses* as a Practical Handbook," 255.

45. Wharton and Codman, *The Decoration of Houses,* 15.

46. In *A Backward Glance,* Wharton refers to an architectural style known as "Hudson River Gothic." This is, in fact, a conflation of two architectural styles that were popularly employed in late 1800s Hudson Valley construction: the first being "Carpenter Gothic" (also known as "American Gothic"), and the second being "Hudson River Bracketed." The architect Alexander Jackson Davis, working in cooperation with the landscape designer and decorator Andrew Jackson Downing, popularized both of these styles. Wharton mentions Downing, but not Davis, in *Hudson River Bracketed,* citing an "epoch-making" treatise on this, the Hudson Valley's "indigenous style of architecture," but this is, to some extent, a fictional reference. Downing's best-known work, which he coauthored with Davis, is called *Cottage Residences* (1842); it was highly influential in popularizing the "Carpenter Gothic" style among upper-class elites, though it does not specifically mention the term "Hudson River Bracketed." See Wharton, *A Backward Glance,* 28; Wharton, *Hudson River Bracketed,* 54–56; and Alexander Jackson Davis and Andrew Jackson Downing, *Cottage Residences: or, A Series of Designs for Rural Cottages and Adapted to North America,* 1842 (reprinted as Andrew Jackson Downing, *Victorian Cottage Residences* [New York, Dover, 1981]). Wharton owned an 1859 copy of Downing's *Treatise on the Theory and Practise of Land-scape Gardening,* which she annotated

and underlined heavily; today The Mount retains that copy as part of its library collection.

47. Wharton, *A Backward Glance,* 28.

48. Lee, for instance, misses the point entirely when she states that "Old Miss Lorburn," the deceased former owner of The Willows in *Hudson River Bracketed,* "goes back to the long-ago figure of Wharton's childhood, her wealthy aunt Elizabeth Schermerhorn Jones . . . In the novel, [Wharton] turns the lonely old woman's house into the much prettier, more endearing architectural style of the region—all pointed shingled roofs, curly pillars and fanciful, delicate balconies." Rather, it is certain that Wharton would have hated the architectural style that strikes Vance as "irregular . . . with an irregularity that was unfamiliar to him." As is clear from the opinions that she lays down in *The Decoration of Houses,* Wharton despised this very kind of irregularity, and so situates The Willows (which she does not draw from her imagination but, I believe, from her memory of the Wilderstein estate) as a testament to the architectural fancies and follies of this era. See Lee, *Edith Wharton,* 669–70; see Wharton, *Hudson River Bracketed,* 47.

49. Wharton, 47.

50. In an effort to bolster my case for Wilderstein as the inspiration for The Willows, it is worthwhile to consider three additional facts: (1) that Wilderstein was originally called "The Cedars" (a name that more closely compares to The Willows than Jones's Rhinecliff); (2) that the landscaping at Wilderstein was done by Calvert Vaux, longtime friend and partner of Andrew Jackson Downing, who is responsible for popularizing the Hudson River Bracketed (also known as "Hudson River Gothic") style; (3) that though Wilderstein is, today, painted according to the Victorian "painted lady" tradition (that is, in a brash "polychrome palate"), for most of the 1800s it was painted a uniform, somber brown, just as Wharton describes The Willows in her novel. See Cynthia Owen Philip, *Wilderstein and the Suckleys: A Hudson River Legacy* (Delmar, N.Y.: Black Dome, 2012), 20–48.

51. If Wharton encountered Wilderstein in the 1890s, she would have seen it painted its customary brown, following a brief 1889 polychromatic paint job that, according to some, caused Bessie Suckley "to faint." See Owen Philip, 20.

52. Wharton and Codman, *The Decoration of Houses,* 152.

53. Archer Newland, Wharton's protagonist in *The Age of Innocence* (whose taste, Wharton would have us believe, is conventionally masculine yet decidedly conservative, unrefined, and stultifying) has a very similar library. "Archer settled Mr. Jackson in an armchair near the fire in the Gothic library and handed him a cigar"; meanwhile, downstairs, Mrs. Archer and Janey sit "beside a Carcel lamp with an engraved globe, facing each other across a rosewood work table." Historical photographs indicate that the Wilderstein library featured similar, hallmark

touches of Gothic design (stained glass, archways, dark wood, and faux medieval touches), as well as Carcel lamps. See Wharton, *The Age of Innocence*, 26.

54. Wharton and Codman, *The Decoration of Houses*, 152.

55. This position, of course, compares to William Morris's oft-cited "golden rule," which states, "Have nothing in your house which you do not know to be useful or believe to be beautiful." Earlier in this same essay, Morris argues that, whereas previously "all works of craftsmanship were once beautiful," modernity (and modern methods of production) has enforced a division between "works of art" and "non-works of art." Notice that Morris, in this statement, places emphasis on "non-work" vs. "non-art," indicating that the issue of trained and capable labor is central to a culture's ability to produce "art-works"; this, I think, compares to the previous discussion of Wharton and Codman's view that well-trained labor is a necessary component of well-executed "style." See William Morris, "The Beauty of Life," *Hopes and Fears for Art* (Boston: Roberts Brothers, 1882), 110, 78.

56. Wharton and Codman, *The Decoration of Houses*, 183.

57. Wharton and Codman, 185.

58. I provide a more detailed discussion of the compulsion to hoard in chapter 2. In the case of Wilderstein, Wharton and Codman's design prohibitions appear to have been prophetic: Daisy Suckley became a notorious hoarder, occupying her childhood home well into her nineties amid piles of trinkets and rubbish, closets crammed full of old *New York Social Registers,* dresses left over from her mother's and grandmother's generations, and checkbooks dating back to the 1810s, among other sundries. I am grateful to Duane Watson, Wilderstein archivist, for showing me these portions of the Wilderstein estate, which, today, are not generally available to the public.

59. Wharton and Codman, 190.

60. Lydia Pyne, *Bookshelf* (New York: Bloomsbury, 2016), 8.

61. Pyne, 46.

62. Lefebvre, *The Production of Space*, 89–90.

63. Lefebvre, 90.

64. Wharton, *The Writing of Fiction* (New York: Scribner's, 1925), 6–7, emphasis mine.

65. Bachelard, *The Poetics of Space*, 33.

66. Foucault reminds us that all space, however modern or innovative, "has a history in Western experience, and it is not possible to disregard the fatal intersection of time with space." Wharton's plans for The Mount, I would argue, speak to a kind of layering of time periods and historical spaces that squares with Foucault's insistence on seeing space as shaped by historical fantasy. See Foucault, "Of Other Spaces," 22.

67. Fryer, *Felicitous Space,* 71.

68. Today, this room is designated the Hondecoeter Room, after having been converted to a dining space later in the nineteenth century. See Adrian Tinniswood, *Belton House: Lincolnshire* (London: Trafalgar Square, 1992), 80.

69. The term "enfilade" comes from French military vocabulary and refers to the arrangement of rooms in a straight line (so that they open into and upon each other successively). Judith Fryer, who provides a stunning reading of Wharton and Codman's original plans for The Mount, uses the word "penetralia," a term she takes from Henry James's description of The Mount that characterizes the way that the rooms on the first floor serve as points of entrance and access for each other. See Fryer, *Felicitous Space,* 65, 70.

70. The word "den" is used today in reference to this room, though the more appropriate term might be "study." Wharton and Codman, at least, express disdain for the former, noting, with evident chagrin, that the word "den" "seems to have attained the dignity of a technical term." See Wharton and Codman, *The Decoration of Houses,* 154.

71. Henry James, *The American Scene* (New York: Harper and Brothers, 1907), 162.

72. James, 162.

73. Lefebvre, *The Production of Space,* 102.

74. "The Custom of the Country: *Vogue* Recreates Edith Wharton's Artistic Arcadia," *Vogue,* 16 August 2012, https://www.vogue.com/article/the-custom-of-the-country-edith-wharton-estate-in-the-berkshires.

75. Whitman's *Leaves of Grass* was one of Wharton's all-time favorite books. Her personal copy, which dates from 1897, was a gift from Walter Berry and is filled with Wharton's personal annotations and underlinings. Today it is in very poor condition. When Annie Leibovitz staged the scene for the *Vogue* photo spread in 2012, she wanted to photograph Eugenides holding Wharton's own copy of the Whitman text but was disallowed this request on account of the book's condition. Leibovitz then visited the nearby Lenox Library in order to secure a replacement copy and discovered the exact same 1897 edition in circulation. It is possible, given Wharton's involvement with the Lenox Library and given the date of the edition still held by it, that Wharton purchased and donated this exact copy to the library, as she did many other books. I am grateful to Nynke Dorhout, librarian and curator at The Mount estate, for relating this story. I have visited the Lenox Library and seen the 1897 edition of *Leaves of Grass* sitting on the shelf, awaiting its next borrower.

76. Henri Lefebvre, *Rhythmnalysis: Space, Time, and Everyday Life* (New York: Bloomsbury, 2014), 17, emphasis original.

77. Wharton, *The Writing of Fiction*, 21.

78. Wharton and Codman, *The Decoration of Houses*, 151.

79. Wharton and Codman, 40.

80. Wharton folds this old-world concern for intentionality into her 1913 novel *The Custom of the Country*; in it, Undine Spragg marries a French nobleman, Raymond de Chelles, and relocates with him to his ancestral home, Saint Désert. When Undine learns of the de Chelles's financial troubles, though, she immediately suggests that they sell Saint Désert or, barring that, its ancient tapestries. "In America," she tells Raymond, "we're not ashamed to sell what we can't afford to keep," and Undine proceeds to contact an American collector in anticipation of selling them. Wharton, of course, intends for her readers to be shocked by Undine's selfish and uncouth behavior, yet she is, arguably, sketching a prehistory of her own tapestries at The Mount: she wouldn't own them had not some European noble been forced to swallow his pride and sell them. See Edith Wharton, *The Custom of the Country* (New York: Doubleday, 1998), 384–92.

81. Susan Pearce, in her work *On Collecting*, points out that mantelpieces are part of a suite of household furniture that is meant to accommodate practices of conspicuous display. "Mantelpiece ornaments, by contrast, carry not a greater weight of social meaning but a weight of more greatly regarded social meaning . . . They are, in some way, 'on display'; they have been chosen deliberately from a range of possible material." Richard Wendorf corroborates Pearce's attitudes toward conspicuous display when he asserts that "the physical settings within which objects in a collection are displayed help to shape their significance and meaning." See Susan Pearce, *On Collecting* (New York: Routledge, 1995), 23; and Wendorf, *The Literature of Collecting* (Boston: Boston Athenaeum and Oak Knoll Press, 2008), 46.

82. Wharton and Codman, *The Decoration of Houses*, 87.

83. Wharton and Codman, 88.

84. Baudrillard, "The System of Collecting," 24.

85. Wharton and Codman, *The Decoration of Houses*, 149.

86. Wharton, *The House of Mirth*, 8.

87. Paul Bourget, *Outre-Mer: Impression of America* (New York: Scribner's, 1895), 91, 93.

88. The noted English bibliomaniac Thomas Frognall Dibdin commented in the 1840s on the gendered (and class-specific) nature of book collecting, observing that "it is a remarkable circumstance, that the bibliomania has almost uniformly confined its attacks to the *male* sex, and among people in the higher middling classes of society." Quoted in Henry Howard Harper, *Book-Lovers, Bibliomaniacs, and Book Clubs* (New York: Riverside Press, 1904), 12.

89. The Hatchard Memorial Library in *Summer,* like the Lenox Library in real life, is free to local residents and thus "public." But the Hatchard Library, it is clear, suffers from a lack of financial maintenance, having received only its initial endowment from the Hatchard family. "Old Miss Hatchard" pays Charity personally for her labor; thus, it would appear that the town of North Dormer does not sustain or support the library in a way that would designate it as a "public" institution. See Edith Wharton, *Summer* (New York: Harper and Row, 1980), 41–42, 46–49, 89.

90. Wharton's family, for instance, belonged to the New York Society Library, one of the oldest surviving subscription libraries in the United States. As the NYSL reports in a March 2012 blog post, "Edith's father George Frederic Jones was a Library shareholder who often took out books for himself and his family"— indeed, this is because the NYSL, though it granted women membership and permitted them access to the stacks, discouraged women from congregating in or using the public space of the library. In spite of these prohibitions, though, the NYSL, as Austin Baxter Keep recounts in his 1908 history of the library, considered itself to be ahead of its time in granting any form of access whatsoever to female members in contrast to "the Boston Athenaeum . . . where no women were allowed to consult books prior to 1829 . . . save in one or two exceptional cases." See The New York Society Library, "Edith Wharton's New York City," 15 March 2012, https://www.nysoclib.org/events/edith-whartons-new-york-city-backward-glance; and Austin Baxter Keep, *History of the New York Society Library* (New York: DeVinne, 1908), 188.

91. Wendorf, *The Literature of Collecting,* 4.

92. Wharton's description of this real community of people, who, she explains, "lived beyond the pale of law or church or genteel 'household order'" on Bear Mountain, outside Lenox. Wharton reports that these "mountain people" were rumored to be descended from the railroad laborers who relocated to the Berkshires in the 1860s, but she skirts the details associated with this legend and, in *Summer,* depicts this community as a drunken band of miscreants who live off the land and eschew polite society. This caricature prompted many critics to reject *Summer*; T. S. Eliot dismissed it as "a satire on the New England novel." See Wharton, *Summer,* 11; Wharton, *A Backward Glance,* 360; Eliot, quoted in Lee, *Edith Wharton,* 510.

93. Wharton, *Summer,* 9.

94. Wharton, 10–11.

95. Wharton, 10–11.

96. John Guillory, *Cultural Capital* (Chicago: University of Chicago Press, 1993), 23, 34.

97. Pierre Bourdieu, *Distinction: A Social Critique on the Judgment of Taste* (Cambridge, Mass.: Harvard University Press, 1984), 11.

98. Wharton, *Summer,* 10.

99. Bourdieu, *Distinction,* 11.

100. Wharton, *Summer,* 22, 39.

101. Wharton, 75.

102. Georg Simmel, quoted in Stephen Kern, *The Culture of Time and Space* (Cambridge, Mass.: Harvard University Press, 1983), 40.

103. Wharton, *Summer,* 15.

104. Dewey's launch of the new cataloging system in 1876 was contemporaneous with both the advent of the American Library Association and the resulting push to "professionalize" librarian stewardship. "The time has come," Dewey proclaims in the 1876 inaugural issue of the *American Library Journal,* "when a librarian may, without assumption, speak of his occupation as a profession." This sheds light on another way in which the Hatchard Memorial Library is "behind the times," in Wharton's view; Charity is not a professional librarian and has received no special training in connection with her duties at the Hatchard Library. See Wiegand, *Part of Our Lives,* 49–51.

105. Wharton, *Summer,* 15.

106. Wharton, 16.

107. Harney identifies one library book in particular and tells Charity that "a little air and sun would do this good; it's rather valuable." This is consistent with the way that Wharton often positions male figures like Harney as possessing insight into the subjects of value and worth, particularly where books are concerned. This scene actually plays like a more direct representation of the conflict that underlies Laurence Selden and Lily Bart's interactions in *The House of Mirth,* with which I engage in greater detail in chapter 2. See Wharton, *Summer,* 19.

108. Wharton, *Summer,* 70.

109. Wharton, 23.

110. Wharton, 24.

111. These marks appear on page 152 of Wharton's copy of Hazlitt. Deidre Lynch, meanwhile, views Hazlitt as belonging to a group of nineteenth-century men who "campily mimed . . . the patricians' displays of bookishness" and professed to love literature in order to appear more thoroughly cultured. Lynch, in fact, reads this particular essay as embodying an outlook that is "central to Hazlitt's and his fellow bookmen's bibliographic imagining of the self." See Lynch, *Loving Literature,* 107, 104.

112. See William Hazlitt, "On Reading Old Books," in *Essays* (London: Scott, 1889), 161.

113. For a more detailed genealogy, see Eric Homberger, *Mrs. Astor's New York* (New Haven, Conn.: Yale University Press, 2002), 114–15.

114. Lenox Library Association, "About the Library—History," 2016, Lenox-Lib.org.

115. See Lee, *Edith Wharton,* 143. Cornelia Brooke Gilder also reports that "by the early 1900s, Lenox was a well-established resort with an intellectual history," which helps to explain why figures like Wharton might have been attracted to it during this era. Even more important, though, Gilder offers a detailed history of Teddy Wharton's relationship to the Berkshires, which began decades before he and his wife built their summer home there: Gilder explains that in the early 1870s Teddy's family "began to look to the Berkshires for their American summers" and that Teddy Wharton was installed as a member of the Lenox Club, with his name appearing regularly in its register by the year 1878. See Cornelia Brooke Gilder, *Edith Wharton's Lenox* (Charleston, N.C.: The History Press, 2017), 11, 24–25.

116. Wharton, *Summer,* 47–48.

117. Charity's space at Mr. Royall's is also subject to invasion. Early on in Wharton's novel, for example, Charity recounts the memory of a time when Royall, drunk and seeking sexual gratification, attempted to break into her room in the middle of the night. See *Summer,* 28–29.

118. Wharton and Codman, *The Decoration of Houses,* 11.

119. Wiegand, *Part of Our Lives,* 95.

120. Arthur E. Bostwick, *The American Public Library* (New York: D. Appleton, 1910), 1.

121. Wharton, for example, was involved in the founding of a French-language conversation club, which met weekly at the Lenox Library. Today The Mount estate pays tribute to this side of Wharton's philanthropy by hosting weekly gatherings of the very same club throughout the summer months.

122. Wharton, *Summer,* 53, 62.

123. Wharton, 89.

124. Wiegand, *Part of Our Lives,* 78–79.

125. Wharton reports on this situation in a letter to her sister-in-law, Minnie Cadwalader Jones; her letters to a "Miss Phelps," who was employed as a librarian at the Lenox Library during this time, additionally allude to an all-female cast of volunteers associated with the cataloging project of 1908. Lee corroborates this information in her biography of Wharton and cites Helen and Mary MacDonald's *History of the Lenox Library* (Lenox, Mass.: Lenox Library Association, 1956). See Wharton's letter to Jones, 8 June 1908 (Edith Wharton Collection, Beinecke Library, Yale University, New Haven, Connecticut); Wharton's letter to Phelps,

undated (Grace Kellogg Smith Papers, Smith College, Northampton, Massachusetts); and Lee, *Edith Wharton,* 152, 775 (n. 77).

126. Lee, 152.

127. Wharton, *Summer,* 13.

128. Wharton, 50.

129. Wharton, 14.

130. In particular, Wharton's description of the festivities associated with Old Home Week (which includes a procession of the town's unmarried female residents, who dress in white gowns for the occasion) recalls the village May Dance that occurs in the opening chapters of Hardy's *Tess.* See Wharton, *Summer,* 170–71, 190–91.

131. Lefebvre, *The Production of Space,* 142.

132. Wharton, *Summer,* 39.

133. Wharton, 291.

134. Quoted in Benjamin, *The Arcades Project,* 224.

135. Wharton and Codman, *The Decoration of Houses,* 153.

136. See Dana Goodyear, "Lady of the House," *New Yorker,* 14 September 2009, https://www.newyorker.com/magazine/2009/09/14/lady-of-the-house.

137. Elsie de Wolfe, *The House in Good Taste* (New York: Century, 1913), 249.

138. The combination "knickknack-and-bookshelf" would, by the midcentury, become de rigueur in American interior design. A 1956 decorating manual published by the *New York Times,* for example, asserts that bookshelves "have replaced the Victorian what-not as a logical place to display personal mementos and assorted art objects"—indeed, to the extent that books are not specifically mentioned and so appear subordinate to the knickknacks featured in the "arrangement." See *Books in Your Home* (New York: New York Times, 1956), 47.

139. Pyne, *Bookshelf,* 58.

140. Benjamin, "Unpacking My Library," 67.

141. Benjamin, 66–67.

142. O. A. Bierstadt, in his highly detailed, descriptive account of the personal library collection of Robert Hoe, one of the foremost late-twentieth-century bibliophiles, makes a similar (albeit somewhat hyperbolic) claim regarding the issue of object versus subject where book collecting is concerned. "With a truly reverent spirit the contemporary bibliophile puts his books above himself, and plans for their survival after he shall have done with his life . . . As the custodian of his treasures, he repairs the ravages of time, and assures their future preservation by robing them in substantial beautiful bindings." The notion that the true bibliophile sacrifices his or her self for the sake of a well-preserved collection suggests that the object, or collection of objects, is designed to supersede the primacy of the

subject more generally. See O. A. Bierstadt, *The Library of Robert Hoe* (New York: Duprat, 1895), 3–4.

143. Baudrillard, "The System of Collecting," 24.

144. In his *The Library at Night,* Argentinian author Albert Manguel comments on the futility of book collecting, observing that bibliophilia springs from a desire to "lend[] the world a semblance of sense and order," but that bibliophiles like himself nevertheless "know[] perfectly well that, however much we'd like to believe the contrary, our pursuits are sadly doomed to failure." Alice Crawford uses this quotation as the epigraph to her introductory essay in *The Meaning of the Library,* explaining that the library, as a "construct," is similarly "doomed to failure," and that the history of libraries and book collections is accordingly characterized by narratives of failure. See Manguel, *The Library at Night* (New Haven, Conn.: Yale University Press, 2009), 6; and Alice Crawford, "Introduction," in Alice Crawford, ed., *The Meaning of the Library* (Princeton, N.J.: Princeton University Press, 2015), xiii.

145. Baudrillard, "The System of Collecting," 24.

146. The spelling of Royall Tyler's name furthermore suggests a link between Wharton's associate and the fictional "Lawyer Royall" of *Summer.* Royall Tyler was a descendent of *the* Royall Tyler, a colonial politician and playwright who was accused of incest, pedophilia, and repeated instances of adultery. That we may furthermore read Mr. Royall's relations with Charity in *Summer* as both quasi-incestuous (he is her legal, though not her biological, father) and pedophiliac (she is more than thirty years his junior and only sixteen at the start of the novel) supports this connection.

147. "Royall Tyler, 1884–1953." Dumbarton Oaks, https://www.doaks.org/resources/bliss-tyler-correspondence/annotations/royall-tyler; John Russell, "Kenneth Clark Is Dead at 79; Wrote 'Civilization' TV Series," *New York Times,* 22 May 1983, https://www.nytimes.com/1983/05/22/obituaries/kenneth-clark-is-dead-at-79-wrote-civilisation-tv-series.html.

148. Clark, quoted in George Ramsden, *Edith Wharton's Library* (York: Stone Trough Books, 1999), xv.

149. Clark, xvi.

150. Colin Clark inherited his portion of Wharton's library at the age of five and can't be directly blamed for the neglect it suffered. In a letter to Bernard Berenson written in January 1938, for instance, his father, Kenneth Clark, writes: "I have Edith's library here which has been installed as well as could be managed," with "here" referring to the Clarks' second home, Saltwood Castle. What's more, Colin Clark explains in his autobiography that he was not made privy to the fact of his inheritance—which he, like his father, views as being intact, calling

it Wharton's "entire library"—until he was eighteen years old. He reports that he was prevented from taking possession of it until after his father's death. Ramsden reiterates this point in a separately released "afterword" that proceeded the publication of his *Edith Wharton's Library* catalog, explaining that Kenneth, not Colin, "became the effective owner of the greater part of Edith Wharton's library." Sir Kenneth Clark died in 1983, and, shortly after, his son Colin's portion of the Wharton library collection was sold at auction, though the sale was orchestrated not by Colin but by his older brother Alan, as I explain in the Conclusion to this book. Many volumes in Wharton's library are marked with the initials "KC" for Kenneth Clark, applied by a childish hand in blue crayon and likely put there by one of the Clark children, if not necessarily by Colin. See Robert Cumming, ed., *My Dear BB: The Letters of Bernard Berenson and Kenneth Clark, 1925–1959* (New Haven, Conn.: Yale University Press 2015), 193; Colin Clark, *Younger Brother, Younger Son* (New York: HarperCollins, 1997), 167; Ramsden, "Afterword," *Additions* (self-published, 2001), 3.

151. Thomas R. Adams and Nicolas Barker, "A New Model for the Study of the Book," in *The Book History Reader* (New York: Routledge, 2006), 55.

152. Jacques Bonnet, *Phantoms on the Bookshelves* (New York: Overlook Press, 2010), 12.

153. James Salter, quoted in Bonnet, 1.

154. Bonnet, 35.

155. Benjamin, *The Arcades Project*, 220.

156. Wharton had two additional reasons for pursuing a French rather than an American divorce: first, she saw France as taking a more friendly approach to the institution of divorce, and she hoped that French laws would protect her claims to her married name (and, by extension, her authorial persona); second, she wanted to shield the episode from the eyes of the American press, which she explains to Morton Fullerton in a 1913 letter: "As you know, the public can't get at the register of the French courts, and the reporters will soon tire of their vain researches." See R. W. B. Lewis and Nancy Lewis, eds. *The Letters of Edith Wharton* (New York: Scribner's, 1988), 301.

157. Benjamin, *The Arcades Project*, 221.

158. Lefebvre, *The Production of Space*, 102.

159. Lefebvre, 97.

2. The Library as Hoard

1. Wharton, *The House of Mirth*, 102.

2. Wharton, 105.

3. Michael Dirda, "Tolstoy and Trollope Fans, Meet Couperus," *Wall Street Journal,* 24 July 2012, http://www.wsj.com.

4. "Three New Novels," *New York Times,* 28 February 1892, 19, https://www.nytimes.com/1892/02/28/archives/three-new-novels-ruling-the-planets.html.

5. The repetition of characters' names in *Eline Vere* and *The House of Mirth* is indeed worth noting. In addition to names like Lili and Paul, Couperus's novel also features a male love interest named Lawrence. Lawrence St. Clare is from New York and is Eline's "last chance," just as Lawrence Selden is Lily's in Wharton's novel. Yet neither of these Lawrences opt to intervene and save the doomed heroines in question—the result of their similar commitments to independence and to selfish bachelorhood.

6. Wharton, *The House of Mirth,* 106.

7. Louis Couperus, *Eline Vere,* trans. Ina Rilke (New York: Archipelago, 2010), 6.

8. Couperus, 8.

9. That is to say, no one has within the field of literary scholarship. A 2010 review of Ina Rilke's updated translation of *Eline Vere* mentions Wharton in passing, though the author does not offer substantive claims about her relationship to Couperus's novel and does not specifically cite *The House of Mirth.* See "Book Review: Eline Vere," *Scotsman,* 23 April 2010, https://www.scotsman.com. I would be remiss if I argued that *no one* has made the connection between *Eline Vere* and *The House of Mirth*: the fact is that I would likely not have heard of the latter if it weren't for Nynke Dorhout, librarian at The Mount, who, being Dutch, first drew my attention to the similarities between these two novels.

10. The most commonly cited sources of influence include Honoré de Balzac, Emile Zola, and Gustave Flaubert, of course, since Wharton's narrative in *The House of Mirth* exhibits aspects of literary naturalism descendent from this tradition in French literature.

11. One such example is Paul Pickrel's comparison of Wharton's *The House of Mirth* to Thackeray's *Vanity Fair* in "*Vanity Fair* in America: *The House of Mirth* and *Gone with the Wind,*" *American Literature* 59, no. 1 (1987): 37–57. More recently, Michael Gorra revives and echoes this comparison in "The Portrait of Miss Bart," *New York Review of Books,* 1 May 2015, https://www.nybooks.com/daily/2015/05/01/house-of-mirth-portrait-miss-bart/.

12. Studies of this kind are, of course, numerous, but I'll mention some highlights here. Elizabeth Ammons places Lily Bart among "second generation" American heroines of her day, so in *Edith Wharton's Argument with America* (Athens: University of Georgia Press, 1980), she locates Wharton alongside Kate Chopin and Theodore Dreiser; Amy Kaplan develops Wharton's relationship to

American literary realism in *The Social Construction of American Realism* (Chicago: University of Chicago Press, 1988); Donald Pizer famously argues for Wharton's relationship to American naturalists like Dreiser and Norris over French naturalists like Zola in "The Naturalism of Edith Wharton's *The House of Mirth*," *Twentieth-Century Literature* 41, no. 2 (1995): 241–48; Lori Merish follows Pizer's lead in "Engendering Naturalism: Narrative Form in Commodity Spectacle in U.S. Naturalist Fiction," *Novel* 29, no. 3 (1996): 319–45; a decade later, Jennifer Fleissner accepts Pizer's and Merish's contentions as de rigueur in her *Woman, Compulsion, and Modernity* (Chicago: University of Chicago Press, 2004); Jennie Kassanoff extends the discussion of Wharton's "Americanness" to the topic of race in *Edith Wharton and the Politics of Race* (New York: Cambridge University Press, 2004).

13. Wharton's library does not currently feature a copy of *Eline Vere*, but there are two reasons to believe that it might have at an earlier point in time. First, as previously explained both in this book's Introduction and in chapter 1, a significant portion of Wharton's fiction collection was destroyed after William Royall Tyler inherited it and stored it in a warehouse in London during World War II; second, the inclusion of comparatively more "minor" works by Couperus—like *The Later Life* (1915) and *Old People and the Things That Pass* (1918)—suggest that Wharton would likely have possessed copies of his "major" works, too. Despite its obscurity, *Eline Vere* is by far Couperus's best-known work, especially among English-speaking audiences. If Wharton read any Couperus at all (and it's clear that she did), she would have no doubt read *Eline Vere* as well.

14. In a February 1892 advertisement for the series, for instance, Appleton proclaims, "In offering this series to American readers the publishers feel that they are opening a field of profit and enjoyment as distinctive and fresh as the fields of Russian fiction and of Spanish fiction twelve years ago." This statement puts Couperus on par with writers like Dostoevsky, who achieved popularity in translation in the 1880s. See "Display Ad 5," *New York Times* (13 February 1892), 5.

15. Pascale Casanova, *The World Republic of Letters* (Cambridge, Mass.: Harvard University Press, 2007), 23.

16. Ton Anbeck reports that Couperus's works sold well in English-speaking countries "at the beginning of the twentieth century" and through the 1920s, "thanks in no small part to [Couperus's] translator," who was well connected throughout British literary circles, in particular. Wharton owned these very editions, released in the late 1910s and translated by A. Texeira de Mattos. From this it would appear that, beginning in the 1930s, *Eline Vere* and other novels by Couperus drifted into canonical obscurity following this thirty-year period of relative popularity. See Ton Anbeek, "Literary Renewal, 1880–1893," in Theo

Hermans, ed., *A Literary History of the Low Countries* (Rochester, N.Y.: Camden House, 2009), 480–82.

17. Benjamin argues that, more than the initial event of translation, new and updated translations crucially establish a literary work's canonical viability and inclusion. "Just as the manifestations of life are intimately connected with the phenomenon of life without being of importance to it, a translation issues from the original—not so much from its life as from its afterlife . . . and since the important works of world literature never find their chosen translators at the time of their origin, their translation marks their stage of continued life." See Walter Benjamin, "The Task of the Translator," in *Illuminations* (New York: Schocken, 1968), 71.

18. Simon During, *Exit Capitalism: Literary Culture, Theory, and Post-Secular Modernity* (New York: Routledge, 2010), 57–58.

19. Pierre Bourdieu, oddly, has very little to say about libraries in his *Distinction*. He mentions them only once and in the same breath as art museums, observing that "the professions, under-represented in use of libraries and museums, are more represented among exhibition visitors than museum visitors." Bourdieu reasons that this is because the objects on display in a museum are not for sale, and so upper-class subjects of "taste" are less likely to be interested in viewing them. Thus, while he does not specifically mention libraries (be they private or public), Bourdieu would appear to see the private library as a "world of objects available for appropriation" that "belong to the status attributes of one's group." See Pierre Bourdieu, *Distinction: A Social Critique on the Judgment of Taste* (Cambridge, Mass.: Harvard University Press, 1984), 273–78.

20. Lily, for instance, wears a "grey gown of devotional cut" in an attempt to woo the conservative Percy Gryce. Eline, similarly, appears early in Couperus's novel in a "simple morning gown of dark grey wool . . . and a close-fitting, plain bodice tied at the waist with a grey silk ribbon." See Wharton, *The House of Mirth*, 45; and Couperus, *Eline Vere*, 25.

21. Couperus, *Eline Vere*, 19.

22. Couperus, 27.

23. Diana Fuss, *The Sense of an Interior: Four Writers and the Rooms That Shaped Them* (New York: Routledge, 2004), 12.

24. Wharton, *The House of Mirth*, 86.

25. Bruno Latour, "The Berlin Key or How to Do Words with Things," trans. Lydia Davis, in Paul Graves-Brown, ed., *Matter, Materiality, and Modern Culture* (New York: Routledge, 2000), 10.

26. Couperus, *Eline Vere*, 132.

27. Scott Herring, *The Hoarders: Material Deviance in Modern American Culture* (Chicago: University of Chicago Press, 2014), 15.

28. Herring, 4.

29. Baudrillard additionally develops the connection between obsessive collecting and guilt or shame, pointing out that fanatic collectors tend to "maintain about their collection an aura of the clandestine, of confinement, secrecy and dissimulation, all of which give rise to the unmistakable impression of a guilty relationship." See Baudrillard, "The System of Collecting," 9.

30. Couperus, *Eline Vere,* 115.

31. Eline's behavior here compares to the ways in which religious devotees and church leaders would, during the medieval era, kiss and handle their prayer books. Kathryn M. Rudy sheds light on this particular practice with relevance to Dutch history, explaining that "a priest would repeatedly kiss the canon page of his missal, depositing secretions from his lips, nose, and forehead onto the page. In the Missal of the Haarlem Linen Weavers' Guild, made in Utrecht in the first decade of the fifteenth century, the illuminators provided an osculation plaque at the bottom of the full-page miniature depicting the Crucifixion . . . designed to bear the wear and tear of the priest's repeated kisses." See Kathryn M. Rudy, "Dirty Books: Quantifying Patterns of Use in Medieval Manuscripts Using a Densitometer," *Journal of Historians of Netherlandish Art* 2, no. 1–2 (2010), https://jhna.org/articles/dirty-books-quantifying-patterns-of-use-medieval-manuscripts-using-a-densitometer.

32. Couperus, *Eline Vere,* 132.

33. Couperus, 125.

34. Lori Merish, *Sentimental Materialism: Gender, Commodity Culture, and Nineteenth-Century American Literature* (Durham, N.C.: Duke University Press, 2000), 305.

35. Piper furthermore argues, as other critics have, that the act of reading, as viewed within the popular consciousness, has been historically structured by sentiment. See Piper, *Book Was There,* xii.

36. Karl Marx and Friedrich Engels, *The Communist Manifesto,* in *Karl Marx: Selected Writings,* ed. David McLellan (New York: Oxford University Press, 2002), 248–49.

37. Marx and Engels, 249. Jonathan Arac interprets Marx and Engels's idea of "world literature" in terms of the word "intercourse," which, Arac points out, is often mistranslated when rendered in English: Marx and Engels use the term *Verkehr* for "intercourse," which, Arac maintains, "means to turn over, with the usual off-key sense carried by the prefix *ver-,* so, to put it colloquially, to screw up." Thus, for Arac, *Verkehr* communicates a sense of alteration or dilution, of "the world turned upside down." This interpretation, I think, squares with my thinking

about Marx and Engels here, since both Couperus's and Wharton's protagonists seem to register and respond to the experience of manipulation at the hands of "new wants" in these novels. See Jonathan Arac, "Global and Babel: Language and Planet," in Wai Chee Dimock and Lawrence Buell, eds., *Shades of the Planet: American Literature as World Literature* (Princeton, N.J.: Princeton University Press, 2007), 21.

Emily Apter clarifies Arac's argument by observing that it is not *exchange* that is meant by Marx and Engels's use of *Verkehr* but rather a kind of screwed-upness that results in a "process of translating untranslatability." See Emily Apter, *Against World Literature* (New York: Verso, 2013), 18.

38. See "Three New Novels."

39. The word "dandy" is the prevailing descriptor of Couperus's person. The Dutch-language Wikipedia page for the term "dandy" even cites Couperus, and multiple books and studies make liberal use of this term in reference to him. See, for example, Michael Dirda's review of *Eline Vere,* "Tolstoy and Trollope Fans, Meet Couperus," and José Buschman's *Een Dandy in de Orient: Louis Couperus in Afrika* (Amsterdam: Bas Lubberhuizen, 2009).

40. Couperus, *Eline Vere,* 237.

41. Baudrillard, "The System of Collecting," 10.

42. Couperus, *Eline Vere,* 151.

43. Couperus, 152.

44. Couperus, 154.

45. Levi R. Bryant, *The Democracy of Objects* (Ann Arbor, Mich.: Open Humanities Press, 2011), 169.

46. Couperus, *Eline Vere,* 153–54.

47. Couperus, 154.

48. Couperus, 95.

49. Richard Ohmann, *Selling Culture* (New York: Verso, 1996), 82. "Bucchi" most likely refers to Ermocrate Bucchi, an Italian artist known in the 1870s and 1880s for his still-life paintings of flowers. Many of Bucchi's watercolors were, according to one source, exported to Holland ("I suoi migliori acquarelli di fiori furono spediti in Olanda"), where he enjoyed relative fame among the wealthy Dutch elites who collected his paintings. Dutch readers in the 1880s, in perceiving the value attached to the Bucchi brand name, would have been able to interpret Otto's giving the Bucchi fan to Eline in this scene as an extravagant and lavish gesture. See Angelo de Gubernatis, "Bucchi, Ermocrate," *Dizionario degli Artisti Italiani Viventi* (Florence: Le Monnier, 1889): 77–78, https://archive.org.

50. This is how Selden describes himself in *The House of Mirth* as he lectures

to Lily, telling her that his "idea of success . . . is personal freedom. . . . To keep a kind of republic of the spirit, that's what I call personal success." See Wharton, *The House of Mirth*, 55.

51. Wharton, 70.

52. Couperus, *Eline Vere*, 107.

53. Wharton, *The House of Mirth*, 8.

54. Couperus, *Eline Vere*, 243.

55. Couperus, 306.

56. Theodor Adorno, *Kierkegaard: Construction of the Aesthetic* (Minneapolis: University of Minnesota Press, 1989), 44.

57. Walter Benjamin, in *The Arcades Project*, makes passing reference to the nineteenth century's obsession with preserving dried flowers. As he reports, "Fashion journals of the period contained instructions for preserving bouquets." This observation seems representative of the desire during this era to convert living organisms into *things* in order to preserve, if not their life, their "presence" in the world. Adorno arrives at a similar contention in his interpretation of Kierkegaard's "*intérieur*": "In the *intérieur* archaic images unfold," including "the image of the flower as that of organic life." See Benjamin, *The Arcades Project*, 220; Adorno, *Kierkegaard*, 44–45.

58. Couperus, *Eline Vere*, 497.

59. Jane Bennett, *Vibrant Matter* (Durham, N.C.: Duke University Press, 2010), 5.

60. Couperus, *Eline Vere*, 495–96.

61. Wharton, *The House of Mirth*, 200.

62. Wharton, 107.

63. Wharton, 106–7, emphasis added.

64. Cynthia Griffin Wolff, "Lily Bart and the Beautiful Death," in Wharton, *The House of Mirth*, 332–33.

65. In her biography of Wharton (published three years after her essay "Lily Bart and the Beautiful Death"), Wolff does use the word "collector" in connection to Selden, observing that Selden has the "lingering, appraising, inventorial mind of an experienced collector." But it's important to note that Wolff does not offer a detailed treatment of collecting in either instance, nor does she directly label Selden in this way. By contrast, she uses the word "collector" repeatedly with reference to Percy Gryce. See Cynthia Griffin Wolff, *A Feast of Words: The Triumph of Edith Wharton* (New York: Oxford University Press, 1977), 117.

66. Wolff, 331.

67. Wharton, *The House of Mirth*, 7.

68. Wharton, 11.

69. Wharton, 10–11.

70. This apparent concern for "quality," in fact, subtly links Selden to Lily's least-likeable suitor, Simon Rosedale. Wharton describes Rosedale's tendency to appraise Lily with his eyes, "as though he were a collector who had learned to distinguish minor differences of design and quality in some long-coveted object." Thus, while Wharton calls out both Gryce and Rosedale for being opportunistic "collectors," she refrains from applying this particular vocabulary to Selden in order to emphasize the depths of Selden's delusions about himself. See Wharton, *The House of Mirth,* 234.

71. Wharton, 12.

72. Judith Fryer beautifully describes this dynamic when she comments that Selden "regards [Lily] with Epicurean fascination: one can almost see him walking round her as if she were some object in a glass case, wondering at her external finish—'as though a fine glaze of beauty and fastidiousness had been applied to vulgar clay.'" See Fryer, *Felicitous Space,* 92.

73. Latour, *Assembling the Social,* 46.

74. Wharton, *The House of Mirth,* 53.

75. Wai Chee Dimock, in her landmark essay on the subject, emphasizes themes of exchange in her reading of *The House of Mirth.* "The fluidity of currencies, . . . the apparently endless business possibilities," Dimock observes, "attest[] to the reduction of human experiences to abstract equivalents for exchange." Dimock then cites, in a very general way, chapters 1 and 2 of Marx's *Capital,* those being "The Commodity" and "The Process of Exchange." Though Dimock does not elaborate on these references to Marx, the citations point, I believe, to Marx's understanding of the commodity as a *receptacle* (or "bearer" [*Träger*]) *of value,* the extent of which is only realizable through processes of exchange. It is my aim, in part, to extend Dimock's discussion of value and exchange here. See Dimock, "Debasing Exchange," 784. See also Marx, *Capital,* tr. Ben Fowkes (New York: Penguin, 1976), 178–81, including the translator's note about "Träger."

76. Wharton, *The House of Mirth,* 11.

77. The mark "Chambolle–Duru" appears on the rear pastedown, indicating that the book was bound by René Victor Chambolle and Hippolyte Duru, two noted French bookbinders who worked in conjunction for only a few years, from 1861 to 1863, but whose joint signature continued to appear on books bound by the Chambolle firm as late as 1915. Chambolle–Duru bindings were viewed as being the gold standard among late nineteenth-century bibliophiles and collectors. They were lavish and thus very expensive; for instance, Henri Eugène Philippe Louis d'Orléans, the Duke d'Aumale, judged Chambolle-Duru bindings to be among only three "worthy" options for the books that he collected in his library

at the Château de Chantilly. And in *The Binding of Books* (1894), which Wharton owned, Howard Horne lists Duru as exemplary of the postrevolution school of bookbinding and says that "the technical accomplishments of this school are quite extraordinary." For the sake of a timely comparison, consider that a reprint, French-language edition of *Don Quixote*—not an early or rare edition, and thus not worth much in and of itself—bound by Chambolle–Duru sold, according to one catalog, for $120 in American currency in the year 1899; today, that would amount to $3,298. See Arthur S. Livingston, *American Book Prices Current* (New York: Dodd, Mead, 1899), 83; and also Howard Horne, *The Binding of Books* (London: Kegan Paul and Trench Trübner, 1894), 158.

78. Wharton, *The House of Mirth*, 11.

79. In the Introduction to this book, I explained Colton and Storm's branding of this period as a "golden age." See Storm and Peckham, *Invitation to Book Collecting*, 33.

80. Johann Wolfgang von Goethe, quoted in Horne, 158.

81. Wharton, *The House of Mirth*, 48, 11.

82. Wharton, 19.

83. Wharton, 20.

84. Wharton, 20–21.

85. Storm and Peckham, *Invitation to Book Collecting*, 43.

86. Here Storm and Peckham contradict Robert H. Wiebe when he says that "what Thorstein Veblen made famous as 'conspicuous consumption' carried a far more exact meaning in the town where everyone look on and cared than in the cities where only squandered millions would attract attention." Wiebe is specifically talking about the 1870s—the era in which Wharton was raised and that forms the basis for her later work *The Age of Innocence.* Percy Gryce, to be sure, is not squandering "millions" on his book collection, yet it is his one true "conspicuous" indulgence. This, I think, helps to explain what Storm and Peckham are getting at: the aspiring bibliomaniac is, in most instances, also an aspiring cosmopolitan, possessing enough means but unskilled in the arts of social ascendancy. See Robert H. Wiebe, *The Search for Order: 1877–1920* (New York: Hill and Wang, 1967), 3.

87. While the difference between the labels *bibliophile* and *bibliomaniac* might appear insignificant, another noted book collector from this era, Henry H. Harper, explains them in this way: "There is as much difference between the inclinations and taste of a bibliophile and a bibliomaniac as between a slight cold and the advanced stages of consumption." See Henry H. Harper, *Book-Lovers, Bibliomaniacs, and Book Clubs* (Boston: Riverside Press, 1904), 13.

88. Wharton, *The House of Mirth*, 55, emphasis original.

89. Wharton, 106.

90. Carl L. Cannon, *American Book Collectors and Collecting from Colonial Times to Present* (New York: H. W. Wilson, 1941), 41, 65.

91. Lydia Pyne, *Bookshelf* (New York: Bloomsbury, 2016), 58.

92. James Russell Lowell, "Spenser," *Literary Essays* (Cambridge, Mass.: Riverside Press, 1890), 222.

93. In a similar way, Frank Kermode identifies the "*querelle* between ancient and modern" when he defines a classic as built on "the assumption that the ancient can be more or less immediately relevant and available" and "contemporaneous" with the modern. See Kermode, *The Classic* (Cambridge, Mass.: Harvard University Press, 1975), 15–16.

94. Van Alstyne remarks that it was a "deuced bold thing [for Lily] to show herself in that get-up." See Wharton, *The House of Mirth*, 106.

95. Wharton, 109.

96. Marx, for example, insists on the link between commodity status and *use* or *wear,* explaining that "the commodity is in reality a use-value; its existence as value appears only ideally, in its price, through which it is related to the real embodiment of its value, the gold which confronts it as its opposite." In this scene, Wharton has Selden witness a conversation in which Lily's bodily assets are literally weighed in comparison to monetary worth ("jewelry," after all, denotes *gold,* a form of currency in its own right during this era in human history). The comparison is unsettling for Selden, because it summons an awareness of Lily's true *cost*: if Lily is a commodity, she must, by definition, cost more or less the same amount as any other woman on the market. Marx explains the ubiquity of commodity pricing in this way via the example of linen, noting that "all the linen on the market counts as one single article of commerce, and each piece of linen is only an aliquot part of it." And if Lily essentially costs the same as other commodities (women) on the market, Selden would be mad to invest in her. See Marx, *Capital,* 197–202.

97. Wharton, *The House of Mirth,* 55.

98. Marx, *Capital,* 179.

99. Wharton, *The House of Mirth,* 237.

100. Wharton, 11.

101. This is not the only instance in which we see Wharton encode her distaste for her own (male) heroes. Judith Fryer argues that Wharton furthermore does this with Newland Archer in the *The Age of Innocence*; Fryer reads Wharton's descriptions of "Newland Archer's preferences in tasteful decoration" and his enthusiasm for "'sincere' Eastlake [furniture]" as a kind of covert but nonetheless "devastating criticism." See Fryer, *Felicitous Space,* 121.

102. Dimock, "Debasing Exchange," 786.

103. Herring, *Hoarders,* 12.

104. Herring, 13.

105. Dimock, "Debasing Exchange," 786.

106. Wharton, *The House of Mirth,* 247.

107. Wharton, 247.

108. Ohmann, *Selling Culture,* 45–46.

109. Fuss, *The Sense of an Interior,* 15.

110. Wharton, *A Backward Glance,* 52.

111. Wharton describes her "great-grandmother Rhinelander" as being "of French descent," thus indicating a modicum of French influence in her ancestral line. But what's likely more important, in this instance, is the fact that Wharton was partially raised in Paris. She spent much of the first few years of her life in France after her parents relocated there during the Civil War. See Wharton, *A Backward Glance,* 15.

112. Casanova, *The World Republic of Letters,* 29.

113. Casanova, 88.

114. Casanova, 88.

115. Casanova, 89, emphasis original.

116. Theodor Adorno, *Minima Moralia: Reflections on a Damaged Life* (New York: Verso, 2005), 52.

117. Adorno, 52.

118. Eric Hayot, *On Literary Worlds* (New York: Oxford University Press, 2012), 9.

119. Hayot, 10.

120. Couperus, *Eline Vere,* 55.

121. Perceptions about value lie, of course, at the very heart of debates over canonicity. John Guillory examines the ways in which the discourse of canonical "value" wavers between "separatist and universalist claims" but argues that the overall "discourse of value emerges out of a pluralist consensus which, in discarding aesthetics, excludes just the sort of question that might be raised by a Marxist aesthetic—the question of the relation of the aesthetic to other domains of the social." Guillory is referring here to Benjamin's famous rewording of the question "What is the attitude of the work to the relations of production of its time?" as "What is the [work's] position *in* them [the social relations of its time]?" Guillory is arguing that dispensing with the "value" of the aesthetic likewise means dispensing with the possibility of seeing and assessing aesthetic–art as socially *valuable,* in turn. See John Guillory, *Cultural Capital* (Chicago: University of Chicago Press, 1993), 275–81; and Benjamin, "The Author as Producer," 81.

122. "Review 1—No Title," *New York Times,* 1 April 1905, https://www.ny times.com/1905/04/01/archives/review-1-no-title.html.

123. Wharton, *A Backward Glance,* 52.

3. The Library as Network

1. With regard to this famous quotation from Gramsci, Said goes on to explain that "the only available English translation inexplicably leaves Gramsci's comment at that, whereas in fact Gramsci's Italian text concludes by adding, 'Therefore it is imperative at the outset to compile such an inventory.'" See Antonio Gramsci, quoted in Edward Said, *Orientalism* (New York: Knopf Doubleday, 2014), 25.

2. "Lily's tale instructs young social climbers what situations they should avoid—or avoid getting caught in," argues Amy L. Blair, which supports my contention that Wharton approaches social entanglements in her earlier works primarily through the vantage points of fear and caution. See Amy L. Blair, *Reading Up: Middle-Class Readers and the Culture of Success in Early Twentieth-Century United States* (Philadelphia: Temple University Press, 2012), 138.

3. J. Michael Duvall highlights discussions of use and waste in *The House of Mirth* and comes to a similar conclusion regarding Lily's "usefulness," observing that Lily has "internalized utility in the abstract as the highest value and has faith in her ability to serve, no matter what the task." See Michael Duvall, "The Futile and the Dingy," in Gary Totten, ed., *Memorial Boxes and Guarded Interiors: Edith Wharton and Material Culture* (Tuscaloosa: University of Alabama Press, 2007), 160.

4. Edith Wharton, "The Other Two," in *Edith Wharton: Collected Stories, 1891–1910* (New York: Library of America, 2001), 433.

5. Wharton, 434.

6. Wharton, 435.

7. Wharton, 434, 442.

8. Wharton, 442.

9. With regard to irony, Millicent Bell claims that it is a study of "the ironic arithmetic of manners" that defines much of Wharton's later works, though Bell notes that the story "Souls Belated" shows Wharton developing this method at an earlier point in time. "She understood the uses of situations which juxtaposed differing social attitudes; one of her favorite themes becomes that of the cost of personal deviation from the dominant code of behavior," Bell observes, but she goes on to argue that "it is this strain of social satire and irony that actually becomes predominant in Edith Wharton's later stories." My contention is actually the

reverse: networks lose their "ironic" edge for Wharton over time, as novels like *The Gods Arrive* illustrate. See Millicent Bell, "Edith Wharton and Henry James: The Literary Relation," *PMLA* 74, no. 5 (1959): 624.

10. Wharton, "The Other Two," 438.

11. Wharton, 439.

12. Wharton, 449.

13. Levine, *Forms,* 122.

14. Levine, 115.

15. Michael Winship, "The Rise of a National Book Trade System in the United States," in Karl F. Kaestle and Janice A. Radway, eds., *A History of the Book in America,* vol. 4 (Chapel Hill, N.C.: University of North Carolina Press, 2009), 57.

16. Eugene Thacker, quoted in Alexander Galloway, *Protocol: How Control Exists after Decentralization* (Cambridge, Mass.: MIT Press, 2004), xiv.

17. Thacker, xiv.

18. Richard Ohmann, "The Shaping of a Canon: U.S. Fiction, 1960–1975," in Vincent Leitch, ed., *The Norton Anthology of Theory and Criticism* (New York: Norton, 2001), 1881.

19. Wharton explains in *A Backward Glance* that her father's library "probably did not contain more than seven or eight hundred volumes." That such an amount should be considered both modest, and as indicative of an undedicated or disinterested reader, says something about Wharton's own historical vantage point: the owning of books—even several hundred of them—was considered "normal" for cultivated Americans during this era. Too, given that less than two hundred of Jones's original seven to eight hundred books survive as part of Wharton's library collection, these estimates lend additional support for my argument that Wharton's library was likely larger (closer to five thousand volumes) than scholars have previously assumed. See Wharton, *A Backward Glance,* 64; Ramsden, *Edith Wharton's Library,* xv.

20. Lee, *Edith Wharton,* 34.

21. Goldman-Price puts the number of books gifted to the young Edith Jones by family and close friends at "well over sixty." See Goldman-Price, *My Dear Governess,* 7.

22. Wharton, *A Backward Glance,* 51.

23. This point rather reveals the gendered implications of Benjamin's claims regarding inheritance, which he dubs the "soundest" means of acquiring a collection (especially a library collection) and which I discussed in chapter 1.

24. I employ the term "Franco-American" and categorize this group of contacts as French not because they were, in fact, French nationals but because France

provided the setting for the majority of their interactions. This is in keeping with the way that Lee relies on similar terminology when she describes one of Wharton's earliest meetings with Fullerton, which occurred in Paris in 1907 in the company of Henry James. Fullerton and James were, of course, American, while Lapsley was British, yet they all convened at the Whartons' Parisian apartment in the Rue de Varenne. See Lee, *Edith Wharton*, 227.

25. Emphasis original.

26. Wharton's library includes more than a hundred volumes that previously belonged to Walter Berry (George Ramsden claims the number is ninety, but my own experiences with the library holdings suggest that the number is actually higher: see Ramsden, *Edith Wharton's Library*, xix).

27. Wharton, *A Backward Glance*, 172.

28. Wharton, 173.

29. Wharton, 181.

30. Another such example is Wharton's set of Henry of Fielding's *Works*, which dates from 1762 and features an impressive array of ownership signatures and bookplates, beginning with the bookplate of James Heywood Markland, FRS (1788–1864), though Markland could not have been the set's first owner. As Ramsden explains, Markland was a member of the Roxburghe Club, which boasts that it is the "oldest society of bibliophiles in the world." Markland's armorial bookplate is followed by a series of other, identifying markings that includes: J Toulerton Leather (bookplate); John Edwin Biscoe (signature on reverse fly); R. Donald Fraser (signed and dated, "14 11 1917"). Wharton must have therefore acquired this set much later in her life, which helps to explain the absence of any markings she might have added to it. Like the Gibbon set, though, this collection sketches a whole history of ownership and transference, in light of which Wharton looks like a rather unlikely figure in being the only woman and the only American to come into possession of it. See Ramsden, *Edith Wharton's Library*, 47; "The Roxburghe Club," http://www.RoxburgheClub.co.uk.

31. Richard Wendorf, *The Literature of Collecting* (Boston: Boston Athenaeum and Oak Knoll Press, 2008), 22–23.

32. Wharton, "The Other Two," 444.

33. Wharton, 444.

34. Levine, *Forms*, 118.

35. Gilder, *Edith Wharton's Lenox*, 37.

36. The database can be accessed at http://www.EdithWhartonsLibrary.org and includes metadata records for each individual item in the library.

37. Naomi Wolf extends this conversation about the influence of Wharton's various professional relationships on her reading. Wolf credits certain writers (like

Vernon Lee and Henry James) with drawing Wharton "away from American discourses about sexuality in fiction (which were generally moralistic in this period, regardless of the gender of the writer), and toward British and European aestheticism and sexual liberation." According to Wolf, this shift in Wharton's reading and thinking led to a marked interest in the work of Oscar Wilde, which can be furthermore seen in her attempts during this era to "imitate[] Wilde's phrasing" and to concoct "Wildean paradoxes." While Wolf's arguments to this end strike me as overly deterministic and causal, she usefully interprets Wharton's reading during this era in light of networks of social exchange. See Wolf, "Sex and Intellect," *Times Literary Supplement,* 12 December 2017, https://www.the-tls.co.uk/articles/public/edith-wharton-oscar-wilde.

38. Pound went on to popularize this phrase, which he took from the work of Confucian philosophy known as *Da Xue,* years later, in 1928. But modernist writers in the early 1900s were already putting its basic tenets to practice, experimenting with new stylistic and formal approaches that were designed to disrupt and displace nineteenth-century literary conventions. For example, Gertrude Stein's *Three Lives* appeared in 1909, and in a subsequent review published in January 1910, a writer for the *Chicago Record Herald* proclaims that "Nothing could be concretely more unlike the work of Henry James than [] this work of Miss Stein's," indicating the extent to which critics saw Stein as creating something new. See Michael North, "The Making of 'Make It New,'" *Guernica* 15 August 2013, https://www.guernicamag.com/the-making-of-making-it-new/; "Some Early Reviews," in Gertrude Stein, *Three Lives* (New York: Penguin, 1990), xxiv–xxv.

39. Lynch, *Loving Literature,* 214.

40. Older texts are, of course, primed for consecration in having "survived" throughout multiple generations of judgment and in appearing as testaments to previous generations' good taste. "The embodied cultural capital of the previous generations," Bourdieu explains, "functions as a sort of advance (both a head-start and a credit) which enables the newcomer to start acquiring the basic elements of the legitimate culture." In other words, the consumption of already consecrated forms of culture (like classic texts) means less work (i.e., a "head-start") for the contemporary consumer, since that work has already been subjected to systems of historical judgment. See Bourdieu, *Distinction,* 70–71.

41. Wharton owned works by both of these writers, who, in spite of their distance from her own generation, guided much of the reading that she was doing in the late nineteenth and early twentieth centuries. Her edition of Hazlitt's *Essays* (1889) dates from 1918, and its author's analyses center on historical figures like Shakespeare, Wordsworth, and Coleridge: see, for example, the discussion of Wharton's reading of Hazlitt's essay "On Reading Old Books" in chapter 1. Like-

wise, her library retains sixteen volumes by Arnold, some of them much marked; see the discussion of Arnold in chapter 4.

42. Gordon Hutner, *What America Read: Taste, Class, and the Novel, 1920–1960* (Chapel Hill, N.C.: University of North Carolina Press, 2009), 2.

43. Hutner, 37.

44. Ronald Zboray, for instance, does an admirable job of examining large-scale data sets in concert with individual readers' accounts in his analysis of patron borrowing records from the New York Society Library (to which Wharton and her family belonged). See Ronald J. Zboray, *A Fictive People: Antebellum Economic Development and the American Reading Public* (New York: Oxford University Press, 1993).

45. Hutner, *What America Read,* 39, 3.

46. Hutner sees Howells's death in 1920 as a watershed moment for American writers working in the realist vein. He notes how the emergence of writers like "Sherwood Anderson and Sinclair Lewis," who emerged during this same time period "as forerunners to Fitzgerald, Hemingway, and Faulkner," took up the mantle of realism in a way that speaks to Howells's influence, but that Howells's death nonetheless helped to clear the way for the creation of a more ambitious literary style. He neglects to mention how Edith Wharton became the first woman to win the Pulitzer Prize that same year, also in 1920; that event, arguably, had a greater effect on the field of literary realism than Howells's passing, given that the latter's work was quickly forgotten (and never succeeded in becoming an enduring part of the American literary canon), whereas Wharton's realist novels remained commercially successful into the 1930s and, in many cases, retain canonical significance today. See Hutner, 37–38.

47. Goldman-Price, *My Dear Governess,* 30–32.

48. Kenneth Clark, who had a tendency for exaggeration where Wharton's library was concerned, argues otherwise. In a short piece titled "Portrait of Edith Wharton," which was meant to serve as a lasting accompaniment to the library collection, he claims that "there is a higher proportion of books on religion, allied philosophies, mysticism, and histories of religious orders than on anything else." See Clark, "Portrait of Edith Wharton," Box 62, Folder 1749, YCAL 42, Series 4 Edith Wharton Papers, Beinecke Rare Books and Manuscript Library, Yale University, New Haven, Connecticut.

49. The graph of Wharton library volumes by subject was drafted from a representative sample of roughly 1,600 titles (65 percent of the total library collection). The number of actual books included in the sample is actually higher, given that many of these titles—like the two sets of Gibbon's *Decline and Fall*—comprise multivolume sets.

50. Ramsden, *Edith Wharton's Library,* xvi.

51. Tyler, quoted in Ramsden, xv.

52. Pizer, "The Naturalism of Edith Wharton's *The House of Mirth,*" 242.

53. Winship, "Rise of a National Book Trade System," 60.

54. Wharton, *A Backward Glance,* 66.

55. See John Stuart Mill's "On the Subjection of Women" (1869), which kick-started much of the controversy surrounding the expansion of coeducation during this era.

56. D. H. Clarke, *Sex in Education: or, A Fair Chance for Girls* (Boston: Houghton-Mifflin, 1873), 152, https://archive.org/details/sexeducationor00cla riala.

57. Some of Wharton's acquaintances were educated in this manner, as Irene Goldman-Price explains; see Goldman-Price, *My Dear Governess,* 3–4.

58. Not least among the figures associated with that discussion was the poet and activist Julia Ward Howe, who published her own rejoinder to Clarke's work, called *Sex and Education,* in 1874.

59. Friedrich Schiller, *The Piccolomini,* in *Schiller's Works,* vol. 2 (London, George Barrie, 1883), 166. Clarke represents this quotation differently in his *Sex and Education,* substituting the "thou" for "though," among other inconsistencies. See Clarke, *Sex and Education,* 161.

60. Clarke, 161.

61. Goldman-Price, *My Dear Governess,* 4.

62. Cynthia Jay, quoted in Goldman-Price, 4.

63. Wharton, *Hudson River Bracketed,* 282.

64. Wharton, 282.

65. Wharton, *The Gods Arrive* (New York: Appleton, 1960), 48.

66. Mary Suzanne Schriber argues in her reading of *The Gods Arrive* that Vance is actually irritated by Halo's intellectual training and expertise and that this is why he appears to "prefer the company of his pseudo-intellectual male companions to that of the far more perceptive Halo." In other words, like Halo herself, Vance appears all too aware of the intellectual distance between the two and rejects Halo's company for this very reason. He thus becomes "essentially the type of male character, not infrequent in Wharton's fiction, who wheels out the culture's ideology of woman when it serves his needs." See Mary Suzanne Schriber, *Gender and the Writer's Imagination* (Lexington: University of Kentucky Press, 1987), 164–65.

67. Lionel Trilling, *The Liberal Imagination* (New York: New York Review of Books, 2008), 206.

68. Trilling, 207.

69. This view is particularly common among midcentury critics. Millicent

Bell (1951) insinuates that *The Age of Innocence*, which many critics consider to be Wharton's "masterpiece," might be "a final monument to [Henry James's] influence" on her work and that, following the publication of this work, we see Wharton getting further and further away from James (and thus further away from the standards set by him), an observation that she applies to her treatment of *The Gods Arrive*; see Bell, "Edith Wharton and Henry James," 636. Similarly, Richard H. Lawson (1977) groups these novels among what he calls Wharton's "slick-magazine fiction" and argues that Vance Weston amounts to an "inferior" version of the sort of protagonist seen in the works of Thomas Mann; see Lawson, "Thematic Similarities in Edith Wharton and Thomas Mann," *Twentieth Century Literature* 23, no. 3 (1977): 293–94, www.jstor.org/stable/441258. More recently, critics like Robin Peel (2005) have reinforced such views, as when Peel observes that Wharton's "rhetoric" in these novels "verges on melodrama"; see Peel, *Apart from Modernism: Edith Wharton, Politics, and Fiction before World War I* (Vancouver, B.C.: Farleigh Dickinson University Press, 2005), 158. Wharton's biographers have added their own share of complaints on the subject: Benstock, in her *No Gifts from Chance*, labels the ending of *The Gods Arrive* "all too hopeful" and criticizes Wharton for departing from more realistic narrative standards, while Lee laments a quality of "decreasing vividness" in *The Gods Arrive* that remains unrelieved by occasional "flashes of Wharton's old lightness." See Benstock, *No Gifts from Chance*, 440, and Lee, *Edith Wharton*, 680–81.

70. Wharton, *The Gods Arrive*, 206.

71. Wharton, 292.

72. Wharton, 211.

73. Wharton, 209.

74. Foucault, "Other Spaces," 22.

75. Wharton, *The Gods Arrive*, 346.

4. The Library as Tomb

1. Wharton, *A Backward Glance*, 69.

2. Alberto Manguel, *The Library at Night* (New Haven, Conn.: Yale University Press, 2009), 305.

3. Ray Bradbury, "Libraries, the Love of My Life," *Logotopia: The Library in Architecture, Art, and the Imagination*, ed. Sascha Hastings and Esther E. Shipman (Montreal: Cambridge Galleries/ABC Art Books Canada, 2008), 60.

4. Wharton, *Summer*, 13.

5. Wharton, 11, 16.

6. Wharton, 13.

7. Wharton, 49, 50.

8. Wharton, 13.

9. Wharton, *A Backward Glance,* 69.

10. Wharton, 70.

11. This has to do with the way that libraries appear linked with the history of gothic *architecture,* as well. "Practitioners of the gothic mode," as Lynch explains, "seem to enjoy thinking about how, housed within deserted libraries that seem requisite architectural features of this mode's châteaux and abbeys, a book can survive for ages without anyone lifting up its cover—and yet still be available to the readers who might just happen along and select it from the shelf." See Lynch, *Loving Literature,* 209.

12. Lefebvre, *The Production of Space,* 33.

13. Lefebvre, 221.

14. Thomas Laqueur explains that Eleanor Marx was cremated following her suicide in 1898, and because no family members claimed her ashes, they were then handed over to the Socialist League and, later, to the Marx Memorial Library. The library later went on to fund a new gravesite for the entire Marx family, located in London's Highgate Cemetery, which replaced the previous, unmarked site that had been the original resting place of Karl Marx's body. See Laqueur, *The Work of the Dead* (Princeton, N.J.: Princeton University Press, 2015), 18–20. The remains of less well-known deceased figures, meanwhile, also appear installed in libraries. For example, the Annmary Brown Memorial Library, located at Brown University, houses both the personal mementos and physical remains of its benefactors, General Rush C. Hawkins and Annmary (Brown) Hawkins. What's more, the Library showcases the way that, in early twentieth-century America, a synonymous link formed between the terms "library" and "collection," for the library does not contain any books and, indeed, was not originally designed for the purpose of housing them. I'm grateful to Elizabeth Scharf for drawing my attention to this library. And lastly, let's not forget that Hollywood's favorite professor-cum-tomb-raider, Indiana Jones, discovers the tomb of a knight from the First Crusade beneath the floor of a Venetian library in *Indiana Jones and the Last Crusade* (1989).

15. Barbara Johnson, *Persons and Things* (Cambridge, Mass.: Harvard University Press, 2008), 38.

16. Riegl, like Benjamin, may be viewed as a near contemporary of Wharton. He was born only four years before her (in 1858) and lived and wrote during the same period, making his theories of monumentalized space all the more significant to a discussion of monuments to the dead in Wharton's fiction.

17. Alois Riegl, "The Modern Cult of Monuments: Its Essence and Its De-

velopment," in Nicholas Price and M. Kirby Talley, eds., *Readings in Conservation* (Los Angeles: Getty Conservation Institute, 2016), 69, emphasis original.

18. Baudrillard, "The System of Collecting," 7, emphasis original.

19. In a very similar way, journalist William Garibaldi points out, books convey a right to the occupation of space. As a physical object, a book takes up space in the life of the consumer who purchases or acquires it and, in so doing, insinuates that the ultimate objective of human existence might be "to build something worthy of being bound and occupying a space on those shelves, on *all* shelves." As such, Garibaldi argues, books are seen as having earned the space that they occupy. See William Garibaldi, "Why We Need Physical Books," *New Republic,* 19 April 2015, https://newrepublic.com/article/121560/bibliophiles-defense -physical-books.

20. Riegl, "The Modern Cult of Monuments," 70.

21. See Gillian Silverman, *Bodies and Books: Reading and the Fantasy of Communion in Nineteenth-Century America* (State College: University of Pennsylvania Press, 2012), 52–53. Silverman's comments echo those of John Milton, who, in his 1644 speech "Areopagitica," views books as living and productive, as when he says, "Books are not absolutely dead things, but doe contain a potencie of life in them to be as active as that soule was whose progeny they are; nay they do preserve as in a violl the purest efficacie and extraction of that living intellect that bred them." See Milton, "Areopagitica: A Speech for the Liberty of Unlicenc'd Printing for the Parliament of England," John Milton Reading Room, Dartmouth University, Hanover, New Hampshire, 2016, https://www.dartmouth.edu/~milton/reading _room/areopagitica/text.html.

22. Silverman, *Bodies and Books,* 54.

23. Anne-Sophie Springer and Etienne Turpin, eds., *Fantasies of the Library* (Cambridge, Mass.: MIT Press, 2017), iv.

24. Wharton, "The Angel at the Grave," in *Edith Wharton: Collected Stories, 1891–1910,* 254.

25. Wharton, 254.

26. Wharton, 256.

27. Wharton, 256.

28. Wharton, 256.

29. Wharton, 257.

30. Wharton, 255, 257.

31. Wharton, 256.

32. Wharton, 254.

33. Orestes Brownson never actually resided in Concord, though he was

a close associate of many of that town's most noteworthy residents. Brownson founded the *Boston Quarterly Review,* which he published himself and which featured regular contributions from the likes of George Ripley, Margaret Fuller, George Bancroft, and Elizabeth Peabody. Brownson was a founding member of the Transcendentalist Club, which formed first in Boston in 1836 and included Ripley, Fuller, Bancroft, and Peabody as members, along with Emerson, Thoreau, and others. For more on Brownson, and on the history of the *Boston Quarterly* in particular, see R. W. B. Lewis, *The American Adam: Innocence, Tragedy, and Tradition in the Nineteenth Century* (Chicago: University of Chicago Press, 1955), 174–93. Later in "The Angel at the Grave," when the strange visitor named Corby comes to visit the Anson house and library, he tells Paulina that "he got on the trail" of Anson's work "through some old book on Brook Farm." This reference to George and Sophia Ripley's experiment in communal living, which took transcendentalist philosophy as its basis and chief inspiration, cements the associations between Wharton's story and the transcendentalist community at Concord. See "The Angel at the Grave," 266.

34. Joan W. Goodwin, *The Remarkable Mrs. Ripley* (Boston: Northeastern University Press, 2011), xviii.

35. Lee, *Edith Wharton,* 19.

36. Wharton, "The Angel at the Grave," 258.

37. Wharton.

38. Ralph Waldo Emerson, "Character," *Essays: Second Series* (New York: Houghton Mifflin and Company, 1884), 103–4.

39. Emerson, 104–5.

40. Emerson's essay "Character" would continue to hold special significance for Wharton. Lee explains that, many years later, Wharton would employ a phrase from this essay to describe her relationship with her lover, Morton Fullerton, in a letter written to him. See Lee, *Edith Wharton,* 309.

41. Lewis, *The American Adam,* 236.

42. Wharton, "The Angel at the Grave," 262.

43. Wharton, 256–57.

44. Wharton, 258.

45. Wharton, 258.

46. Wharton, 259.

47. Wharton, 259.

48. Wharton, 259.

49. Jules Michelet sees the historian as subject to a pacifying instinct, wherein they feel compelled to please, or to do justice to, the dead subject. As Carolyn Steedman puts it, "Michelet understood the Historian's task as pacifying the spir-

its of the dead, exorcising them 'by finding the meaning of their brief existences.'" This compares to the way in which Wharton's Paulina seems to fear the censorious appraisals of her dead grandfather: she has not yet completed her work on *Life,* and has not yet fulfilled her debt by "finding the meaning of his existence." As a result, she must reject any commitments that would impinge on that larger project—even if doing so means rejecting her own opportunities for happiness. Paulina thus epitomizes the fate of the historical researcher who, in Michelet's words, is so besotted with her historical quest that she becomes "remote" to herself. See Michelet, quoted in Steedman, *Dust,* 70–71.

50. The connection between communications *media* and the human subject as spiritualist *medium* has, of course, proven to be an exceptionally fruitful ground for scholarly analysis. Jill Galvan, in *The Sympathetic Medium,* "tracks [the] pervasive and versatile literary presence" of the female spiritualist medium, and Jonathan Sterne, in *The Audible Past,* links early sound recording technology to the Victorian "cult" of death. Yet Sterne, in focusing on sound recording's role as an "archival medium" for late nineteenth-century audiences, likewise explains how audiences' fears about its technological durability resulted in a "momentous battle against decay." I would argue that, via Paulina Anson, we see Wharton channeling similar fears about "decay," since the living medium is destined for eventual decomposition. Written works, Wharton is suggesting, do not continue to "live" by virtue of their material existence: they require living *users.* See Jill Galvan, *The Sympathetic Medium: Feminine Channeling, the Occult, and Communication Technologies, 1859–1919* (Ithaca, N.Y.: Cornell University Press, 2010), 2; and Jonathan Sterne, *The Audible Past: Cultural Origins of Sound Reproduction* (Durham, N.C.: Duke University Press, 2003), 287–92.

51. Wharton, "The Angel at the Grave," 260.

52. Wharton, 260.

53. Wharton, 260.

54. Wharton, 261.

55. Wharton, 261.

56. Wharton, 251.

57. Wharton, 262.

58. Wharton, 263.

59. In *The Buried Life of Things,* Simon Goldhill provides a nuanced reading of the way that actual human remains became part of an archival arrangement and exhibit at Knebworth House in England, the former home of Robert Bulwer Lytton (who, in the mid-nineteenth century, wrote under the pen name Owen Meredith). In a glass case at Knebworth House, according to Goldhill, one can view a set of human skulls that are purported to be the skulls of two *fictional*

characters from Lytton's writing. Goldhill refers to these objects as "The bones of literary inventions" and surveys how "objects became conceptualized within particular regimes of knowledge and perception" and how these skulls, in particular, "epitomize an important era of transition" with regard to such regimes. I bring up this example because the skulls in the case provide a literal counterpart to Paulina Anson's hypothetical encasement in "The Angel at the Grave." Paulina is aware of being part of Anson's archive to the same extent that an object or set of human remains might also be, and, what's more, Goldhill's study suggests that such a view is consistent with the way that late nineteenth century audiences—a population of which Paulina is a representative—were "thinking about display and the body." See Simon Goldhill, *The Buried Life of Things: How Objects Made History in Nineteenth-Century Britain* (New York: Cambridge University Press, 2014), 10–11.

60. Wharton, "The Angel at the Grave," 254.

61. Wharton, 260.

62. Wharton, 263.

63. Wharton, 264.

64. Wharton, 264.

65. Emerson, "Character," 98.

66. Wharton, "The Angel at the Grave," 264.

67. Wharton, 265.

68. Wharton, 265.

69. Wharton, 267.

70. Wharton, 267.

71. Wharton, 268.

72. Corby speculates that Anson must have written the pamphlet in the early 1830s based on research he was doing in the 1820s, and he tells Paulina that the pamphlet was concerned with "describing the notochord of the *amphioxus* as a cartilaginous vertebral column." Here it seems likely that Wharton is relying on complex scientific terms in order to emphasize Paulina's feelings of confusion (and convey those feelings to the reader, too). But what she is describing, in effect, are early efforts made within the fields of biological science to understand the evolution of the cellular being (the "universal" type of being). This puts Wharton's fictional references to Anson's research on the *amphioxus* nearly in step with Matthias Schleiden and Theodor Schwann's groundbreaking research on cellular theory. Schleiden's and Schwann's theories were first publicly presented in 1838, and they subsequently appeared in the 1839 volume *Microscopical Researches into the Accordance in the Structure and Growth of Animals and Plants*. This work is described in the 1881 *Proceedings of the American Academy of Arts and Sciences* as "marking an

era in biological science" from a "physiological point of view," though the proceedings note that "[Schwann and Schleiden's] views in regard to the origin of cells have been entirely supplanted by those of more recent investigators," proof that, with fifty more years, science had advanced even far beyond the "era of biological science" defined by Schleiden and Schwann's initial investigations. See Wharton, "The Angel at the Grave," 267; and "Theodor Schwann," *Proceedings of the American Academy of Arts and Sciences* 17 (June 1881–June 1882): 460–61.

73. Wharton, "The Angel at the Grave," 268.

74. Wharton, 269.

75. Wharton, 270.

76. Barbara A. White's reading compares to Lee's. White claims that, at the end of the story, it appears that Orestes Anson's reputation *will* be successfully recuperated thanks to Corby and, even better, "Paulina can share in the work" of that resuscitation. As I point out here, though, Paulina is clearly unprepared for anything that might resemble "sharing" so far as that work is concerned; her only capabilities include acts of domestic maintenance, transmission, and custodianship. See Barbara A. White, *Edith Wharton: A Study of the Short Fiction* (Woodbridge, Conn.: Twayne, 1991), 54.

77. Lee, *Edith Wharton*, 189.

78. The term "Mechlin cap" refers to a cap that has been trimmed with Mechlin lace. Such caps were fashionable in the early part of the nineteenth century; an example of this is an 1816 account of the marriage of Princess Charlotte that lists multiple "Mechlin lace caps" as part of the princess's millinery. But as Wharton gives us no reason to assume that the temporal setting of "The Angel at the Grave" is not contemporaneous with the time of its writing, we can assume that Paulina's cap, like her grandfather's philosophy, would be viewed as outmoded by the year 1900. As C. Willett Cunnington additionally explains, by the year 1884 lace caps were "only worn by old ladies." Such references, though, are furthermore characteristic of the way that Wharton often uses fashion as a vehicle for conveying criticisms of obsoleteness. She does precisely this in *New Year's Day*, when the narrator describes his grandmother as wearing "lace lappets and creaking '*moiré*.'" In both instances, terms like "Mechlin cap" and "lace lappets" are used to highlight old-fashioned sensibilities. See *Hone's Account of the Royal Marriage* (London: W. Hone, 1816), 40–41, https://www.books.google.com; C. Willett Cunnington, *English Women's Clothing in the Nineteenth Century* (New York: Dover, 1990), 358–59; Wharton, "The Angel at the Grave," 264; and Edith Wharton, *New Year's Day*, 230.

79. Wharton, "The Angel at the Grave," 265.

80. Wharton, 265–66.

81. Wharton, 255.

82. Wharton, 270.

83. Jennifer Fleissner, *Women, Compulsion, Modernity: The Moment of American Naturalism* (Chicago: University of Chicago Press, 2004), 23.

84. Lauren Berlant, *Cruel Optimism* (Durham, N.C.: Duke University Press, 2011), 1.

85. This pattern of behavior also squares with Berlant's discussion of the "precocious" or "intellectually oriented" child. Berlant, working from Adam Phillips's arguments about intellectual subjectivity, speculates that such children are believed to harbor feelings of "diffuse resentment" (Phillips's term) for the world and so tend to feel a "sadistic thrill" when brought face to face with a familiar "scene of optimism and disappointment." Such an assertion furthermore bolsters Berlant's overall arguments about "cruel optimism"—namely, that the modern subject experiences a kind of pleasure, sadistic or otherwise, when he or she recognizes a set of conditions that feel familiar, regardless of whether or not those conditions are, in fact, desirable, pleasurable, satisfying, and so on. The point is that the recognizing of them is itself pleasurable. See Berlant, 144.

86. Josephine Donovan, *After the Fall: The Demeter–Persephone Myth in Wharton, Cather, and Glasgow* (State College: Pennsylvania State University Press, 1989), 53.

87. Emily J. Orlando, *Edith Wharton and the Visual Arts* (Tuscaloosa: University of Alabama Press, 2007), 151.

88. Orlando, 152.

89. Wharton, "The Angel at the Grave," 256.

90. Orlando, *Edith Wharton and the Visual Arts,* 150.

91. Marx, quoted in Benjamin, *The Arcades Project,* 209.

92. Wharton, "The Angel at the Grave," 270.

93. Riegl, "The Modern Cult of Monuments," 77.

94. Johnson, *Persons and Things,* 40.

95. Foucault observes that is the concept of the sacred that helps to mediate between public and private where such spaces are concerned. Because it pertains to the body, death is viewed as a private and intimate affair yet as an event that must be reassembled and repackaged for polite, public consumption. Such oppositions, Foucault points out, are "nurtured by the hidden presence of the sacred." See Foucault, "On Other Spaces," 23.

96. Riegl, "The Modern Cult of Monuments," 82.

97. Michel Foucault, "Fantasia of the Library," in *Language, Counter-Memory, Practice: Selected Essays and Interviews by Michel Foucault,* ed. Donald F. Bouchard (Ithaca, N.Y.: Cornell University Press, 1977), 90–91.

98. William Wordsworth, "Monuments to Literary Men," in *The Prose Works of William Wordsworth*, ed. William Knight (London: Walter Scott, 1893), 109, https://books.google.com.

99. June Howard, "Regionalism and Cosmopolitanism in Wharton's *Old New York*," in Emily J. Orlando and Meredith L. Goldsmith, eds., *Edith Wharton and Cosmopolitanism* (Gainesville: University of Florida Press, 2016), 171.

100. Wharton, *False Dawn*, in *Old New York*, 27.

101. Wharton lists Ruskin as being among those figures whose works had been "added to the French and English classics" that comprised her father's version of a nineteenth-century "gentleman's library." And while Wharton speculates that Ruskin's books, like those written by some of the other "new" authors in her father's collection (including Coleridge and the Brontës), were not likely read, it is nonetheless clear that she was familiar with Ruskin's work from a relatively young age. In an 1887 letter to her governess, Anna Bahlmann, she comments on having recently given one of Ruskin's books to the latter as a birthday present. See Wharton, *A Backward Glance*, 52; and Goldman-Price, *My Dear Governess*, 76. Too, Wharton's close friend, Bernard Berenson, was a devotee of Ruskin, as was his protégé, the art historian Kenneth Clark. When Wharton willed half of her library collection to Clark's son, Colin, she did not include art history books or works by Ruskin, banking on the assumption that the Clarks already owned them.

102. Howard, "Regionalism and Cosmopolitanism," 168.

103. Wharton, *False Dawn*, 74.

104. Wharton, *The Spark*, in *Old New York*, 226.

105. Wharton, *New Year's Day*, 246.

106. Wharton, "The Pelican," in *Edith Wharton: Collected Stories, 1891–1910*, 77.

107. Wharton, *A Backward Glance*, 68–69.

108. June Howard additionally explains that Wharton uses this same phrase in her essay "The Vice of Reading," which appeared in 1903 in the *North American Review*, to refer to "those who come effortlessly, admirably, to culture." But this characterization oversimplifies the case with Lizzie, who might not be a "born reader" but who is, significantly, a reader nonetheless. In her essay, Wharton actually praises this quality of reader, stating that being a less accomplished (or less automatically inclined) kind of reader "is certainly not a fault" and that there is "little harm in the self-confessed devourer of foolish fiction." If anything, Wharton argues, this type of reader improves upon the figure of the moralist reader who decrees what must and should be read and who views "the desire to keep up" as the strongest incentive for reading. See Howard, "Regionalism and Cosmopolitanism,"

181; Wharton, "The Vice of Reading," *North American Review* 177, no. 563 (October 1903): 514–15.

109. Wharton, *New Year's Day*, 245, 266.

110. Wharton, 299.

111. Wharton, 229, emphasis original.

112. Wharton, 284.

113. "While Wharton's fiction does indeed provide a horror gallery of marriages," Eby nevertheless argues that Wharton "believed in the institution and was interested in what could make marriage work." In particular, Eby reads a line from the novel *The Glimpses of the Moon* (one character's remark that "everything's changed nowadays; why shouldn't marriage . . . too?") as proof of Wharton's interest in "modernizing" the institution of marriage. Eby views *Glimpses* as an account of a failed experiment at modernized marriage, though I would argue instead that *Glimpses* is less about "experimental" forms of marriage than about *traditional* marriage (and about revealing it as an outmoded institution that is prone to clashing with modern values and social standards). See Clare Virginia Eby, "*The Glimpses of the Moon* and the Debate over Marital Reform," *Edith Wharton and Cosmopolitanism*, 20–21.

114. Wharton, *New Year's Day*, 239.

115. DeVries's *Plant Breeding* is only one of many books in Wharton's library devoted to the subject of botany. Others include H. Drinkwater's *A Lecture on Mendelism* (1910), Sir J. William Dawson's *The Geological History of Plants*, and Alexander McDonald's touchstone work of early nineteenth-century horticulture, *A Complete Dictionary of Practical Gardening* (1808). What is additionally interesting is that Wharton's allusion to plant breeding in *New Year's Day*—which is supposed to take place in the 1870s—is subtly anachronistic. Gregor Mendel, whose experiments with plant breeding began in the 1860s, did not gain popularity during his lifetime, and it was only later, in the 1890s, that scientists working in similar areas rediscovered and popularized his ideas. William Bateson used Mendel's theories to coin the term "genetics" in 1905. Wharton, having read early twentieth-century texts (like those by Drinkwater and DeVries) would have been acquainted with theories of plant genetics by the time that she wrote *New Year's Day* in the 1920s, but Wharton's character, Lizzie Hazeldean, would have been unlikely to encounter a "new" species of hybridized rose in the 1870s. Though the first "hybrid tea" rose appeared in 1867, the practice of hybridizing roses did not become popular until the early twentieth century. Too, France was, for decades, the center of activity with regard to rose hybridization, and Wharton lived exclusively in France after her relocation there in 1911. New species of hybrid roses would have been slower to reach the United States during this period, but they would have been common in

France. I thank my mother, Sandra Liming, for teaching me so much about roses, without which I would have missed this connection entirely.

116. Hugo Devries, *Plant Breeding: Comments on the Experiments of Nilsson and Burbank* (Chicago: Open Court Publishing, 1907), 187.

117. Wharton, *New Year's Day,* 242.

118. Wharton, 243.

119. Wharton, 281.

120. Wharton, 282.

121. Wharton, 291.

122. Wharton, 296–97.

123. The narrator additionally explains that Lizzie speaks French and Italian, inviting comparison between Lizzie and Wharton (who also spoke these languages), thus casting further doubt on Lizzie's inabilities as a reader. If Wharton's intention was to establish Lizzie as uneducated and disinclined toward intellectual tasks, she does a poor job of it here. See Wharton, *New Year's Day,* 297.

124. Wharton, 301–3.

125. The original passage reads in French as "Je vois avex joie la solitude se faire autour de moi: c'est mon élément, ma vie. On ne fait rien qu'avex la solitude: c'est mon grand axiome. Un homme se fait en dedans de lui et non den dehors." The English translation is my own. See Lacordaire, quoted in Matthew Arnold, *Notebooks* (New York: Macmillan, 1902), 17.

126. Wharton, *New Year's Day,* 304.

127. Howard also pronounces Lily Bart to be a "non-reader," but—as is the case with Lizzie Hazeldean—this pronouncement is untrue. Both of these characters read; Lily, for instance, can be seen "cut[ting] the pages of a novel" in one of the very first scenes of *The House of Mirth,* and she reflects fondly on her father's penchant for reading poetry, even as her mother equates reading poetry with laziness. See Wharton, *New Year's Day,* 181, and *The House of Mirth,* 17, 30.

128. Wharton, *New Year's Day,* 306.

129. Stephanie Copeland, the former director of The Mount and its associated nonprofit, Edith Wharton Restoration, was heavily criticized for her decision to purchase the library books at Ramsden's stated price of $2.6 million. We ought, however, to greet any statements regarding the collection's "worth" in relation to that price—such as those issued by Mead in her *New Yorker* article—with generous skepticism. Since its installation in 2008, the library has succeeded in drawing new generations of visitors (including scholars) to The Mount while also generating publicity and helping to attract high-profile donors (like former First Lady Laura Bush). Copeland resigned as director in 2008, at the behest of the estate's board, who were eager to pin The Mount's continued financial difficulties

on someone in particular; at that point, members of the board (including the critic Louis Auchincloss, who edited Wharton's poems and published a biography about her) suggested selling the library books and replacing them with convincing copies. To this, Copeland responded by saying that "the Met could hang copies of paintings," too, which suggests that discussions of "worth" are, to a very great extent, null and void when claims to authenticity are at stake. See Rebecca Mead, "Restoration Drama," *The New Yorker,* 28 April 2008, https://www.newyorker .com/magazine/2008/04/28/restoration-drama; Kate Bolick, "Save the Mount!," *Slate.com,* 21 April 2008, http://www.slate.com/articles; and Michelle Dean, "The Fight to Save Edith Wharton's Beloved Home from Itself," *The Guardian,* 18 October 2015, https://www.theguardian.com/books.

130. Wordsworth, "Monuments to Literary Men," 108–10.

131. In her Introduction to *Illuminations,* Hannah Arendt observes that Benjamin had a variety of reasons for ending his own life (which he did in September 1940); among those reasons was a fear of the loneliness that he might encounter in being viewed as an endangered species. Whereas many of his Frankfurt School associates had emigrated to America during the 1930s, Arendt describes Benjamin's reluctance to do the same, explaining that "nothing drew him to America where, as he used to say, people would probably find no other use for him than to cart him up and down the country to exhibit him as the 'last European.'" See Hannah Arendt, Introduction to Benjamin, *Illuminations,* 18.

132. Lee, *Edith Wharton,* 322.

133. Updike, who founded the Merrymount Press, was based jointly out of Boston and Providence and became a good friend of the Whartons, visiting them often at their first residence in Newport. Updike's Merrymount Press oversaw the printing of Wharton's earliest books for Scribner's, including *The Greater Inclination*; he went on to print other books for her, like *The Book of the Homeless* (1916), in addition to designing the bookplates for her two French residences in 1924. He is furthermore well known among book historians for his 1922 work *Printing Types: Their History, Forms, and Use* and for his own personal library collection, which features works on the history of type and is held at the Providence Public Library in Rhode Island. See Lee, *Edith Wharton,* 426, 547; Goldman-Price, *My Dear Governess,* 174–77.

134. Wordsworth, "Monuments to Literary Men," 109.

135. Wordsworth, 110.

136. Wordsworth, 129.

137. Laqueur, *The Work of the Dead,* 390.

138. Wordsworth, "Monuments to Literary Men," 110.

139. Lee, *Edith Wharton,* 761.

140. Lee, 762.

141. Laqueur, *The Work of the Dead,* 215.

142. Ramsden, *Edith Wharton's Library,* 38.

Conclusion

1. Sarah Lyall, "Alan Clark, a British Scold, Is Dead at 71," *New York Times,* 8 September 1999, http://www.nytimes.com/1999/09/08/world/alan-clark-a-british -scold-is-dead-at-71.html. The "Turner" in question was an original 1845 painting by the artist J. M. W. Turner called *Seascape Folkstone,* which had belonged to Kenneth Clark. Alan sold it to Sotheby's in 1984, the same year that he sold the Wharton library materials to Maggs Bros. See "Turner Painting to Be Auctioned," *New York Times,* 14 March 1984.

2. Lyall, "Alan Clark."

3. Maggs Bros., Ltd., "The Library of Edith Wharton: Auction Catalogue," 1984, The Mount Archives, Lenox, Massachusetts.

4. Maggs Bros., Ltd. Maggs's decision to do this becomes more with the help of Richard W. Oram, who reports having corresponded with Ed Maggs in preparation for writing his *Writer's Libraries.* Oram points out, via that correspondence, that "although the book trade has sometimes been criticized . . . for 'breaking' libraries, it is actually advantageous to sell the collection as a unit: 'Commercially speaking . . . a sale en bloc is nearly always better, as long as the price has a reasonable relationship to the melt value, so authors' libraries aren't necessarily broken in the interests of gain.'" To this, though, Oram adds a rather important caveat: "However, when the library is extremely bulky or contains a substantial amount of 'non-literary' material, the equation changes." See Richard W. Oram, *Collecting, Curating, and Researching Writers' Libraries: A Handbook* (Lanham, Md.: Rowman and Littlefield, 2014), 20–21.

5. George Ramsden, "Alan Clark and Edith Wharton's Library," *Matrix* 25 (2005): 7.

6. George Ramsden, personal interview, March 15, 2017.

7. Ramsden; Alan Cowell, "After a Century, an American Writer's Library Will Go to America," *New York Times,* 15 December 2005, http://www.nytimes .com.

8. Heywood Hill opened his bookshop in 1936, and its early successes were due in part to the presence of Nancy Mitford, who worked in the shop in the 1940s and later went on to become a novelist. Mitford's sister, Deborah, became the

Duchess of Devonshire after marrying Andrew Cavendish, the eleventh Duke of Devonshire, who was a renowned bibliophile. The Duke became a majority shareholder in the shop in the 1990s, and his son, Peregrine "Stoker" Cavendish, twelfth Duke of Devonshire, assumed his father's interests and subsequently became the sole owner of the shop in 2013, solidifying the store's ongoing connection to the British gentry. See "About Heywood Hill," HeywoodHill.com.

9. Ramsden, personal interview.

10. Ramsden, "Library as Autobiography," *A Book of Booksellers,* ed. Sheila Markham (privately printed, 2004), 235.

11. Ariane Bankes, "Horn-rims and Baggy Chords," *Slightly Foxed* 5 (Spring 2005): 27.

12. Ramsden, personal interview.

13. Bankes, "Horn-rims and Baggy Chords," 27.

14. Ramsden, "Library as Autobiography," 235. Staff members at The Mount are fond of repeating the story of the time when one of Ramsden's children threatened to destroy items from Wharton's library—a few duodecimo volumes of poetry—just to get his attention. Ramsden's daughter, apparently exasperated by the depth of her father's absorption in the cataloging process, snatched the volumes and carried them off to the garden, though they were later safely returned.

15. Ramsden, "Alan Clark," 8. Orpen's *Onlooker in France* has since been reunited with the rest of Wharton's library books and is now on display at The Mount. The postcard that Ramsden describes here, though, remains at large.

16. Wharton had her bookplates for both of her French residences, Pavillon Colombe and Sainte-Claire-du-Château, designed at the same time by Daniel Berkeley Updike; see chapter 4.

17. Lyall, "Alan Clark."

18. Ramsden, "Alan Clark," 8.

19. The text is in French, but the title translates to *A Morality without Obligation or Sanction.* This volume was not included in the original Maggs auction sale, nor was it discovered by Ramsden. It was sold to The Mount only recently, in 2017, by a British donor who is related to the person ("Norman") who had, years previously, received it as a gift ("birthday card") from Alan Clark. Whatever the incident that prompted the gift, and Clark's apology, it must have been momentous: he was evidently not big on apologizing.

20. Ramsden, "Alan Clark," 9, emphasis original.

21. The "young woman" is named Cornelia Brooke Gilder, and she is the author of the book *Edith Wharton's Lenox* (Mount Pleasant, S.C.: History Press, 2017). In that book, Gilder draws from archival records in addition to personal and family history: her mother, Louisa Ludlow Brooke, grew up in Lenox during

the period that immediately followed Wharton's residency there, at a time when people still remembered her presence in the Lenox community. Gilder went on to marry George Gilder, another Lenox resident with a storied familial history that appears time and again throughout the pages of *Edith Wharton's Lenox*. George Gilder's great-grandfather, Richard Watson Gilder, edited *The Century Magazine* and so oversaw the publication of some of Wharton's earliest poems. I met Cornelia Brooke Gilder during the summer of 2017 and am grateful for the additional information she was able to share with me about her connections to both Wharton and Ramsden.

22. This volume was also not included in the Maggs auction collection, nor was it included among the books that Ramsden sold to The Mount in 2005. It surfaced a few years later, in 2007, as the gift of an anonymous donor. I am grateful to my colleagues Eric Ross and Lauren Kaplow, who translated the inscription for me; Ross correctly identified Meleager's *The Greek Anthology* as the source of the quotation.

23. Lee, 340. I think Gilder puts it best, though, when she describes Fullerton as "unworthy"—of Wharton's affection and devotion, of her intellectual gifts, and of her society. See Gilder, *Edith Wharton's Lenox,* 16.

24. The inscription is in Italian and translates as "For you, always for you." For additional discussion of this pair of inscriptions, see Ramsden, *Edith Wharton's Library,* 9, and Lewis and Lewis, *The Letters of Edith Wharton,* 256. The latter work claims that Wharton's "Ogrin the Hermit" contains a "passionate and triumphant defense to herself of her adulterous conduct."

25. Henry James, *The Portrait of a Lady* (New York: Oxford World Classics, 1998), 124.

26. Ramsden, personal interview.

27. Shelagh Hancox, "Introduction and Question," email to the author, July 26, 2017. I am grateful to Shelagh Hancox—who succeeded the Sheelagh Hancox (spelled with two e's) mentioned here and became Alan Hancox's second wife—for the information she shared with me regarding this book and its previous owner. Alan Hancox died in 1992, and Ms. Hancox explained that her late husband had been professionally acquainted with Ramsden through their mutual dealings in the book trade.

28. Ramsden, personal interview.

29. Lynch, for instance, cites a similar response from the nineteenth-century collector Brayton Ives, who observes, "My acquaintance with my books has not been confined to their exteriors. . . . They have comforted me after many a weary day, and have stood often in the place of friends." See Brayton, quoted in Lynch, *Loving Literature,* 103.

30. Lee's staggeringly detailed biography of Wharton would not appear until 2007, but she was hard at work on it during this time and keen to view the library materials in connection with that project. Her introduction to Ramsden's catalog permitted her one means of doing that.

31. Lynch explains how, in the beginning of the nineteenth century, "descriptive bibliography" (such as the kind that Ramsden employed in building his catalog) "suffer[ed] in public opinion as a result of its perceived proximity to the irrational, exuberant, amorous world of the collector." In other words, bibliography was viewed as a collector's pastime and not as a serious scholarly enterprise. In reviving and relying on many of the standards of nineteenth-century descriptive bibliography (including an emphasis on material considerations like "typeface, paper, [and] printers' marks"), Ramsden's catalog, to a very similar degree, flatters the collector's agenda while downplaying or neglecting that of the scholar. See Lynch, *Loving Literature,* 104.

32. Wharton's two-volume set of the French writer Boileau's *Oeuvres Diverses*—both first editions dating from 1701—is handsomely bound in full crimson morocco leather by Lortic. This celebrated binder is erroneously referred to as "Lortig" in Ramsden's *Edith Wharton's Library.* What's more, in a set of Gibbon's *The Rise and Fall of Ancient Rome* (ed. 1816), a bookseller's note appears tipped into the pages of volume 4. It advertises a set of volumes by the Italian writer Benedetto Varchi that are for sale, "bound in a full brown morocco . . . by the great French binder Lortic." This last phrase appears handwritten in pencil and has been added to the bookseller's typewritten letter. For more about Marcellin Lortic (1852–1928) and his accomplishments in the field of bookbinding, see such sources as Cyril Davenport, *The Book: Its History and Development* (New York: D. Van Nostrand, 1908), 231, 241. Joris-Karl Huysmans, in his 1884 work *Against Nature,* mentions both Lortic and Chambolle-Duru directly: "He had succeeded in procuring unique books, adopting obsolete formats which he had bound by Lortic, by Trautz-Bauzonnet or Chambolle": see Joris-Karl Huysmans, *Against Nature* (New York: Lieber and Lewis, 1922), 12. See also "Lortic, Marcellin, of Paris (1852–1928)" in the British Library's Database of Bookbinding, https://www .bl.uk/catalogues/bookbindings/Default.aspx.

33. Ramsden, personal interview.

34. Interestingly, the restoration of the gardens at The Mount ended up costing EWR almost the exact same amount during this time, totaling $2.7 million. See Mead, "Restoration Drama."

35. Lynch, *Loving Literature,* 105.

36. Cowell, "After a Century."

37. Ramsden, personal interview.

38. James H. Billington, "The Modern Library and Global Democracy," in Alice Crawford, ed., *The Meaning of the Library* (Princeton, N.J.: Princeton University Press, 2015), 255.

39. T. S. Eliot, "Choruses from 'The Rock,'" *The Complete Poems and Plays of T. S. Eliot* (London: Faber and Faber, 1989), 147.

40. *Reader's Digest*, which promised quality reading "in condensed and compact form," in fact launched during the same period, with the first issue appearing in 1922.

41. William H. Wise and Company, advertisement for *The Elbert Hubbard Scrap Book, Time*, December 1927. Box 50, Folder 1504. YCAL 42, Series 4 Edith Wharton Papers, Beinecke Rare Books and Manuscript Library, Yale University, New Haven, Connecticut.

42. T. S. Eliot, "Burnt Norton," in Cary Nelson, ed., *Anthology of Modern American Poetry* (New York: Oxford University Press, 2000), 310. Critic Andrew Goldstone labels such anxieties as constitutive of "late style," or of an artist's desire to view his or her productive tendencies as separate from those of their contemporary moment, as out of sync. Goldstone argues that Eliot reveled in this feeling of being out of sync and so took refuge in thoughts of posterity, which promised "the freedoms of disembodiment" and release from "the limitation imposed by biographical contingency." Eliot, in other words, sensed that his work might be most at home in the libraries of the future, even though that meant that he might not live to witness his own attainment of that canonical prestige. See Andrew Goldstone, *Fictions of Autonomy: Modernism from Wilde to de Man* (New York: Oxford University Press, 2013), 68–69.

43. Lefebvre, *The Production of Space*, 102–3.

Index

···················

Adams, Henry, 201
Adorno, Theodor, 84, 101, 230n57
Age of Innocence, The (Wharton),
   215n53, 233n101
Americana, textual artifacts, 36, 86,
   91–93
anachronism, 250n115
"Angel at the Grave, The" (Wharton),
   13, 141–59, 167, 169, 246n72
Appleton (publisher), 72–73, 226n14
architecture, 18, 37–38, 42–45, 50,
   57–61, 67, 137; Gothic, 38, 40, 43,
   135, 214n46, 215n53; "Hudson
   River Bracketed," 214n46; Italianate,
   28, 42–43
archives, 8, 19–23, 26–27, 33, 52, 132,
   141–42, 146–47, 151, 156, 159;
   maintenance of, 58, 149–51, 157,
   167–68
Arendt, Hannah, 252n131
Arnold, Matthew, 122, 168, 170
association copies (books), 115–17
authenticity, 36, 50, 92, 95, 98–99,
   102–3, 151, 163
autodidacticism, 5, 8, 12, 34, 125,
   130, 144, 156. *See also* self-making

Bachelard, Gaston, 33, 42, 212n18
Backward Glance, A (Wharton),
   34, 103, 112, 115, 137–38, 163,
   214n46, 219n92, 234n111, 236n19,
   249n101
Bahlmann, Anna, 18–19, 30, 47,
   63–64, 81, 139–40
Barker, Nicholas, 196–97
Barnes, Djuna, 123
Baudelaire, Charles, 21
Baudrillard, Jean, 18–19, 30, 47,
   63–64, 81, 139–40
Bayley, John Barrington, 37
beauty, feminine, 76, 92; possession of,
   76–78
Bédier, Joseph, 188
Beethoven, Ludwig van, 120
Belton House (England), 43, 217n68
Benjamin, Walter: on Baudelaire,
   21–22; bibliomania, 6, 208n8; collecting, 5–9, 11–12, 60–61, 74, 117,
   173, 209n23, 230n57; inheritance,
   29–30, 48, 252n131; translation,
   227n17; value, 234n121; as Wharton's contemporary, 207n7
Bennett, Jane, 85

Berenson, Bernard, 28, 223n150
Berlant, Lauren, 155, 248n85
Bernard Quaritch, Ltd., 195
Berry, Walter, 28, 44, 114, 118, 120, 124, 135, 217n75, 237n26
best sellers (literature), 121–22
bibliomania, 2, 6–7, 11, 92, 103, 218n88
bibliophilia, 2–3, 7, 11, 62–66, 75, 86–87, 91–93, 174, 192, 237n30
Billington, James H., 202
Boit, Edward, 115
Bonnet, Jacques, 66
bookbinding, 5, 8, 16, 24, 28, 46, 65, 89, 116, 186, 196, 222n142, 231n77, 256n32. *See also* Chambolle-Duru; Lortic
Book Collector, The (magazine), 196
bookplates: as epitaphs, 173–78; in Wharton's books, 23, 68, 89, 116, 173–74, 184–89, 237n30, 252n133, 254n16
bookshelves, 35, 40–41, 61
Bostwick, Arthur E., 55
botany, 165–66, 250n115
Bourdieu, Pierre, 50, 74, 122, 227n19
bourgeois, 38, 76, 80, 83, 122–23. *See also* class; taste
Bourget, Paul, 47, 114
Bradbury, Ray, 137
brands (consumer goods), 82–83, 229n49
Brownson, Orestes, 144, 243n33
Bryant, Levi R., 82
Bucchi, Ermocrate (Italian painter), 82–83, 103, 229n49

Cannon, Carl L., 92–93
canon (literature), 7, 73–76, 99–101,

123–24, 226n16, 227n17, 234n121, 239n46, 257n42
capitalism, 77, 80, 98–99, 133, 157
card catalog, 51, 221n104
Carlyle, Thomas, 168
Carnegie, Andrew, 15, 33, 55
Casanova, Pascale, 73, 100–102
Caswell, Edward (illustrator), 160–61
Chambolle-Duru (bookbinder), 89, 196, 231n77, 256n32
Chanler, Daisy (Margaret Louisa Terry), 129
Clark, Alan, 181–83, 185, 197–98, 202, 254n19
Clark, Colin, 25, 64–65, 125, 181, 223n150
Clark, Lady (Elizabeth Winifred Martin), 116–17, 256n32
Clark, Sir Kenneth, 64, 116, 181, 223n150, 239n48
Clarke, Edward H., 127–28
class (socioeconomic), 99–100, 115, 122, 129, 132–33
classic literature, 29, 93–94, 99, 124, 249n101
Clifford, William Kingdom, 168
Colette (Sidonie-Gabrielle Colette), 120
collecting: "Americana" print materials, 92–93; anti-social behavior, 46, 139; and architecture, 40–41, 46, 218n81, 222n138; books, 6–7, 12, 16–17, 30, 36, 62–64, 103, 124; as education, 209n23; in general, 17, 75–78, 86–98, 115–17, 160, 168–69, 174, 183–89, 192; "golden age" of book collecting, 89. *See also* hoarding; paranoid accumulation

commodity, 98, 157

compulsion, 153–55, 174, 248n85

Concord (Massachusetts), 144, 243n33

Copeland, Stephanie, 193–201, 251n127

cost, 65, 86–87, 95, 97–98, 172–74, 193. *See also* price

Couperus, Louis, 18, 72–85, 97–101, 226n16

cultural capital, 48, 50–51, 74–75, 101, 122–23, 174, 234n121

curation, 4, 28, 62, 65, 141–42, 157, 163, 167–69, 176

Custom of the Country, The (Wharton), 44, 218n80

cutting (opening) books, 24–25, 114, 120, 168, 211n49, 251n127

d'Aurevilly, Jules Barbey, 120–21

Davis, Alexander Jackson, 214n46

death, 18, 137–41, 147, 149–50, 170–71

Decoration of Houses, The (Wharton and Codman), 31, 33, 36–47, 55, 60–61

de Vries, Hugo (botanist), 165, 250n115

Dewey Decimal System, 170–71, 220n104

de Wolfe, Elsie (interior designer), 61

Dickens, Charles, 108

Dickinson, Emily, 118

Dimock, Wai Chee, 96–97, 231n73

domesticity, 108, 152–55, 165, 169

Donovan, Josephine, 155–56

Dorhout, Nynke, 177–78, 217n75, 225n9

Dostoevsky, Fyodor, 226n14

Downing, Andrew Jackson, 43, 214n46, 215n50

Drinkwater, William H., 130, 250n115

drugs. *See* overdose

Dunsany, Lord (Edward John Moreton Drax Plunkett), 119

During, Simon, 74

Eby, Clare Virginia, 165

Edda (Norse mythology), 124

Edgeworth, Maria, 111

Edith Wharton Restoration, Inc., 26, 123, 251n127

EdithWhartonsLibrary.org, 22, 54, 90, 161, 166, 210n43

Elbert Hubbard Scrap Book, The, 203

Eliot, George, 25, 124, 177–78, 186

Eliot, T. S., 203–4, 257n42

Emerson, Ralph Waldo, 112, 120, 144–46, 150, 170, 243n33

Engels, Friedrich, 80, 103

ephemera (print materials), 93, 151; in Wharton's books, 25, 116, 187–90, 196, 256n32

Epictetus, 24

Ethan Frome (Wharton), 53, 121

eugenics, 23. *See also* race

Eugenides, Jeffrey, 217n75

evolution (science), 125, 151–52, 246n72

exchange value (economics), 10, 14, 51, 88, 94–95, 99, 193, 231n73. *See also* commodity

exile, 67, 120

False Dawn (Wharton), 160–62, 167–69

fandom, 78

Fielding, Henry, 237n30
first editions, 88–90, 96, 114, 119, 123, 165, 172, 201, 256n32
Flaubert, Gustave, 25, 101, 119, 123, 177
Fleissner, Jennifer, 154–55
form, 12–14, 20, 67, 108, 113, 118
Foucault, Michel, 31–32, 134, 159, 167, 212n18
France: literature, 100, 120, 130, 169; revolutions, 100
Friedlaender, Ludwig, 120
Fruit of the Tree, The (Wharton), 35–36, 53, 208n18
Fryer, Judith, 43, 217n69, 231n72, 233n101
Fullerton, Morton, 28, 44–45, 114–15, 118, 188, 224n156, 236n24, 255n23
Fuss, Diana, 77, 99

Galloway, Andrew, 110, 113
gender, 9, 47–48, 55–56, 59–60, 84, 87, 124, 127–31, 164; and book collecting, 218n88
ghosts, 27, 138–40, 147, 150, 167, 169–71
Gibbon, Edward, 116, 125, 256n32
Gilder, Cornelia Brooke, 118, 191–92, 254n21, 255n23
Glimpses of the Moon (Wharton), 165
globalization, 74, 80, 102, 129, 133, 197, 228n37
Gobineau, Comte de, 23
Gods Arrive, The (Wharton), 10, 18, 105–8, 130–35
Goethe, Johann Wolfgang von, 25, 89–91, 124

Goldman-Price, Irene, 34, 36, 128–29, 143
Gramsci, Antonio, 105
Greece, literature, 188
Grein, J. T. (translator), 74
Guillory, John, 50, 54, 234n121
Guyau, Jean-Marie, 187

hair, in books, 25
Hancox, Alan, 190
Hancox, Sheelagh, 189–90
Hardy, Thomas, 59
Hart-Davis, Rupert, 192
Hayot, Eric, 101
Hazlitt, William, 52, 122, 220n111
hegemony, 98
Hensley, Nathan K., 14–15, 26
Hercules (mythology), 46
Herring, Scott, 78, 97–98
heterotopias, 212n18
Heywood Hill (bookshop), 183–84, 253n8
hoarding, 7, 15–18, 28, 41, 46–47, 75–77, 84, 103, 117, 160, 168, 174, 216n58; books, 12, 91, 96–97, 157, 179; institutional, 17, 28, 63. *See also* collecting; paranoid accumulation
Holland, literature, 72–80
Horne, Howard, 89
House of Mirth, The (Wharton), 10, 11, 16, 24, 36, 47, 67, 71–78, 83–88, 99–103, 105, 208n18, 251n127
Housonville, Comtesse de (Pauline d'Harcourt), 116
Howard, June, 160–61, 164, 170
Howells, William Dean, 123, 239n46

Hudson River Bracketed (Wharton), 10, 13, 35–36, 38, 48, 67, 129

Hutner, Gordon, 122–23, 239n46

Huxley, Thomas, 168

Huysmans, Joris-Karl, 256n32

individuality, 80, 84, 94–95, 99

inheritance, 9, 29–32, 48, 64, 113–14, 125, 160–61, 252n131

inscriptions, in books, 30, 111, 114–15, 120, 188–93, 201, 255n24

intellectualism, 8, 12–13, 34–38, 48–52, 59, 80, 118, 126–31, 143–52, 162–65, 173, 209n23

interior design, 15, 17, 27, 30–33, 36–48, 55, 58–60, 76

investment, 86–87, 89, 95–97, 169

Irish Literary Revival, 119

Italy: art, 28, 82, 160–62, 167, 229n49; literature, 125, 169

James, Henry, 28, 43–45, 114–15, 118, 120–21, 123–24, 189–91, 201, 236n24

Johnson, Barbara, 138, 158

John the Apostle (St. John), 146

Jones, Adeline Schermerhorn, 53

Jones, Elizabeth Schermerhorn, 38, 52

Jones, Frederic, 112

Jones, George Frederic, 29, 111, 127, 135, 137–38, 141, 236n19, 249n101

Jones, Lucretia, 28, 112

Joyce, James, 114, 121

Keats, John, 112

Kierkegaard, Søren, 84, 230n57

Kippis, Andrew, 196

knickknacks, 40–41, 45–47, 61, 97, 222n138. *See also* hoarding

labor, 20, 27, 37–38, 41, 52–53, 55, 61, 63, 155, 163, 193, 216n55

La Bruyère, Jean de, 88–89, 95–96, 101

Lacordaire, Jean-Baptiste Henri-Dominique, 170

Land's End (house), 23, 68, 174, 186, 211n47

Lapsley, Gaillard, 114, 242n14

Laqueur, Thomas, 18, 175–76, 242n14

Latour, Bruno, 78, 88, 209n35

Leaves of Grass (Whitman), 217n75

Lee, Hermione, 145, 153, 185

Lefebvre, Henri: on reading space, 212n18; social space, 31–34, 41, 45, 69–70, 138–39; superimposed space, 13, 31, 42, 59, 205

Leibovitz, Annie, 44–45, 217n75

Lenox Library (Massachusetts), 33, 48, 51–58, 64, 69, 217n75, 219n89, 221n121

Lesjak, Carolyn, 20–22

Levine, Caroline, 12–14, 108, 118

Lewis, R. W. B., 146

libraries: circulating, 48; exclusion of women, 48, 56; "gentleman's," 111, 124, 127, 236n19, 249n101; institutional, 111, 124, 127; memorial, 137–38, 242n14; private, 15, 30, 35, 47, 61, 75, 86–92, 137–38, 141–48, 162–65; public, 15, 48, 55–56, 59, 109, 219n89; subscription (social), 15, 56, 219n90

library, as corpus, 109, 125–26

London Blitz (1940–41), 1–2, 65, 125

Lortic (bookbinder), 116–17, 196, 256n32

Lowell, James Russell, 93–94, 124
Lynch, Deidre Shauna, 7, 8, 18, 122, 138, 198, 220n111, 242n11, 255n29, 256n31

Macaulay, Rose, 1–2
Machiavelli, 120
Madame Bovary (Flaubert), 178
Maggs Bros., Ltd., 181–85, 194, 253n4
Mallock, William Hurrell, 168, 170
Manguel, Alberto, 137
manners, 132–34, 235n9
marginalia, 23–24, 52, 89, 145–46, 150, 165, 170, 196
Markland, James Heywood, 237n30
marriage, 78, 81, 87–88, 97, 105–8, 147, 164–65, 189
Marshall, Kate, 33
Marx, Karl, 10, 20, 80, 88, 95, 103, 138, 157, 228n37, 231n75, 233n96, 242n14
material culture, 75, 78–82, 98–99, 160, 164
materialism, 14–15, 19, 80, 110
Mead, Rebecca, 171
Meleager, 188
Mendel, Gregor, 130, 250n115
Meredith, George, 189, 206–7
Merish, Lori, 80
Middlemarch (Eliot), 177
Mill on the Floss, The (Eliot), 178
Mistral, Frédéric, 120
modernism, 36–37, 121, 123, 257n42
modernity, 67, 100, 122–23, 141, 151, 157, 164–65, 174, 214n43, 216n55
monuments, 18, 67, 77, 103, 137–73, 242n14

Morris, William, 216n55
Mount, The: architecture, 3, 10, 22, 26, 31–32, 41–47, 73, 173; institutional finances, 171–72, 256n34; lack of custom bookplates, 68–69; library, 73, 120, 171–74, 251n127; as museum, 171. *See also* Edith Wharton Restoration, Inc.
museums, 18, 26, 139, 142–50, 171, 227n19

national identity, 120
networks: abstract vs. material, 110, 113; hubs, 106–8, 144; publishing, 109; social, 18, 105–13, 132–35, 146–47, 149–50, 235n9, 237n37
New England, 142, 144, 154, 219n92
New Formalism, 14
New Year's Day (Wharton), 10, 11, 35, 160–69, 247n78, 250n115, 251n123, 251n127
New York City, 31, 38, 53, 99, 102–3, 106–7, 112, 147, 160–67
New Yorker, The, 61, 171
New York Times, 72–74, 171
Nietzsche, Friedrich, 8, 20, 208n18

Ohmann, Richard, 83, 98–102, 110, 229n49
Old New York novellas (Wharton), 160, 173. See also *False Dawn; New Year's Day*
opera, 77–82
Oram, Richard W., 253n4
Orpen, William, 185, 254n15
Orlando, Emily J., 155–56
orphanhood, 34–36, 49, 143–46
Ouida (Maria Louise Ramé), 168
overdose, 85, 106, 208n18

Paget, Violet (Vernon Lee), 28
paranoid accumulation, 75, 98, 102.
    See also collecting; hoarding
Paris, 5, 21, 27, 68, 100–101, 108,
    115, 118–20, 174
Pavillon Colombe (house), 5, 68, 174,
    186
Peckham, Howard, 17, 91
Perkins, F. B., 71, 97
philology, 130
philosophy, 143–44, 153, 157, 163,
    182, 200
photography, 44–45, 79, 81–82,
    84–85, 117
Piper, Andrew, 34
Pizer, Donald, 125
plant-breeding. *See* botany
Poe, Edgar Allan, 36
poetry, 21, 36, 124–25, 129, 162, 169
price, 8, 16, 87, 93, 98, 171. *See also*
    cost
Price, Alan, 24, 210n46
printing technology, 16, 24, 65, 89, 93,
    109, 121, 211n49
prostitution, 164–65
Pyne, Lydia, 41, 62, 93

race, 14, 23, 120, 165
Ramayana, The (Valmiki), 25
Ramsden, George, 5, 19, 65, 125,
    176–79, 182, 254nn14–15
Ramsden, James Edward, 183
realism, 42, 121–23, 154
Red Cross, 116
Regniér, Henri de, 119
reification, 30, 99, 127
Reinach, Salomon, 188
religion, 125, 143, 146–47, 161, 200,
    228n31

Relph, Edward, 29
Reynolds, Joshua, 71, 120
Riegl, Alois, 138–40, 158–59, 242n16
Rilke, Ina (translator), 74
Ripley, Sarah Alden Bradford, 144
Roxburghe Club, 237n30
Ruskin, John, 161, 168, 249n101

Sainte-Claire-du-Château (house), 5,
    23, 68
Saltwood Castle, 65, 181–82, 185–87
Sand, George, 120, 124
Santayana, George, 120
Sassoon, Siegfried, 192
Schiller, Friedrich, 128
Schofield, William Henry, 120
science, 125, 130, 151–52, 157, 246n72
Seillière, Ernest, 120–21
self-making, 45, 69, 142–44, 156, 163,
    174. *See also* autodidacticism
Selley, Peter, 194
Settle, Smith, 195
Silverman, Gillian, 140
Simmel, Georg, 51
Smith, John Hugh, 120
Smith, John Saumarez, 183
Sontag, Susan, 174, 209n23
Sotheby's, 194–95
space: monumental, 139–42; private,
    11, 15–17, 31–35, 41–42, 47–48,
    61–70; public, 11, 27, 33, 43, 54,
    58; social, 31–34, 41, 45, 69–70,
    138–39. *See also* Lefebvre, Henri
Spark, The (Wharton), 162
Spectator, The (magazine), 1
spinsterhood, 145–47, 156
Springer, Anne-Sophie, 142
Staël, Albertine de (Baroness de Staël
    von Holstein), 115–16

Staël, Madame Germaine de (Anne
  Louise Germaine de Staël-Holstein),
  115–16
statuary, 158
Steedman, Carolyn, 26–27
Stendhal, 146
Stone Trough Books, 183–85, 199
Storm, Colton, 17, 91
Stroobant's (book binder), 28
style, 45, 216n55. *See also* taste
Suckley (family), 40
Suckley, Daisy, 216n58
Summer (Wharton), 10, 13, 48, 49–60,
  138, 142, 219n89, 221n117
symptomatic reading, 20–21

tableaux vivants, 71–75, 86, 92,
  94–95, 97–98
taste, 36, 41, 77, 80, 83, 149, 160
Tennyson, Alfred, 124
Thacker, Eugene, 110, 113
Thoreau, Henry David, 137, 144–45
tradition, 9–10, 20, 37, 50–52, 67,
  129–31, 155, 164–65; hatred of,
  101
Transcendentalist Club, 243n33
Trilling, Lionel, 132
Tugendhat, Christopher, 197–200
Turner, William (painter), 181, 253n1
Turpin, Etienne, 142
Tyler, Elisina Grant, 2
Tyler, Royall, 2
Tyler, William Royall, 2–3, 64–65, 125
Tyndall, John, 168

Ulysses (Joyce), 114, 172, 201
Updike, Daniel Berkeley, 174,
  252n133, 254n16

value, 75, 86, 96–97, 100, 161,
  171–72; of books, 16, 49, 51, 65,
  73–74, 86–97, 100, 234n121
Vaux, Calvert (landscape architect),
  215n50
Villa Madama (Raphael), 42
Vogue (magazine), 44, 217n75

Wendorf, Richard, 48, 117
Wharton, Edith: ancestry, 145,
  234n111; as bibliomaniac, 6–7, 11;
  charities, 116; divorce, 68, 174; education, 12, 29, 124, 127–29, 202;
  foreign language fluency, 129–31;
  grave, 176; as library benefactress,
  33, 53–54, 58, 221n121; as reader,
  8, 12, 25–27, 125–27, 134–35,
  203–4; poetry, 115; travel, 4, 67–68,
  174. *See also* Land's End; Pavillon
  Colombe; Sainte-Claire-du-Château
Wharton, Edward (Teddy), 53, 67–68,
  115, 118, 174
Whitman, Walt, 44, 162, 191, 217n75
Wiegand, Wayne A., 15, 55–56
Wilderstein (estate), 38–42, 46,
  215n53
Wilson-Patten, John, Baron of
  Winmarleigh, 116
Winship, Michael, 109, 126–27
Winterkorn, Joan, 195–96
Wissler, Susan, 191
Wolff, Cynthia Griffin, 86
Woolf, Virginia, 192
Wordsworth, William, 159, 172–75
Wren, Christopher, 43

Yeats, William Butler, 119

Zola, Émile, 123, 130

SHEILA LIMING is assistant professor of English at the University of North Dakota.

Made in the USA
Monee, IL
20 June 2023